JOHN WISDEN

JOHN WISDEN

A Steadfast Friend

Stephen Baldwin

Foreword by David Frith

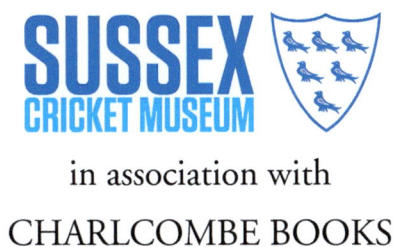

in association with

CHARLCOMBE BOOKS

Sussex Cricket Museum
1st Central County Ground, Eaton Road, Hove BN3 3AN

Charlcombe Books
125 Garnet Street, Bristol BS3 3JH

The picture on the front cover of this book shows John Wisden at Lord's in about 1850. It is from a painting by William Bromley in the MCC collection and is reproduced with the kind permission of MCC.

First published 2025

ISBN: 978 1 7399293 9 8

Printed and bound in Great Britain by
CPI Group, Chippenham, Wiltshire

Contents

John Wisden

FOREWORD

David Frith

Whose is the most renowned name in cricket? W.G.Grace? Don Bradman? Garry Sobers? Ian Botham? Sachin Tendulkar? The possibilities are far-reaching, inevitably, and heavily subject to personal prejudice. In the wake of the breath-taking 2019 English season there may even be some cricket-lovers who would vote for Ben Stokes.

But time shrinks everything. Meanwhile, there's also a little chap whose influence is still strongly evident 141 years after his death, and this is John Wisden. He is remembered for much more than taking all ten wickets in a North v South first-class match at Lord's in 1850 – cutting the ball up to a yard down the slope, in similar fashion to Sri Lanka's own shortish quickie Lasith Malinga. John Wisden had no rainbow hairdo but bowled a similarly roundarm and nippy delivery.

Not least interesting in this overdue biography is the manoeuvring and sharp rivalry of the professional touring teams that travelled all over England, intensifying interest in the game while making a hard-earned profit and enduring fatigue. William Clarke's name looms large in this, and the rivalry between the professional camps conjures up visions not only of the Packer revolution so many years in the future but also today's tug-of-war between the traditional game and the garish Twenty-20 tournaments that have sprung up all around the world. This narrative makes it clear that John Wisden maintained his dignity throughout the money-making ventures.

Of course, he is remembered for much more than just his bowling. Wisden took part in the first major international cricket tour, when a team of intrepid Englishmen in 1859 crossed the wild Atlantic Ocean to play in a pioneering tour of North America, colourfully described here. And he established a flourishing sports shop in London. Further, he was a highly respected coach. What a man.

Little John Wisden, all 5 ft 4 ins of him, has long been immortalised by the *Almanack* which bears his name. He founded it in 1864, unwittingly triggering what became an immensely precious and all-embracing annual record of cricket's scores and development and controversies, subsequently assembled by his numerous successors. That first edition was very slim, and priced at a shilling and a penny (5p in today's bloated money: the average weekly wage in England at that time was £2). The little *Almanack* and its succeeding and ever-expanding annual volumes faithfully record almost all that matters in cricket, embracing today much detail from a vast global game. Even though he saw off the challenges of other cricket publishers, notably the Lillywhites, Wisden could never have anticipated his *Almanack's* massive growth as the decades unfolded.

A long time ago I searched for John Wisden's grave. This chronicling was another of my cricket hobbies. I was stunned to discover that such a significant figure had no clearly marked final resting place. Bill Gray, a true gentleman who then had control of Wisden publishing and had supported me in the establishment of the original *Wisden Cricket Monthly*, agreed to finance a handsome headstone, and the unveiling was duly celebrated.

Few have looked upon that admirable memorial, but here Stephen Baldwin has done a superb job of gathering together just about all that might reasonably be of interest concerning John Wisden, from birth to death, as family member, cricketer, coach, sports-shop proprietor and publisher. The depth of research is impressive and the presentation pleasing. Running through a cricketer's career performances often generates tedium for the reader. But not in this case. Stephen has a light touch and has stitched an elegant tapestry. Immerse yourself in this colourful tale. Spend a while in mid-19th Century England, away from the modern horrors that surround us.

As for conjecture about cricket's most famous name, it truly is hard to gainsay the opinion that John Wisden's continues to be the most frequently uttered across the years from among cricket's crowded ranks of players and writers. Hence his life story: welcome, entertaining, significant.

INTRODUCTION

Roger Packham

Of all the famous cricketers in the pre-W G Grace era, the name of John Wisden (1826-1884) is the most enduring, mainly through the *Almanack* that he started in 1864. Throughout two world wars and a pandemic it has never failed to appear in 158 years. Even non-cricket folk are largely aware of its existence.

Robert Winder, in 2013, wrote a very good account of the almanack and included a short biography of John Wisden. Many other authors, covering the history of Sussex cricket especially, have provided biographical details of this remarkable man. These historians include Arthur Haygarth, Alfred Gaston, Alfred Taylor, Arthur Gilligan, John Marshall, Christopher Lee and John Wallace but, disappointingly, a quick glance at the references to John Wisden would soon convince the read that discrepancies abound. Biographical information from these sources on 'The Little Wonder' is contradictory and in many cases patently incorrect. He is allocated the wrong father and the wrong place of birth, and even his 'ripping' tearaway fast bowling has been demeaningly represented as slow underhand on Cricket Archive.

The oft repeated story of an impoverished, youthful John Wisden working for Tom Box as a pot boy in a Brighton public house is also a myth. In producing this work Stephen Baldwin has examined primary sources such as Brighton census records, street directories, birth, marriage and death certificates and newspaper files to build an accurate story of Wisden and to establish his family as prosperous builders and developers in a boom time for Brighton, following the arrival of the railway in 1841.

There is much to admire about John Wisden's cricketing exploits. His rapid bowling brought him over 1100 wickets in first-class matches, and his exploits for firstly the All England Eleven and later the United (All) England Eleven gained a further 1730 wickets. His batting was always useful and his slip fielding exceptional. In 1855 his 148 v Yorkshire in the match to open the Bramall Lane ground at Sheffield was the only century that season by anyone. Beyond statistics, though, John Wisden consistently showed himself as an able administrator. The story of how a group of professional cricketers broke away from Clarke's All England Eleven to form the United (All) England Eleven revolves around Wisden. His secretaryship/leadership of UEE is a milestone in cricket development and when the first overseas tour was arranged to North America in 1859 it was organised by George Parr and Wisden. He turned down an invitation to join the first tour of Australia.

His later involvement with the Cricketers' Fund Friendly Society is another indication of his administrative skills and the respect in which he was widely held. His dedicated coaching at Harrow School was highly successful and set new standards for this task. His work with UEE contributed significantly to the popularity of cricket and the establishment of county-based professional cricket.

The author succeeds in correcting many of the errors and misconceptions but has also tried to illustrate the great contribution made by John Wisden to promote cricket in the British Isles and beyond and to establish the welfare of the professional cricketer. The *Cricketers' Almanack* is a lasting tribute but his cricketing and business achievements also deserve to be loudly applauded.

ACKNOWLEDGEMENTS

When I was about to start on this project I surmised that a good starting point in my search for information would be the *Almanack,* so I contacted the then editor, Matthew Engel. Matthew quickly put me into contact with Roger Heavens who, in turn, introduced me to Roger Packham. At that time Roger and Nicholas Sharp were busy establishing a museum on the County Cricket Ground at Hove. Quickly, I now had access to a substantial network of cricket historians. More of these people later.

John Wisden & Co, principally through Christopher Lane and Hugh Chevallier, have continued to have an interest in the project and have given most welcome support and encouragement across many years, for which I am most grateful.

Margaret Rushton quickly proved to be a valuable resource. She lives in Leamington Spa, is married to a very able and enthusiastic cricketer and is secretary to the town's local history group. Through her unrivalled knowledge of Victorian England I was able to build up a picture of both the Leamington and Brighton in which John Wisden had lived. I have been continuously grateful for her interest and support.

The Nottinghamshire village of Radcliffe-on-Trent made a significant contribution to Victorian cricket. The Manor House, opposite the village church, was the lifetime home for both George Parr, JW's business partner, and his sister Anne, JW's fiancée. Richard Daft was to become a lodger in the Manor House. Radcliffe is blessed with a highly-skilled local history group, at an important time led by Pam and Neil Priestland. I have been most grateful for the background information that their work has provided.

England is blessed with a wonderful network of record offices. I first used Warwickshire's when a hand-turned scroll through reels of microfilm revealed the 1851 census record for 'John Wisdoe, Creekitor'. This entry would have escaped the now more common electronic searches. From Warwick we moved to Lewes (East Sussex), Chichester (West Sussex), Marylebone and then the National Archives at Kew. Leamington Library was a rich source of maps and other local information. All these offices are staffed by skilled and helpful people. Given that is was located in Wisden's home town, the Local History Centre at Brighton was particularly useful in building up a picture of his early years. This centre was welcoming, accessible and, again, staffed by skilled and supportive people. The centre is now part of the 'hi-tech' facility The Keep located close to the University of Sussex – perhaps the future face of historical records.

Cricket is blessed not only with a long history and excellent records, but with a series of people and places to curate those records. Lord's with its pavilion, library and museum is surely the best in the world – although, this being cricket, there will surely be someone who would contest that status. Again the staff, particularly Neil Robinson, have been welcoming and supportive. Other county cricket clubs are establishing museums/ libraries and I have been fortunate in being an easy drive away from Trent Bridge, Nottingham. It is often said of Sir Christopher Wren and the City of London that if you want to see his monument look around you. Peter Wynne-Thomas was also an architect and the same tribute could very appositely be said of him and the museum-library which he created and over which he presided, a rich and homely sanctuary for cricket records.

Yvonne Dedman was born and raised in Crown Street, Brighton – on the other side of the street and a little further up the hill from the Wisden home. Very many years after him, Yvonne followed JW to Middle Street School where she became a member of Wisden House. She has kindly made available copies of plans and documents relating to her family home which have been helpful in understanding the street in which JW was born and raised. I am most grateful to her.

Middle Street School is over 200 years old and hemmed in by the streets of the old Brighthelmstone, the historic core of the modern city. They are rightly proud of their famous alumnus and were generous in allowing us access to their records.

JW was always ready to make use of the law in pursuit of what he felt to be a just cause. At times this led to complications and one case lasted 15 years before the High Court demanded an end to it. I am most grateful to Kevin Mitchell and his colleagues and staff at Blythe Liggins, Solicitors for their time and assistance in helping me to understand the issues within the cases.

In the late 1840s Henry Gray was a rackets professional/coach in Cambridge at a time when Wisden went each spring to the University to help the students prepare for the coming cricket season. Given Wisden's enthusiasm for rackets the two must surely have met. Henry not only played cricket but he also launched the eponymous sports goods firm which is currently in safe hands of five brothers one of whom, Richard, was generous in his provision of materials about sports goods and in particular on William Gilbert, the Rugby School boot-maker whose name is perpetuated every time international rugby appears on television. Gilbert became a key person in the establishment of the sports goods industry. Gray's were later to become publishers of *Wisden's Almanack*. Our thanks to them all.

As well as agreeing to write a foreword to the book, David Frith has been ever ready to offer friendly advice and encouragement during the writing process. His kind words have often given reassurance at critical times either by e-mail or telephone. I hope that I shall one day meet him face-to-face.

One of the challenges of our research is that most of the records for which we were researching were housed at least 100 miles away in either London or Brighton & Hove. We have been fortunate that Andrew, John, Judy and Ros, friends from schooldays in Chichester, continue to live in West Sussex. Mr & Mrs Howard and Mr & Mrs Woodhead have taken a continuing interest in the project, offering encouragement and hospitality, along with keeping a local eye out for photographs and other resources. We remain grateful for their kind support.

Sussex Cricket Museum and Educational Trust came to the rescue of a partially completed manuscript which had 'no home to go to'. I am grateful to Jon Filby, chairman of SCMET, for agreeing that the Museum would publish the book. My involvement with the Museum has brought me into contact with kind people such as Norman Epps and the late Nicholas Sharp who not only offered kind words and advice but also made available their valuable artefacts. Phil Barnes is the Museum's in-house book designer and deployed his knowledge and skills to begin the process of turning the typed manuscript into a book before passing it to Stephen Chalke to make it ready for printing. Thank you, gentlemen.

Finally, a word about three people without whom there would never have been a book. Roger Heavens was already researching Wisden's life when I was introduced to him, but he was also working on Wisden's fellow Victorian cricketer, Arthur Haygarth. We agreed that I would develop the Wisden work while Roger would focus on Haygarth, Harrow School and the publication of further volumes of the most valuable *Scores & Biographies*. The footnotes to the following chapters show how vital

S&B volumes are. Haygarth was happy to add his own observations to the scorecards he published and these have provided an unequalled insight into cricket during the second half of the 19th century. Beyond the books, Roger has a deep and wide-ranging knowledge of Victorian cricket, particularly relating to Harrow School, where Wisden was a successful coach. Roger has been a willing correspondent and a generous supplier of information and encouragement.

It is very true to say if Roger Packham had not come to my rescue there would not have been a book. He took on the daunting task of converting a rambling, disjointed very early draft into a viable book. He used his deep and extensive knowledge of Victorian Sussex cricket to bolster the skeleton text. Roger has a keen eye for such as rigour, accuracy and consistency and he steered the text along a more coherent, straighter path. The text now had a structure against which to build the narrative. His commitment to the book included spending a cold January day, during pandemic 'lockdown', sitting on the concourse of Reading railway station outlining a set of illustrations (we classified it as an out-of-doors working meeting and thus permissible!). He has, also, eliminated 'a thousand' commas. I am, and will ever, be grateful to him for his invaluable support, knowledge and commitment.

My wife, Barbara, concedes that she is 'not particularly interested in cricket'. However, in the cause of supporting me in producing this book, she has spent whole days watching county cricket, trailed through Brompton Cemetery on a bleak winter day and photographed a wide range of buildings, documents and events across half of England. During many hours of indoor research she has become adept at reading reels of microfilm records in the spidery handwriting of Georgian and Victorian clerics. Barbara has a wide and detailed knowledge of the wider Wisden family and their friends and neighbours during Brighton's nascent years.

1

THE WISDEN FAMILY

Brighton has always been much associated with the railways and the service which connects it to the capital. This runs from Sir Laurence Olivier and his theatrical companions taking the late night Brighton Belle back home after evening performances to the notorious Pinky in Graham Greene's *Brighton Rock*. And then there is that iconic four-minute film of the train journey, so often repeated on television. So a good place to start this story might be at the front entrance of the Brighton Railway Station. In front of you the road runs down the hill to the water of the English Channel which, on a fine day, sparkles away to the horizon. Following the road downhill brings you to a crossroads close to which is a clock tower. Turn right to walk past the clock tower and then bear left towards the concourse in front of the Churchill shopping centre. Now look to your left and you will see a narrow roadway. The road is clearly labelled 'Farm Yard'.

Farm Yard is an unusual street name to be found in the centre of a bustling, vibrant, university City. But in 1800 it was exactly that, an old farm yard which marked the north-west corner of Brighton. It was also the location of Simon Wisden's blacksmith's business. At that time the settlement was known as Brighthelmstone, but I shall just use the modern name. In the next 50 years both Simon Wisden's family and his business interests as well as the town of Brighton were to expand rapidly to the north and west of this corner. All would be to the ultimate benefit of the game of cricket and to the professional players who developed it.

The Wisden family had been well established in the town for several centuries, over which time they had displayed a remarkable lack of originality in the Christian names that they gave to their children. Every generation had a Simon and most seem to have had a Thomas and a William, with Mary and Elizabeth for the girls, as well. However, the same can be said of the families with whom they were often joined by marriage, amongst them the Howells and the Walls. A greater variation was to be found within the fluctuations of the spellings – but this was a time when most communication was oral. Thus, the husbandman who was buried on 27th February 1660 was recorded as Symonn Wesden.

The Wisden family tree (abridged)

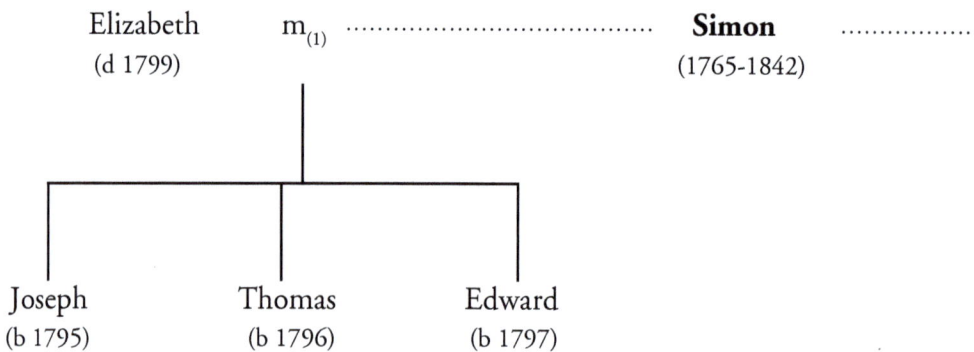

Elizabeth — m(1) ⋯⋯⋯⋯⋯⋯⋯⋯⋯⋯⋯⋯⋯ **Simon** ⋯⋯⋯⋯⋯
(d 1799)   (1765-1842)

Joseph   Thomas   Edward
(b 1795)   (b 1796)   (b 1797)

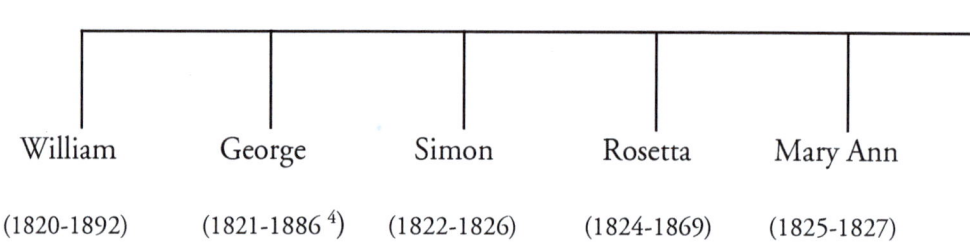

William   George   Simon   Rosetta   Mary Ann

(1820-1892)   (1821-1886 [4])   (1822-1826)   (1824-1869)   (1825-1827)

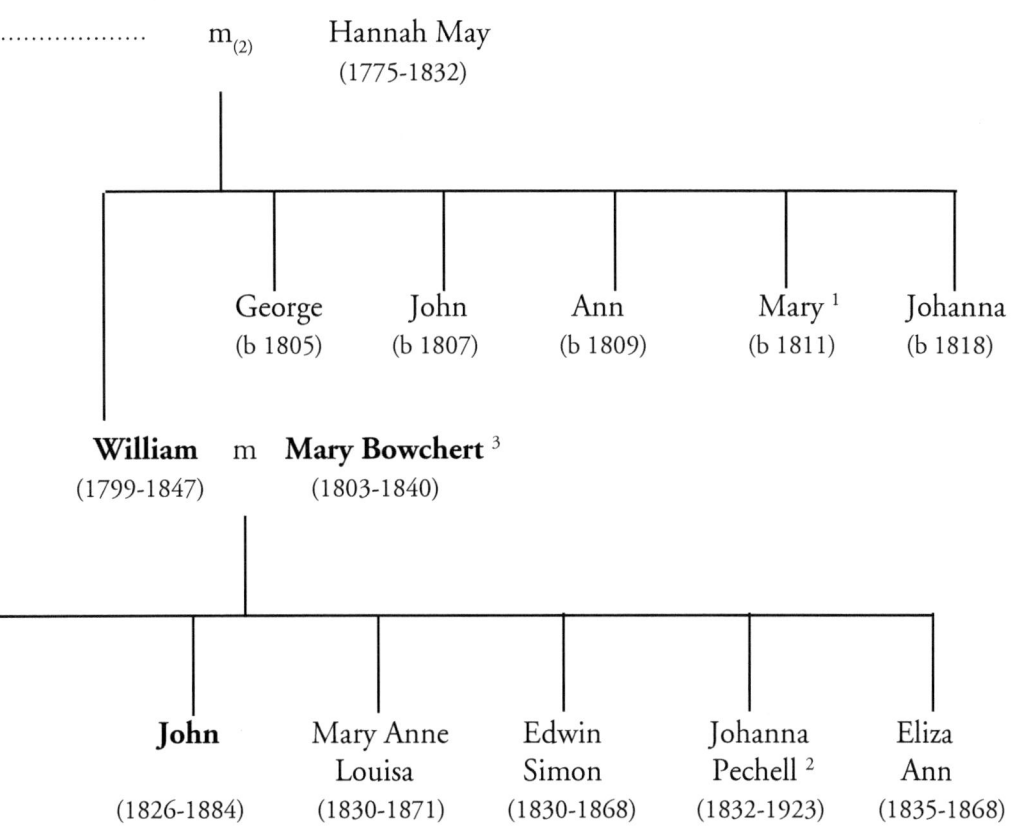

.... m(2) Hannah May
(1775-1832)

George   John   Ann   Mary [1]   Johanna
(b 1805)   (b 1807)   (b 1809)   (b 1811)   (b 1818)

William m **Mary Bowchert** [3]
(1799-1847)   (1803-1840)

John   Mary Anne   Edwin   Johanna   Eliza
              Louisa   Simon   Pechell [2]   Ann
(1826-1884) (1830-1871) (1830-1868) (1832-1923) (1835-1868)

---

[1] Mary married Caleb Hornby who was an executor of Simon's 1765 will

[2] Johanna Pechell married William Games and inherited John Wisden & Co in 1884

[3] All evidence of the spelling of this name is handwritten. The exact spelling is uncertain.

[4] Unvalidated death in Australia

Fortunately other supporting evidence assures us that the Thomas Wisden, who on 1st July 1764 married Mary Walls, was the great-grandfather of the cricketer, publisher and businessman, John Wisden. On 1st December 1765 they christened their son Simon – the man who would become the Farm Yard blacksmith. In November 1767 Thomas and Mary Wisden christened a daughter, Sarah. However, young Simon's life now entered a more turbulent and traumatic phase. The parish records of St Nicholas's Church record that on the same day in December 1768 both Mary Wisden, wife of Thomas, and an infant were buried. With young children to care for, Thomas remarried the following year, to Elizabeth Ade. Young Simon survived the upheaval until he was married and left home but his father was not so lucky. Reports in 1772 tell of his death following a fall from his cart. There was the suspicion that he was drunk at the time.

Simon Wisden began to appear regularly in the town's records around the time of the turn of the century. The north-western corner of the town was often described as the location of 'Simon Wisden's Smithy', and he also frequently appeared in transfers of title as he began to buy and sell land. This was the beginning of the building business which, by the time of his death, might be described as a 'property empire'. He was very much a man in the right place at the right time.

Brighton was about to embark on a boom – in activity, popularity and thus, of necessity, property. Between 1801 and 1851 its size, in terms of buildings, increased by 793% (i.e. it became nearly 9 times as big as it was). There were two principal reasons for that. Firstly it was becoming a militarised town; ever since around 1792 the country had been in fear of an invasion by revolutionary French forces. The beach at Brighton was thought to be ideal for what, in today's terms, might be described as an amphibious landing. A local militia was raised and quartered in the town, requiring not only the building of barracks and fortifications but also accommodation for those tradesmen and women who were required to support the militia. Interestingly, the arrangements were in the hands of a cricketer. The 4th Duke of Richmond had captained Sussex county teams in matches against Hampshire/Hambledon but now as part of his military 'day job' was required to secure the south coast against invaders. As part of his defence preparations the Duke was also mapping the coastal areas of the county, a project which led directly to the inauguration of the Ordnance Survey.

A second cause of the expansion was the presence of royalty. The Prince Regent, later to become King George IV, came to the town and brought the fashionable set with him. In the right season the town greeted and needed to accommodate hundreds of visitors. There was a growing demand for high status 'buy to let' property. All these properties had service needs and their tenants needed to be fed, watered and have their other needs catered for, all increasing commercial activity within the town. Whilst much of the society property was built at the eastern end of the old town, around the Steyne and the Royal Pavilion, housing for the town's people was built to the west, literally outside Simon's front door (or, perhaps, gate!).

The expansion of Simon's property business can be followed through those rate books which survive today. For instance in 1826, as well as his blacksmith's forge and shop (£5-15-0) he had rates levied on numbers 76 & 77 North Street (each at £3-10-0) and 23 & 24 Upper Russell Street (£2-10-0 each). Properties around numbers 76 & 77 North Street were to remain the 'headquarters' of the Wisdens' property businesses for many years. On his death in December 1842, Simon's will listed over 20 properties, both commercial and residential, which were to be distributed amongst his children. The surviving children listed in his will were (year of birth has been added): Joseph (c 1795), Thomas (1796), Edward (1797), William (1799), George (1805), John (1807), Ann (1809), Mary (1811) and Johanna (1818). Johanna, the daughter of his later years, lived with him until his death and received special provisions within his will.

As Simon's business empire increased, so did his personal and social status. Whereas the early, turn of the century, directories listed him simply as 'blacksmith', he was soon also being described as a builder and by 1824 he was one of the commissioners fulfilling the function that, today, would be carried out by the City Councillors. By 1837 he was being listed as 'Gentleman'.

Four of Simon's sons, Joseph, Thomas, William and George, followed him into the business of building houses, etc. Of these Thomas and William (JW's father) went on to achieve a status that would today be described as a 'developer'. Thomas was to become the leader of his generation. Beginning his life as a blacksmith, he gradually expanded his business and it soon included more general building work, including general construction work. Surviving contracts, invoices, cash books, etc., show him undertaking much work for the Corporation of Brighton, including construction of a new fish market and erection of the groynes which were essential to slow the erosion of the beach and the cliffs behind them. As Thomas's business grew his status within the commercial and civic communities within the town rose; he became, firstly, a guardian and then later a commissioner.

Entries in the lists of builders in local directories of the time, show the rise of Allen Anscombe within the North Street building operation; in 1843 Messrs Wisden and Anscombe were recorded erecting educational schools at the rear of the church in Bedford Place. Some deeds dated 1849 indicate that Thomas Wisden was by then living in Henfield. Having converted from blacksmith to builder to surveyor, Thomas was now listed as a gentleman. His move to Henfield marked his retirement from active management of the affairs of the company, which were passed to Anscombe, though it appears that Thomas retained a financial interest. In his later years Thomas was a man of sufficient status and standing within the town to make common cause with one Charles Scrase Dickens in campaigns for and against developments within Brighton. Thomas built St Peter's Church, Brighton and Holy Trinity Church, Hurstpierpoint.

Not only were Simon and his sons all engaged in the same type of business, they also lived and worked in and around the same set of streets. Much of the expansion of Brighton was along Western Road. From this main road a number of side streets were built northwards, up the hill towards the Downs. Amongst these streets was the succession of Marlborough, Crown, Dean, Spring and Hampton ending in Hampton Place. The Wisden family had a strong presence within these streets.

Thomas Wisden had a builder's yard on the corner of Marlborough Street and Western Road. Late on the night of Monday 12th May 1834 a fire broke out in the yard. Fortunately a passer-by quickly noticed it and raised the alarm at 11.45pm. While one neighbour was told to run to the Town Hall to notify the fire engine others began to address the blaze. The yard gates were broken down and the two horses were rescued from their stables. The neighbours had difficulty raising Thomas Wisden who lived in the house next to the yard and eventually resorted to throwing a brick through his bedroom window. With the business acumen typical of the Wisden family, he rushed down to his office and rescued his account books, plans and cash tin, while his neighbours began retrieving other valuables. After 45 minutes the town fire engines arrived. An hour later a second engine arrived.

Soon all of the neighbours were aware of the fire and were beginning to take precautions in case the fire spread. From the back bedroom windows in his home in the next street, young JW would have been able to watch the drama. At 2.00am Major Martin of the 1st Royal Dragoons brought 80 of his men and their fire engine up the hill to help with the fire-fighting. The combined efforts meant that the blaze was restricted to Thomas Wisden's home and yard, and a neighbour's greenhouse. There were no injuries.

The Wisden yard and business were important to both the immediate community and the town. Such was the significance that three days later a report of the fire in *The Times* ran to 14 column inches. The craftsmen employed by Wisden lost all their tools. The local community rallied round and collected funds for replacements. Just 10 days later the craftsmen were able to have a notice in the *Brighton Gazette* thanking their neighbours for their support and say they were now able to get back to work.

JW grew up in the community centred around an extended family of successful businessmen. In an age when formal schooling was infrequent this would be valuable training and education.

In order to build all these new houses there was an urgent and ever increasing need for bricks. It was this need that led the wider Wisden family to make a great, though inadvertent, 'gift' to cricket. They became listed as 'Builder & Brickmaker' and owners of a brickyard in Hove. However, the family needed an experienced man to run the yard for them and they recruited a master brickmaker called Frederick William Lillywhite who lived in the village of Westhampnett, just outside the city of Chichester, where he made bricks for the Duke of Richmond's Goodwood Estate. Besides being a master brickmaker, William Lillywhite was also English cricket's master bowler. Such was his superiority that he had the sobriquet 'Nonpareil'. Being now based in Brighton allowed William to develop both his brick-making and cricket careers. There were summer days when he rose at 3am to put in time setting up the yard ready for production before going off to play cricket for Brighton or Sussex or England.

Just as important, in terms of the benefit to cricket, William brought with him his new wife Charlotte. They had a large number of children, amongst whom were the cricketers James (b 1825), John (b 1826) and Frederick (b 1829). The lives of these boys ran parallel to, or were intertwined with, JW's for almost all of their years.

The wider Wisden family were not only closely located but also close-knit. There is evidence of them supporting each other, so when son Joseph (JW's uncle Joseph) was declared bankrupt his father Simon bailed him out and set him back in business. The cost of this rescue was clearly set against Joseph's inheritance in Simon's will.

SKETCHES AT LORD'S GROUND
Nº 2.
WILLIAM LILLYWHITE,
DEDICATED TO THE MEMBERS OF THE MARY-LE-BONE CLUB.
LONDON : THOMAS C LEWIS & Cº 96 CHEAPSIDE.

William Lillywhite was, arguably, the foremost
bowler of his generation. He was brought to Hove
by the wider Wisden family, to make bricks.

2

GROWING UP

John Wisden was born and brought up in Crown Street, Brighton, which is one of a series of parallel side streets running northwards, up the hill, from Western Road. The street still exists, as do many of the original houses. Sadly the house that was JW's home has been demolished. By the early 1930s Western Road had become a major east-west thoroughfare linking the centre of Brighton into Church Road, Hove. The carriageway was no longer wide enough for all the traffic making use of it. To facilitate the necessary widening of the road the shops and some of houses on the north side of the road were demolished. What had been small local shops were now replaced with buildings to accommodate stores. The stores were deeper than the shops and so houses at the southern end of the side roads were demolished. The site of the Wisden family's former home is now occupied by a large store fronting on to Western Road. At the time of writing the building is occupied by Primark.

Site of the Wisden family home
Crown Street, Brighton

JW's branch of the extensive Wisden family was first recorded as living in the street in a directory for 1822, when they are listed as living at No. 2 (with a note that it is on the west side). The family later moved across the street to No. 26 and rate books from the 1830s show William Wisden (variously listed as either carpenter or builder) being levied

23

a rate of £2-10-0 on this house but £3-0-0 on No 25 which also had 'a yard'. In other directories 25 Crown Street was given as the works/business address of William Wisden (either carpenter or joiner or builder). Originally Crown Street was developed as two short, parallel and facing rows of houses, open at the top end to fields, with the downs behind them. Later the top was closed off with further building and in the subsequent, necessary, renumbering Nos 25 & 26 became Nos 31 & 32.[1]

In April 1820 William Wisden married Mary Bowchert at St Nicholas's Church, Brighton. When John was born on 5th September 1826 he joined a rapidly growing family comprising older brothers William (junior, born 1820), George (b 1821), Simon (b 1822) and sisters Rosetta (b 1824) and Mary Ann (b 1825). Sadly Simon died that year and Mary Ann died the following year. There was now a pause in new arrivals until the twins Simon Edwin and Mary Louisa were born in the spring of 1830. Each of the twins was given the name of one of the children who had died in infancy, but they became generally known as Edwin and Louisa. Later they were to be joined by Johanna Pechell (b 1833) and Eliza Ann (b 1835).

JW was fortunate in his time and place of birth. In the 1820s and 1830s Brighton was a fashionable, prosperous and rapidly expanding town, providing much work and a steady income for the many branches of the extensive Wisden family, all greatly involved in building and development.

Of a similar age to JW were the three sons of William Lillywhite who were to make their mark in the world of professional cricket. John Lillywhite, the best player amongst the brothers, was born just a couple of months after JW, in November 1826. James was one year older, while Frederick was born in 1829. Little is known of JW's earliest years but clearly the cricket taking place 'just up the road' at William Lillywhite's Montpelier ground was a great attraction.

In his tribute to JW published in *Bell's Life* on 14th June 1884, Charles Francis Trower recalled:

> Anyhow he was a native of Brighton, and my first personal recollections of him were on Old Lillywhite's cricket ground, then on the site now covered by the upper portion of Montpellier-terrace, when I was doomed as a schoolboy

[1] The houses in Crown Street are numbered in a single sequence, not with an odd side and an even side. No. 1 was at the southern end of the west side and the numbering then progressed up the west side, across the northern top and down east side. The highest number was 34.

to pass part of my Midsummer holidays in Brighton, and fled for occupation and amusement to that beautifully-kept greensward, fed down by the bite of a few sheep and deer, and in which, for the moderate sum of 5s per season, one had the privilege of having one's middle stump upset by the first bowler of the age. Wisden, then a little boy of slim and slight proportions, was one's long-stop, glad to pick up an honest 6d and, silently, no doubt, taking in what he saw and learned from the great master of attack. Occasionally even then he would "send up" a good round hand ball himself (but was not yet strong enough to keep it up) in a style which foreshadowed his future greatness in the line.[2]

It seems reasonable to imagine that James, John and Fred Lillywhite might also have been there, helping their father with his coaching classes, and the well-known 'Lillywhite at Home' engraving would seem to show father bowling to a son on the grass outside the family home in an area now occupied in part by Wilbury Road. Who else might have been there? Brother George Wisden certainly became an able cricketer, reaching a standard that might in today's terms be described as 'good club'. In the 1850s he made repeated appearances in the cricket columns of *Bell's Life*, playing for various London-based clubs. The Lillywhite cricket ground was just a short walk from the Crown Street home.

There were clearly some cricketing genes in the Wisden family. As well at JW and brother George, one William Wisden appeared in a team of five local cricketers to take on the mighty William Lillywhite in a single-wicket match in October 1832. William Wisden is recorded as dismissing the 'Nonpareil' for low scores in each of two innings helping the local five to win the contest. When Lillywhite suggested 'best of five' with adjusted playing conditions William was reported to have said 'No Thanks!'. Other information confirms this William to be JW's father. In 1795 a Brighton cricket team to play rivals Lewes had included a Simon Wisden – perhaps JW's grandfather.

Evidence from his later life would suggest that JW was astute and aware. He would have valued his own time and efforts and gladly accepted the sixpences as a fair reward. This, I suspect, is a more accurate portrayal

---

[2] Charles F Trower was a cricketer and a Sussex historian. This quote is an extract from an obituary for JW that he wrote. The full obituary can be found at Appendix E.

of the situation than the 'hungry looking lad grateful for a sixpenneth of coppers' style of comment found elsewhere. He would have 'watched and learned' about bowling, but also watched the Nonpareil's coaching style. Before becoming commercially successful, JW was also a successful, well-respected and highly effective cricket coach.

Although they would not have realised it at the time, the association of JW with the four cricketing Lillywhites was to last for the rest of their lives, firstly in the playing, reporting and recording of the game and then as cricket outfitters and equipment suppliers. Also, they all took on administrative roles as the professional player became an increasing influence on the development of the game.

Later achievements would suggest that JW was developing more than just his cricketing skills. In an age before formal schooling was the norm we can assume that he was picking up skills and knowledge at home. With the centre of his father's expanding and successful business housed next to his home JW had the opportunity to learn from watching and helping his parents. This was in effect an apprenticeship in business management.

During the 1830s, as his status grew, William became increasingly active in civic affairs and became an associate of Capt. George Pechell the local MP. William appears to have named one of his youngest daughters, Johanna Pechell, after the politician in 1833.

It was in November 1837 that JW first experienced formal schooling, joining Middle Street School along with his younger brother Edwin. Middle Street School had been extended that year and it may be that

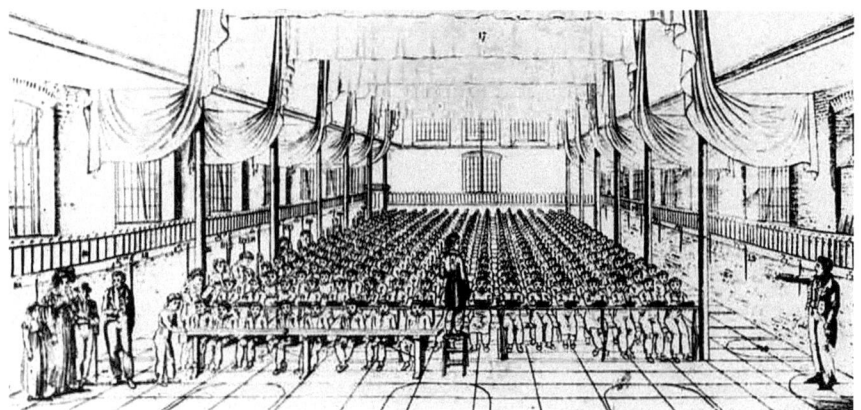

A view inside the Middle Street School classroom. The figures near the walls are the older boys awaiting their turn to pass the lesson on to the younger ones. High windows and all facing front to deter dreaming and to aid concentration.

brothers John and Edwin were able to take up two of the newly created places. JW had already had his eleventh birthday by the time that he started school which was old in an age when few boys stayed at school beyond the age of twelve. The school was supported by donations and sponsorship from churches and chapels within the town. JW was assigned one of the places allocated to The Countess of Huntingdon Chapel.

At this time the school operated in accordance with the Lancaster model of teaching. By this method initially the older boys were instructed by the master on the day's teaching and they then repeated the lesson to other boys arranged in groups by academic progress rather than age. At this time education was generally organised on a single sex basis. JW's entry groupings are recorded in the school log; standard 6 for reading and standard 4 for arithmetic. No record seems to have survived to indicate when he left school. However, his entry groupings and his subsequent success in business and administrative life would confirm that he was both literate and numerate and probably had received some tuition at home before joining the school.

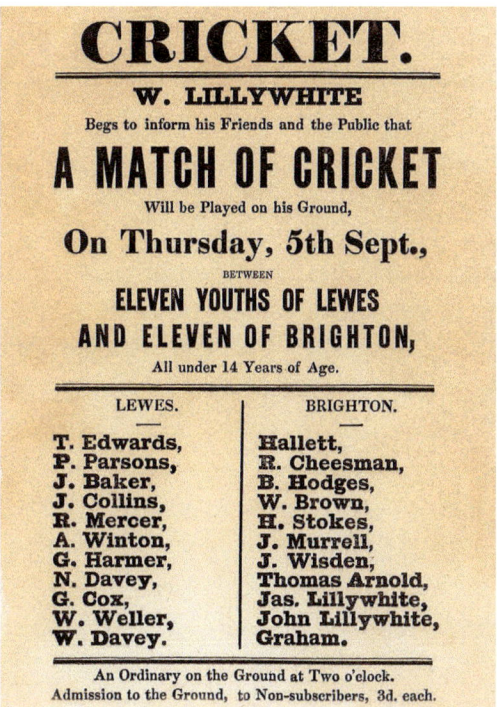

Window Bill 1839
The first public reference to JW as a cricketer. Brighton Boys were well beaten.

The school continues today, still on the same site at the corner of Middle Street and Boyce's Street – though in new buildings! It is a highly successful primary school with places much sought after amongst families from across the city.

In September 1840 JW turned 14 years old, an age when many boys would be starting their careers, possibly receiving their training as apprentices. Certainly this was the plan; in his will (1845) his father clearly stated that after his estate had been liquidated, monies were to be set aside to fund an apprenticeship for those of his sons who had not already received one. Trower said of JW:

> His father was, I believe, a carpenter in West-street, Brighton, and he himself was brought up to the trade.[3]

By this time his eldest brother William was already being listed in town directories as a carpenter and elder brother George was an apprentice at an international trading company in the City of London.

1840 was to be the start of a downhill phase for the family. On 11th October their mother Mary Wisden died. The cause of death was listed as 'consumption' so her passing may have been long anticipated.

The following summer the first ever National Census was conducted recording people in their location on the night of 6th June. William Wisden, the younger, was listed as living with his wife and child in Dean Street, Brighton and brother George was listed in his City of London hostel with myriad other young people. William Wisden, senior, was listed as the head of the household at 32 Crown Street, followed by Rosetta, now aged 17, and probably running the household. She was followed by Mary Anne Louisa, Edwin Simon, Johanna Pechell and Eliza Ann. At this time there was a lack of rigour in the recording of names. Mary Anne Louisa was often recorded as Mary Louisa or just plain Louisa. In his father's will Edwin was listed as Edward Simon. All the family are accounted for in the census except John. One possibility is that in this first ever census he is inaccurately recorded elsewhere, possibly living in the household of his apprentice master.

The census only just caught the family in their Crown Street home. The *Brighton Gazette* of 18th March 1841 indicates that the family were preparing to move home. The layout of the property can be seen from the following announcement:

---

[3] We must assume that a combination of carpentry and cricket left little time for the collection and washing of beer glasses.

```
┌──────────────────────────────────────────────────────┐
│                   Sales by Auction                     │
│                      BRIGHTON                          │
│            A DESIRABLE FREEHOLD PROPERTY               │
│                    BY MR RIDLEY                         │
│                                                        │
│  Without reserve, at the Clarence Hotel, North Street, │
│  on Friday, April 2, 1841, at one for two in the       │
│  afternoon, in one lot, by order of the Mortgagee      │
│  under a power of sale, consisting of                  │
│                                                        │
│  A NEAT DWELLING HOUSE, with four chambers, parlour,   │
│  kitchen, scullery, engine pump, etc. and a most       │
│  convenient Carpenters' Yard, workshops, deal shed and │
│  sawpit adjoining, being No. 32 Crown Street, Western  │
│  Road, and now in the occupation of Mr William Wisden, │
│  the Mortgager.                                        │
│                                                        │
│  Particulars and conditions of sale may be obtained    │
│  seven days prior to the auction of Messrs Colbatch,   │
│  Upperton and Co. Old Steyne, or of the Auctioneer,    │
│  Mr Ridley, 155 North Street, Brighton                 │
└──────────────────────────────────────────────────────┘
```

Number 31, essentially the headquarters of the building operation, may well have provided additional sleeping accommodation on the upper floor. Having his father's business run from next door to his home may well have facilitated JW's early business education. By 1845 *Kelly's Directory* lists 32 Crown Street as the home of John Southon a dairyman. There is no listing for No 31 but No 30 is occupied by Thomas Patchin described as 'plumber, glazier and painter'. At this time the street seems to have had a fairly high concentration of residents working in house maintenance. In the 1848 edition of *Folthorp's Directory* No 30 Crown Street is occupied by Churchman Field who is listed as carpenter & joiner. Other evidence suggests that Field was more than just a carpenter and joiner, at one time he is listed as owning some of the land on which Crown Street was built. By this time builder and surveyor might be a better description for him. No 31 is noticeably missing from this listing of occupants so it may be that it was again being used as the base of a building operation, this time managed by Field.

On 12th December 1842 the family suffered another bereavement, this time grandfather Simon, essentially the founder of the now extensive and prospering family. He was 77 years old. His will illustrates his success as builder, property developer and businessman, listing the distribution of his 20 plus properties and businesses to be shared between his nine surviving children. Some of these houses would be in the million pound range in today's market. JW's father, William, was assigned the properties 81, 82 & 83 North Street. Today, these buildings remain shops and feature the recently established Metro Bank.

The will also illustrates the support the collective family had given to individual members facing difficulty. Some years previously Simon's son Joseph had been declared bankrupt. His father had provided £750 to discharge his bankruptcy, this being seen as an advance of his inheritance. Joseph was assigned three houses with the proviso that he firstly repaid the cash loan, which was viewed as a form of mortgage.

Many of the properties listed had sitting tenants and it would appear that in his later years Simon had not been too diligent in collecting the rents. Many of the tenants were in arrears, some of them having not paid for nearly two years. JW's father, William, was chosen to undertake the task of bringing some order to the estate. He began by bringing the collection of rents up to date and his notebook recording the arrears and payments survives today. The National Archives retains a (copy) hand written notice to quit issued to one tenant. The estate was of such value that the resolution of the will rumbled on through the courts for more than 15 years. The choice of William from amongst Simon's many sons to bring some commercial order to this estate gives a clue as where the young JW might have gained his business skills.

A young JW would have noted the benefits of a self-supporting and business-wise family from the help given to Joseph and also his father's diligent approach to administering business affairs. Although, even at his death, William was described as a carpenter, he was now much more, moving to become a builder and a property developer. In both roles he needed to be a businessman with attributes and skills that he seems to have passed on to at least one of his sons.

Sometime towards the end of 1842, the remaining members of the household moved out of Crown Street and into 2 Suffolk Place.[4] There may have been a couple of reasons for this move. William had moved on from being simply a carpenter. In his book on the development of the estates to the north of Crown Street, Steve Myall makes mention of William Wisden being involved in the buying and selling of land for development purposes. This would make him more of a businessman and less of a craftsman. Part of the value of the Crown Street home was having the builder's yard next door. With little or no need now to

[4] Suffolk Place is now 'under' Churchill Square.

live beside the yard, and with a reducing number of children to house, the move made good sense. The residents of Crown Street had always included a strong representation of building trade craftsmen and others soon moved in to make good use of the facilities.

The family did not stay long in Suffolk Place. In March 1847 William died in the Brighton Workhouse. This seems an unlikely place for such a successful businessman to spend his final days but, like his wife, he died of phthisis/consumption/tuberculosis and it would seem likely that he may have used the workhouse for palliative care, the sort of support that today would be sought from a hospice. William was clearly not destitute. His will, made two years earlier, gave clear instructions as to the administration of his estate and his two eldest sons, William (jnr) and George, were charged with the task. Firstly they were to liquidate the fixed assets. After calling in all of his dues they were to use the cash to pay off his debts and make provision to fund apprenticeships for any of his children who had not yet embarked on one. After this the remaining cash was to be divided equally amongst his carefully-listed surviving children.

By the time of the 1851 census the family seems to have dispersed. William (jnr) had his own young family settled in Brighton. Both George and Johanna are recorded as being in central London and JW is recorded as a 'Creeketer' in a lodging house just off Bath Street in Leamington Priors (now Spa). Younger brother Edwin is listed as a carpenter boarding in a house in Crown Gardens in Brighton.

When JW actually received the funds from his father's estate is unclear. Part of the assets that were to be sold were the properties left to William in grandfather Simon's will. However, Simon's will was the subject of repeated challenges in the High Court in London as late as 1857. It appears that JW had to wait for ten years after his father's death before all of his inheritance was realised.

There are very few surviving negative comments about JW. One of them, though, was a gripe by Fred Lillywhite in the later 1850s, about JW being 'given' his business whereas others, presumably including Fred, had to work for theirs.

3

THE YOUNG CRICKETER

JW's cricketing deeds were first reported in the press when announcing his selection for Brighton Boys under 14 XI. This was in 1838 and he had not yet reached his 12th birthday. In the same side was an equally young John Lillywhite and his older brother James. Despite the inclusion of two future England cricketers the Brighton side suffered a heavy defeat at the hands of their Lewes opponents. The match was played on father Lillywhite's Montpelier ground.

JW next came to the notice of the newspaper readership of Brighton when he appeared for Brighton Juniors in 1840 and 1841. In 1844, the year of his 18th birthday, he frequently turned out in club matches within the town. In general, at this time, he was more successful as a bowler than as a batsman; in most innings he batted at either No 10 or No 11. This makes it difficult to assess the true impact that he was having in matches. Scorecards were limited by 21st century standards. Batsmen had their run totals and modes of dismissal recorded but bowlers' achievements were only recorded when an opponent was dismissed 'bowled'.

JW played for the Brighton Clarence club during the 1844 season and in a match with Hurstpierpoint he achieved easily his highest score of the season when he was 55* in the second innings. From the Clarence club he went on to play for a representative Brighton team having earlier in July played in a Juniors v Seniors preparatory match making the town team to play Lewes later in the month. At the end of August he again played for Brighton, this time against Henfield. In all of these matches he must have bowled several overs and was usually recorded as having dismissed (bowled) two or three batsmen.

Whatever his match figures he must have created a good impression because he was selected for the East Sussex side that for 16th & 17th September travelled to Shillinglee[5], near Chiddingfold, to play against West Sussex. This might be viewed as his break-through match. Batting

---

[5] Shillinglee House and estate was an important cricket venue during the 19th century. In 1908 it became the summer residence of Ranjitsinhji in a season when he was playing cricket for Sussex. Further information can be found in Chris Arnot's book *Britain's Lost Cricket Grounds*.

at No 11 he scored a useful 13 and then took six wickets in West Sussex's first innings. Ten days later he was a member of the Sussex Players team to play the county's Gentlemen. The Players had the better of the unfinished match with *Scores & Biographies* reporting that JW 'was too unwell to bowl'. That was his last recorded match for the season.

JW's first recorded match for 1845 was when he was a member of the Brighton side to visit Henfield for a match on 9th and 10th June. Although he got a duck in the first innings he scored a useful 17 in Brighton's second innings. The bowling figures for the match are virtually non-existent but do record that JW took one of the only two wickets that fell in Henfield's second innings as the hosts scored the required 20 runs for an easy win. At the end of the scheduled match a three-a-side single-wicket match was arranged. JW was not selected for either side; he was not yet a first pick in contests such as these. His next match was the return when Henfield came to play on the ground variously described as Royal New Ground and Tom Box's Ground; Box had recently taken over the running of the ground. Again bowling figures were incomplete but they do record that JW took four wickets in the first Henfield innings and three in the second. He scored 33 in Brighton's first innings but was not required to bat in the second as his team turned the tables on Henfield and won by seven wickets.

The following day the MCC brought a team down to Box's ground for a match with 17th Lancers. Possibly because they were readily available JW and Tom Box were given men for the Lancers' team. Sadly bad weather meant that little of the match was played thus denying JW a further chance to show his developing talents. His pleasant demeanour made him a popular choice over the years as a given player in these high-social status matches. In coming seasons he would go on to play for Eton College, Cambridge University and even for the House of Commons.

A week after the Lancers' match he made his 'first-class'[6] debut when he was in the Sussex team to play Kent, again on Tom Box's ground. His match figures of 6/46 and 3/59 show that he played a crucial role in setting up a three wickets win for Sussex. Slightly surprisingly he opened the batting in Sussex's first innings, scoring just four runs, but did not bat in the second. The match began with JW bowling with James ('Jemmy') Dean. In future years they were to form a strong partnership both on and off the field – and not just at cricket.

---

[6] 'First-class' first appears as a universal classification in the 1850s.

Also in the Sussex team, and also having a good match, was George Picknell. Picknell came from a family of cricketing-farmers with a base in Chalvington, a village a few miles to the east of Lewes. JW must have impressed George because the following week he was invited to be a given man for the village team in their match against East Sussex. He was in good company as Tom Box, Alfred Mynn and William Hillyer were amongst the other given men on either side. Chalvington were well beaten totalling only 60 and 68 in their two innings, leaving East Sussex to score just 10 in their second innings to win the match by seven wickets. JW took two of the three wickets to fall in that innings having taken five in the first innings. He scored only four and nine in his two innings but with his wickets in this company he was making his mark as a coming player. George Picknell would later join JW as a founder member of the United England Eleven.

Tom Box was a well-established figure in Sussex cricket when JW began to play. He was supportive of JW during his early career and many years later ran the Bear Inn just around the corner from JW's Cranbourn Street shop.

In mid-September a Gentlemen v Players match was staged on Box's ground and when Dorrinton pulled out of the Players' XI on the morning of the match, JW was drafted in. However, when the Players had reached 119-3 rain stopped play. Further rain meant that the game never re-started so JW did not get a chance to either bat or bowl.

In the later years of the 1840s William Lillywhite travelled to Cambridge University early each spring to help the students get their cricket season underway. In 1846 he took his two sons, James and John, as well as JW with him. The young men joined in some of the early season preparatory games and assisted with the practice bowling and the coaching. It would seem that they also watched and learned when the Master, the Nonpareil, was coaching. In just a few years time all four of them would hold coaching posts at one or other of England's leading public schools.

JW's time at Cambridge gave him the opportunity to play in a number of matches. The first of these was on 7th May when he turned out in Pell's XII to play Gruggen's XII. This was part of a sequence of matches to launch the Earl of Stamford's new private ground. The next match to involve JW was when the Earl of Stamford and Lord Burghley jointly raised a side to play I Zingari in a one-day match. JW took a single wicket and was left undefeated on 19 when William Lillywhite was run out for a duck to bring their lordships' innings to a close.

Three days later JW played for Earl of Stamford's Club in a match against Haileybury College and then at the end of the month he played for a team raised by Lord Burghley to play the same college. In all of these matches he had moderate success and as well as enhancing his coaching skills it was valuable preparation for the coming season. At the same time he would be developing his personal contacts. Back in Brighton the gentlemen who followed the fortunes of the Sussex team were hoping that all was well at Cambridge. Clearly great hopes were now attached to JW so to allay their fears William Lillywhite had the following letter published in the *Brighton Gazette* of 14th May 1846:

TO THE EDITOR OF THE BRIGHTON GAZETTE

Sir, – You may inform the Sussex Gentlemen that young Wisden is a first rate bowler; I have had him under my eye ever since he has been here, and have got him to bowl in accordance with the new law, not getting his arm too high. He lives with me, is very steady, and highly respected by the gentlemen here.

I am yours, etc.,

Cambridge, May 11. W. LILLYWHITE

By June JW had returned to Brighton but his cricket continued to be for teams of higher social status. On 17th June he turned out for the 12th Lancers in their fixture with I Zingari. He took four wickets and scored 11 runs towards a Lancers' total of 110. Three days later he was the given man for Cambridge University when they visited Eton College. He had a good match, making the top score in each innings (16 & 19) and then taking 7 wickets in one innings and 2 in the other as the university team won by 43 runs.

It was in June 1846 that JW can be said to have become established onto the county cricket scene. On 29th he made his first appearance at Lord's being a member of the Sussex team playing MCC. Once again batting at No 11 JW made just 4* and 5 but took four wickets in the first innings and two in the second. Set 277 to win MCC were reduced to 49 for 8 at the end of day two, at which point they conceded defeat. The Sussex players then travelled back to Brighton to face Kent. JW took only three wickets and scored just 12 runs as Kent won by a massive 144 runs. When this match finished early a single-wicket match was 'got up' on the third day. JW and Edmund Sopp from Sussex were selected to take on Martin and Hinkly from Kent. JW was in the process of developing skills which led to him being recognised as the unofficial single-wicket champion of England. Kent batted first and after 96 balls were dismissed for 12. JW batted first for Sussex and by eight o'clock he had faced 280 deliveries and was 34*. At this point the match ended and Sussex were declared the winners. JW had won £5, a useful amount for a young player. In two or three years' time JW's skill and reputation at single-wicket cricket became a problem for him.

At the end of July Sussex travelled to Tunbridge Wells for the return match with Kent. Kent won again but this time Sussex made a better fight of it going down by 59 runs. JW was still last man in and scored 4 and 6 in the two Sussex innings. However, his bowling achievements in the two Kent innings are less clear. The scorecard in *Scores & Biographies* shows him taking three wickets in Kent's first innings and five in the second. However, a footnote to the scorecard notes that in a Maidstone newspaper he is credited with two more wickets in each innings. The *S&B* scorecard gives no bowling figures which is still quite usual. The game was still controlled by the amateur gentlemen who were predominantly interested in batting with the bowling done by the professionals simply being there to facilitate the batting. In coming years JW would be greatly involved in efforts to address this shortcoming.

After a day's rest JW moved to Canterbury to again play against the powerful Kent side, this time for an MCC-selected England – his first appearance for them. He was promoted to No 10 in the batting order but possibly only because William Lillywhite was settled in at No 11. He was, though, part of an impressive England bowling quartet: William Lillywhite, William Clarke, James Dean and himself. For once JW's full bowling figures were recorded – in today's style they would be 24-9-30-4. Because England batted so poorly (totals of 49 and 42) Kent did not need a second innings.

There now followed two matches for Sussex. JW opened the batting in the first one against MCC, but was run out for 2. Run-outs were to become an increasingly frequent occurrence while he was batting. Despite eight wickets from JW, MCC won by 21 runs. A week later England were the visitors to Brighton. Their side was strong enough to have George Parr batting at No 9. Parr was to be one of JW's victims as he took 4/39 from 30 overs. Sussex followed their innings 106 runs behind but a more determined effort in their second innings saw them bat out a draw with an innings of 162, in which JW was top scorer with 40. This was his first big score in a county level match.

JW completed the season by umpiring at Lewes in the Priory Club v East Sussex match on 27th and 28th August. This brought to a close a highly successful, introductory season; JW was now on the radar of the people who mattered. Three days later William Clarke's newly created All England Eleven played their first match at Sheffield and what would become an important new aspect of JW's career was being launched.

Before the 1847 season was underway JW suffered a bereavement. On 17th March, his father died in the Brighton Workhouse. By this time William was already a widower and many of his children were grown-up. His death seems to have precipitated the final dispersal of his family and so JW no longer had a family base in Brighton. By the time of the 1851 census there is no evidence of a family home.

In April 1847 JW, together with the three Lillywhites, was back at Cambridge helping the University cricketers prepare for another season. As ever, JW 'got fully involved' in the preparation, for instance by joining William Lillywhite and the 'Next Nine' to make a side to take on the University team in a three day match at the end of the month. At the end of May he and John Lillywhite were in McNiven's side that defeated Fitzwilliam's side which included James Lillywhite.

By the beginning of June JW was back in Sussex playing in local matches. He turned out for Brighton in matches with Sompting and Henfield and took just a few wickets in each. However, these matches gave him an opportunity to develop his batting. In each match he batted in the middle order and scored 91 in his only innings in the first match and 62 and 10 in the other. One of the consequences appears to be promotion within the county team's batting order. Having scored 4 and 0 batting at No 10 in the first county match, he again batted at No 10 in the second fixture but made 17* and, promoted to open, 28. In the third county match he went in at No 3 and made 29 and 4. In the first of these county matches Sussex had a convincing 108 run win over MCC, JW taking 9 wickets in the match. The latter two matches were both against the very powerful Kent team. In the first of these he had figures of 56-?-95-4 in Kent's only innings. In the return fixture he took at least 3 wickets in each innings.

Within days JW lined up against Kent again, this time for an MCC-selected England side. Despite having a bowling attack in which JW joined William Lillywhite, William Clarke and James Dean England lost to Kent by 3 wickets. JW acquitted himself well, taking four wickets in each innings, although he was back to batting at No 10! But a week later he played for Sussex in the return match with MCC and batted at No 3. In his only innings he made 12 before he was run out. With bowling figures of 23-?-36-4 and 23-?-28-5 he made a major contribution to Sussex's win by an innings. Conceding only a little over one run per over he was beginning to show one of his key attributes as a bowler.

JW spent August 1847 playing in a series of local games: for Wiston v I Zingari (9 wickets in the match), Gentlemen of Petworth v Players of Sussex (12 wickets in the match) and then Brighton versus Henfield.

Early in September a significant development took place when JW made his first appearance in one of the peripatetic elevens. He travelled to Leeds to play for All England Eleven in a match against Sixteen of Yorkshire (reduced from the Eighteen of the previous year – William Clarke was always eager to avoid defeat). A team containing nine professionals would always be strong in bowling and JW took a single wicket in the first innings as Clarke and Martingell bowled out the Yorkshire side. He batted at No 4 and after the first three batsmen had made just five between them his 45 led the recovery and was the top score of the match. His four wickets in the second innings included that of

George Armitage, whom he later asked to join George Parr and himself at Leamington. AEE were set just 31 to win which they achieved for the loss of two wickets.

Returning to Brighton JW accepted a challenge from Thomas Sherman to a single-wicket match for £20 a side. This he won convincingly by an innings and 12 runs. A collection was made on the ground to fund a second match and JW won this one too although by a much smaller margin.

1847 was to see the last match played on what was at that time called Tom Box's Ground. The site had a long history as a cricket venue but was now to be taken for house building. To mark this end a special match was staged at the end of September between Sussex with the addition of Alfred Mynn and England. JW's improved form with the bat had clearly been noted and he batted at No 3. His first innings 49 turned out to be the highest score of the match which was played over four days, with Sussex winning by 27 runs.

JW's reputation was spreading and he was becoming much in demand. Late in the season he played for Portsmouth in a pair of matches against a Hampshire team. In the first of them, played at Southampton on 20th & 21st September, he took seven wickets but scored no runs in a match dominated by Thomas Adams; Portsmouth won by 10 wickets. The return match was staged at Southsea on 4th & 5th October. This time Portsmouth won by an innings and 65 runs. Adams was again dominant and JW collected six wickets and 16 runs. *Scores & Biographies* added the caveat 'so called' to the name Hampshire.

In between the two matches for Portsmouth JW travelled to Mitcham, Thomas Sherman's home town, to play yet another single-wicket match. JW won again. The published scores so closely matched those of the second of the Brighton encounters, that *Scores & Biographies* saw fit to wonder at their authenticity.

By the end of 1847 JW was recognised as an established county cricketer. His improved batting performances meant that he was now regarded as a genuine all-rounder.

In the spring of 1848 the quartet from Brighton once again made their way north to assist the students of Cambridge, but now changes were in hand. At the instigation of Lords Burghley and Stamford, Francis Fenner had created a new ground in the town – away from the rowdy clamour that had become Parker's Piece. The new ground had been used for a couple of private matches during the two previous years (JW had played against a Lord Stamford XI), but this May there was to be the formal opening of the ground. One of the events to mark the opening was a single-wicket match between John Wisden's team and OC Pell's team. The two Lillywhite brothers joined JW in his side while Pell's side included Guy and Diver. JW's side batted first and scored a creditable 24, of which John Lillywhite contributed half. Pell's side were then reduced to the unusual achievement of all five of them being dismissed 'b. Wisden 0'. This was the first instance of JW's ability to 'wipe-out' an opposition, an ability he was to display at intervals over the coming years.

At the end of the month JW further emphasised his status as 'Best in the Land' at single-wicket when he took all of the wickets, bowled, as he and Guy beat Arnold and Cornell by an innings. In 1846 Felix had played Mynn in a match at Lord's to determine the Single-Wicket Champion of England. Although he had not engaged in any such match there was little doubt that JW was now assuming that crown.

It was not until near the end of June 1848 that JW began his county cricket programme for the year. His first match was for MCC v Sussex at Lord's where he scored 0 and 24 and also took four wickets in each innings. A noteworthy event at this match was the first appearance of Fred Lillywhite's tent, housing his printing press that was being used to produce up-to-the-moment scorecards.

During July 1848 JW had markedly more success in bowling than batting. Playing for an England side that beat Kent by 55 runs he scored only 5 runs in two innings but took 12 wickets in the match as part of an England attack that again included the strong combination of William Clarke, William Lillywhite and James Dean. Two days later he was in the Sussex team that had a fixture with Nottinghamshire for the first time in five years. The match was played at the new Gausden's Ground, Hove, the successor to Box's Hanover Ground which had been in Brighton. JW contributed just 12 runs to Sussex's then massive total of 243 but he then took 14 wickets as Sussex won by an innings and 32 runs. The wickets continued to fall to him; when Sussex beat Kent at Tunbridge Wells by one wicket he took 11 of the Kent wickets. He also scored a valuable 16* to see Sussex home in a tight match. In the return match at Hove he took 15 wickets, 12 of which were dismissed bowled – a testimony to his accuracy. Once again frustration is expressed by *Scores & Biographies* at the lack of bowling figures. JW was steadily increasing his importance as a player in the Sussex team.

JW first met James ('Jemmy') Dean on the cricket field in September, 1844 when they were on opposing sides in the West Sussex v East Sussex match. They were to become team-mates, colleagues, business associates and the firmest of friends up until the very day that James died – Christmas Day, 1881.

In the Gentlemen v Players match at Lord's at the end of July, JW batted at No 7 and made acceptable scores of 12 and 10 but surprisingly went wicketless in each innings as the Players suffered a rare defeat by 27 runs in a low-scoring match.

In 1848 JW was 'engaged at the Auberies' to use a 19th century expression or contracted to Captain C Alexander to use more modern phraseology. The Captain was unusual as a patron in that he saw himself as a bowler rather than a batsman, often batting at No 11 in his own side. During July and August JW interspersed his county matches with six two-day matches for The Auberies, based on Alexander's Suffolk estate and was on the winning side every time. He took at least 10 wickets in four of the matches and seven in each of the other two. His 55 wickets in the six matches showed that he gave good value for his employment. He usually opened the batting but with only moderate success. However, the opportunities to develop this aspect of his game, against good sides, would have been valuable. The batting performances confirmed that there was still scope for improvement. Playing in these matches JW met a number of influential people, including two of the Grimston brothers and Fred Ponsonby. He was steadily building up a network of useful contacts. Before he left East Anglia JW helped Norfolk beat MCC by taking 14 wickets.

After his successful year at the Auberies, JW recommended to Captain Alexander that William Caffyn be engaged for 1849. Caffyn was struggling to establish a career as a professional cricketer in the face of opposition from his family. This is an early example of JW acting in the role of player's agent, a role he was to develop in the next decade.

By 1848 the AEE fixtures were no longer restricted to their original slot within the final two months of the season but had now moved to the middle of the season. In mid-June JW spent a week in the Midlands playing in two AEE matches. In a low-scoring match he and William Clarke bowled out Twenty-Ttwo of Birmingham for 64 and 80 to set up a six wickets win. For the second half of the week the party moved to Powick Ham, which lies on the road between Worcester and Malvern. In this match JW and William Hillyer opened the batting (scoring just 12 between them across two innings) but then bowled out Worcestershire twice for AEE to win by 123 runs. This match was part of the formation of the Gentlemen of Worcestershire side that year[7] and from there a Worcestershire county team. These two AEE matches fitted into a single week during which JW took 40 wickets.

The week beginning Monday 18th September was to highlight some of the emerging issues generated by the expanding AEE match programme. The Sussex team travelled to Nottingham to play the return fixture against the county team. Batting at No 3, JW made only 3 out of a total of 181 but then took four wickets as Notts were bowled out for 134. In the Sussex second innings JW made 92 out of 243-9, at which point time ran out leaving the match a draw. While Tom Box, James Dean and JW all played for Sussex, William Clarke, George Parr and Joseph Guy were missing from the Nottingham side because they were playing for AEE in Leeds.

Scores & Biographies suggests that the Leeds XX would have been better titled 'Yorkshire'. Determined to put up a good show against the travelling eleven, town-based teams were increasingly drawing players from an ever wider area in a process that would reach its culmination in the formation of county cricket clubs some fifteen years later. Leeds won the match by 14 wickets having achieved a first innings lead and been set only 60 to win. The division of playing resources had weakened both

---

[7] See *Gentlemen, Gypsies and Jesters*, p. 26ff.

AEE and Nottinghamshire. There was already mounting comment in the press asking for official county matches to be allowed to be played without competition for players from the fixtures of the travelling eleven.

After the match in Nottingham JW returned to Sussex to play for Brighton in their return fixture with Mitcham; he had played in the original (where he took 12 wickets), and now took nine wickets in a one wicket win. Meanwhile Tom Box made his way to Leamington to re-join the AEE party. Hopefully he had an easier journey than the rest of the group.

Much is made of the fact that the rapidly expanding network of railways made it possible for cricket clubs and teams to expand the geographical range of their fixture lists. The horror story mail coach rides recorded in various autobiographies were supposed to be a thing of the past. Sadly, it was not quite as simple as that. The opening sentences of the *Bell's Life* report on the match 'Twenty-two of Leamington v Eleven of All England' reads:

> From Leeds the Eleven of England proceeded by the mail train, at eight o'clock, which, on its arrival at Claycross tunnel, was stopped by the engine breaking down, so that they had a two hours' sojourn in the cutting there. The train did not reach Derby till after one, and Rugby, where they were to sleep, about three; and though it was nearly four before they got to roost, they had to leave by the 8.15 train for Leamington. … play commenced at half-past twelve.

I suspect that Tom Box arrived in Leamington more rested than others in the AEE group.

Around this time and in ensuing years there was a rising number of complaints about late starts and early finishes. While Sunday could be used for the week-end move from one fixture to the next the mid-week move was more demanding, and many nights and early mornings like the journey to Leamington soon had a cumulative effect. By 1851 JW was playing almost all week, every week for six months. It was all to become too great a workload.

Two initiatives that JW introduced when he later led the United England Eleven was to plan the team's programme around the first-class programme and to promise that for all matches the UEE would be on the ground ready to play by 11am (weather permitting).

John Corbet Anderson's oft displayed portrait of JW casts him in a fresh-faced almost 'boyish' pose; the young player bursting upon the cricket scene. This may account for the 'little' in his nickname (The Little Wonder); in height terms JW was barely an inch shorter than many of his contemporaries.

Late in September JW completed his programme for AEE with matches for Essex against AEE and for AEE against Hampshire. His performances across the two matches were modest. Even though it had now become October JW made his way to Sheffield to play in a benefit match for the Yorkshire professional Emanuel Vincent. He joined Joseph Guy and George Parr as given men for the Gentlemen of Sheffield who were to play the Players of Sheffield. He did not score many runs but he did take six wickets and hold two catches in the Players' only innings. Not surprisingly for the time of year the weather prevented the Players having their second innings and the game ended in a draw.

1848 had been a good season for JW. Still only 22 years old, he had established himself as a leading player not only in Sussex but across the country. He was about to embark upon further ventures.

4

MESSRS PARR & WISDEN'S GROUND AT LEAMINGTON

The report in *Bell's Life* of the 1848 match Twenty-two of Leamington and District versus Eleven of All England was almost certainly written by Fred Lillywhite. He was a correspondent for the paper, he was known to have been at the match – he paid a local boy sixpence to collect up the spilled type on the floor of the tent – and it showed his acerbic style. After having carefully set out the difficulties that the Eleven had experienced travelling from Leeds to Leamington (not yet commonly 'Spa'), he continued:

> If the ground at Darlington was bad, it was beautiful compared with Leamington, for it consisted of a few yards of mown and rolled ground, in the midst of a ridge and furrow field; the furrows being untouched, and all around long grass.

This was hardly surprising given that in the recent past the space had been part of a market garden. However, this assessment would not have been welcomed by the worthies of the town. Leamington was going through something of an identity crisis; developing a cricket centre was seen as an element of re-branding. Since the beginning of the century it had experienced rapid expansion with fashionable gentlefolk coming to the health spa to take the waters. This rapid expansion of the town had generated public health issues which would culminate in an outbreak of cholera at the end of the decade.

In terms of raising the profile of the sport the match met its objectives. *Bell's Life* commented:

> They however, could console themselves with the large and fashionable assemblage of spectators. The Twenty-two consisted twenty-one Gentlemen and one Player (Langley) from Birmingham given.

The twenty-one gentlemen displayed an impressive array of titles. The batting was opened by two 'Revs', Kittermaster and Brett. Three more

'Revs' were to follow and even though Edward Elmhirst was ordained he is listed as a mere 'Esq'. There were two 'Captains' and Hon Edward Chandos Leigh. Leigh was certainly a local man, hailing from Stoneleigh, but the same cannot be said for A Haygarth Esq who was very much a London man; born in Hastings, educated at Harrow, living in Pimlico and an habitué of Lord's.

Haygarth's presence at the game and that of so many other cricketing dignitaries probably showed the behind-the-scene hand of one notable absentee – Lord Heneage Guernsey. Guernsey was the son and heir of the major local landowner, the Earl of Aylesford. Guernsey was a good cricketer, in today's terms he would probably be a county second eleven player. He was to become both the town's Member of Parliament in 1850 and also President of MCC; he was an influential man who was to be a great friend to the project. The present Earl of Aylesford is the current President of Warwickshire County Cricket Club. As Lord Charles Guernsey he played for Leamington Cricket Club in the 1970s.

Help to improve the ground was soon at hand. In December 1848 both the local and the national press reported that George Parr had visited the town from his Radcliffe-on-Trent home to supervise the levelling of the site and its preparation as a cricket ground. Parr had spent several days in the town assessing a number of possible sites but eventually chose the one on which he had scored 41 runs for AEE in the match that had taken place during the previous September. *The Leamington Courier* reported:

> The field is the property of Matthew Wise, Esq., a gentleman who may be safely "booked" as a patron of all manly recreation – cricket among the number.

At this time Leamington was effectively divided into four zones by the River Leam flowing east-west and the principal thoroughfare running north-south. The Wise family lived in and owned much of the south-west quarter. Well financed, Matthew was anxious to save his land from the rapid housing developments that were covering the rest of the town. The outer boundary of this land was now the recently constructed track of the London & North Western Railway. He may well have seen the proposed cricket ground as affording some protection for the green space. This is largely still the case. Despite many and various plans over the years, just

Leamington in 1849, when JW came to the town

Key to places of note

🟢 *Parr & Wisden Ground*　🔴 *Leamington Tennis Court Club*　🔵 *Adelaide Road Bridge*

🟠 *Abbots Street Bakery*　🟣 *Mrs Williams' Lodging House*　🟤 *Railway Station*

two small streets of houses have been built and most of the space is given over to various forms of sport and recreation. The local public house is named *The Cricketers* and bears a claret coloured 'blue' plaque honouring John Wisden and his partnership with George Parr in the town.

JW had not played in the 1848 AEE match but in March 1849 he had formed a partnership with George Parr to open and operate the ground. Parr had been a core member of the AEE since its early days and JW met him when he began playing for that team towards the end of the 1848 season. On 8th April 1849 *Bell's Life* announced:

When the 'grand' matches began on the ground JW was there to take the lead. The first match took place on 3rd & 4th July and was labelled as Leamington v Worcestershire (Ombersley) Club. Parr did not play, though this may have been by agreement between the teams. Each side had two professionals and Leamington may have chosen to play JW and George Armitage as both were much needed bowlers. Leamington won by 5 wickets having been set just 21 to win largely thanks to JW's efforts. He was top scorer with 60 and took five wickets in the first innings and three in the second. Armitage took the rest of the wickets and scored 30 in his only knock. George Armitage, a Yorkshireman, had been hired by the partnership to be a professional bowler on the ground. He also acted as a professional at the Wellesbourne Club[8], a long established club a dozen miles to the south. Lord Guernsey was rewarded for his efforts in promoting the new ground with a good match. His scores of 14 and 10* were the highest for Leamington bar the professionals and *Bell's Life* reported 'both the batting and fielding of Lord Guernsey were regarded by all as first rate'. The paper also recorded his lordship as Lord Guernsey MP.

As well as being a capable cricketer Lord Guernsey was a local social and political leader. At the time that he was MCC President he was also the local MP. He provided great support to the Parr & Wisden Ground project.

[8] A Rugby School team travelling to play cricket against the Wellesbourne Club features in *Tom Brown's Schooldays*.

Worcestershire were one of the early counties to form 'Gentlemen of ...' teams which became the strongest side representative of their county. Ombersley seems to have been the base club for this initiative, so when JW took the Leamington side there at the end of the month for the return fixture and Leamington won by 82 runs, it was a good scalp. Again the two professionals led the way with JW scoring 30 and 24 and Armitage 38 and 9. JW took nine wickets in the hosts' first innings and five in the second with Armitage taking the rest.

While JW was with the Leamington team at Ombersley George Parr played for AEE in a match against Twenty of Leicestershire whose side included Lord Guernsey. Although Parr had been the one to initiate the project of developing the ground and teams to play on it, it was JW who throughout the partnership provided more of the day-to-day support.

During the following week the first of the important matches was played on the new Leamington ground when I Zingari brought a strong side to play 'Gentlemen of Warwickshire with Wisden and Palethorpe'. The home side included both Lord Guernsey and the young Edward Chandos Leigh whose homes provided accommodation for the visitors. In the way in which IZ match reports always did, *Bell's Life* also noted that Lord Guernsey's Offchurch home had once been a residence of King Offa of Mercia. Picking up the theme the report assigned to JW the 'Prime Ministership of Warwickshire' for his excellent bowling – he took seven wickets in IZ's first innings and six in the second. He could not, though, stop IZ from winning by a comfortable 62 runs in two days. The weather was excellent and the attendance good, especially amongst the fashionable set. Their support would be crucial as the project developed.

Given the steady decline in the competitiveness of the Gentlemen v Players fixtures, in terms of cricketing skill the annual North v South matches were the premier matches of the season. At this time one of the fixtures was normally played at Lord's and the second on a ground south of the Thames, so the staging of the second 1849 match on Parr & Wisden's Ground on 30th & 31st August was evidence of Lord Guernsey's commitment to bring big matches north to Leamington. In a low-scoring match (40 and 87 v 110 and 18-1) the North had a convincing victory and the proprietors had a successful match. George Parr's innings of 50 was easily the highest of the match and JW returned figures of 13-6-13-2 and 22.2-5-27-5 (full bowling figures in the scorecard suggests that Fred

Lillywhite attended the match). The home club was also represented by George Armitage who batted at No 11 (1*) and did not bowl and by Lord Guernsey who opened the North's second innings with Lord Burghley and scored 12* of the required 18 runs.

The last of the great matches at Leamington for 1849 was played on 10th and 11th September when AEE travelled from Manchester to play a match on the ground. The home team were described as 'Eighteen of Leamington & District' (a reduction of four in the odds compared to the first match). The *Scores & Biographies* scorecard notes that W Davis is of Hereford, but neither Arthur Haygarth nor Hon Robert Grimston could really be described as coming from either Leamington or District. It can only be assumed that Lord Guernsey had ensured a strong team was assembled to raise the prestige of the match. However, it was noted in the press that as this match followed so closely the North v South fixture, the attendance was low. The 'ground crew' had a good match. JW and Armitage bowled out AEE for just 69 in their first innings and then JW (52*) and George Parr (22) formed the core of the hosts' 152 in reply. Once again rain washed out the third day's play but this time it did AEE a favour as they were 31-3 in their second innings, still 52 runs behind. This match was to be the last one of the season for JW; he picked up an injury while batting; reportedly taking a blow to his side.

During the late 1840s Leamington's local press had been regularly making a case for a new cricket ground and club on the premise that it would raise the social status of the town. A leading social centre for the sportsmen of the town at this time was the Leamington Tennis Court Club. The club's new premises, part real tennis court, part gentlemen's club had been built in 1846. A leader in that project and of the club around this time was Lord Guernsey. Under his leadership LTCC became strong supporters of the new cricket ground and they held a dinner to celebrate its opening.

One small problem was that LTCC's premises were in Bedford Street, north of the river and the cricket ground off Adelaide Road was to the south of the river. The bridge across the river was in a poor state of repair and when the gentlemen travelled from club to ground for their practice sessions they faced a significant risk of getting wet. The newly formed cricket club wrote to the Town Commissioners[9] about this situation and the necessary repairs were quickly made. It was noted in the local press

[9] The commissioners were the forerunners of the town council.

that this work was more quickly completed than was usual. The Tennis Club and the Cricket Club were clearly closely associated in the minds of the general public. When the treasurer of the Cricket Club wrote to the commissioners about the weak bridge the reply was addressed to the Tennis Club.

The partners realised that the venture was not going to be financially viable solely from the high-status matches. They formed a subscription cricket club, with all kit and facilities provided, which made regular use of the ground. Other clubs both from within the town and further afield hired the ground to stage their major fixtures. This produced a coalescing focus for cricket and cricketers within the town. Pulling all the talent together meant that in 1850 a team simply titled Leamington was able to travel to Lord's and beat an MCC team on their home ground.[10]

The return Leamington v MCC match on 5th August was the first of a sequence of three 'great matches' that were staged on Parr & Wisden's new Leamington Ground in 1850. MCC batted first and were fairly quickly bowled out for 75 by JW (36-25-28-4) and George Armitage (34.3-19-41-4). The ubiquitous Rev Edward Elmhirst (34) and Lord Burghley (44) opened the Leamington innings followed by George Parr (34). Lord Guernsey (27) and Armitage (36), coming in at numbers 9 and 10, saw the Leamington score to 271. JW (36-13-44-6) bowled virtually throughout the MCC second innings as the visitors were dismissed for 130 to leave Leamington winners by an innings and 66 runs. Thus Parr and Wisden's newly organised team had completed the double over MCC in their first season.

The early finish gave a rest day (Wednesday) before the return North v South match was played on the same ground with many of the players appearing again. South batted first and JW took three wickets as he and William Clarke bowled them out for 99. The North's reply was dominated by Guy who scored 98 before he was run out. Although Parr only scored 12, JW batting at No 8 maintained Leamington's prestige with 48. JW and Clarke then shot out the South for just 66, JW taking another four wickets and Clarke taking 12 in the match. This was a good week for enhancing the status of the new ground. The pitch seems to have played well and Lord Guernsey made up a quartet of locally based players all of whom had a good week, performing well with either the bat or ball.

[10] It is probable that this club provided JW with a first opportunity to sell cricket equipment to cricketers.

Richard Daft and George Parr both lived in Radcliffe-on-Trent and were leaders of cricket in Nottinghamshire. At various times across the next three decades they partnered JW in important initiatives.

The following week saw the third of the top level matches to be played on the ground in 1850. At this time the Gentlemen of Warwickshire were the nearest that Warwickshire had to a county team. Previously the Gentlemen had played their matches either at Wellesbourne or on Warwick's Hampton Road ground. For the duration of Parr & Wisden's tenancy they played many matches in Leamington. On this occasion their opponents were I Zingari who fielded a depleted side; one of their players having been taking ill while moving from his previous week's match and they also lost an army officer who was required to remain in barracks. Thus there were only nine of IZ to take the field as the home team took first innings. JW clearly enjoyed playing on his own ground. Batting at No 4 he scored 82* and was grateful that Armitage, who had opened the innings, batted long enough to score 44. The seven players who came in to bat after JW totalled 12 between them with four being the highest individual contribution. During the innings further misfortune befell IZ when Hon Fred Ponsonby had to leave the field with lumbago. JW and Armitage bowled out the eight fit players for 49 in just 29 overs, JW taking five of the seven wickets. Following-on the visitors fared better in their second innings totalling 249, the Hon Fred being sufficiently recovered to end on 12*. This left the Gentlemen needing 106 to win and it was noted in *Bell's Life* that on such a well maintained ground this would have been a small target. However as time ran out the match was left as a draw. JW's second innings figures were 57-14-120-4.

After the initial, start-up seasons the partners spent decreasing amounts of time in Leamington. Both became heavily involved in the match programmes of the emerging touring elevens, requiring them to spend many days travelling all over England (and occasionally to Scotland). The running of the ground and the club was delegated to local people. William Russell, a surveyor with an office in the town centre, became the secretary of Parr & Wisden's Cricket Club and his office made a convenient administrative centre. Chris Page was appointed as groundsman/bowler and there were also the services of George Armitage as match professional.

After the intensive effort to establish the ground during the 1849 and 1850 seasons the partners made few further appearances on their ground. In 1851 and 1852 JW played for Gentlemen of Warwickshire in their now annual fixture with I Zingari. Then at the end of July 1856 a match, Gentlemen of England XV v Players was staged on the ground as a benefit match for George Parr and John Wisden. The press reported that attendance at the match was not as good as it had been in former days. The ground was developing into a good quality local or regional venue. Each of the partners made one further playing appearance on the ground when they brought their respective touring eleven to play there. JW's UEE came in August 1861 to play Leamington and the following year George Parr's AEE played Free Foresters on the ground.

The Free Foresters were formed in 1856 in nearby Sutton Coldfield as an exclusively amateur side with no fixed home ground. They made frequent use of the Parr & Wisden ground to stage their matches and, for instance, in August 1857 they used it for their fixture with I Zingari (who also did not have a home ground). Deddington (Oxfordshire) made frequent visits, in one season meeting Free Foresters there on three separate occasions.

There was also a need to make effective use of the many acres when there was no cricket to be played. JW was ever a smart businessman and other activities soon began to arrive. Lord Guernsey's friends from the Tennis Court Club were encouraged to use the ground to 'exercise their hunters' (horses). The large open space, a short walk from the town centre, was an ideal space for archery competitions, some at regional or national level. The ground was also used for town social events such as fetes and the parades of the local militia.

Parr & Wisden's Cricket Ground, Leamington
'Shooting for the Ladies Prize', Illustrated London News, 5 July 1851
Archery was one of the activities introduced to the site to make it commercially viable.

JW returned from time to time, no doubt to check that all was well. This included a visit in 1852 during the week before the launch of UEE when he came to try to resolve a dispute about the composition of teams for a Coventry v Leamington fixture. He offered to help resolve the matter by playing for Leamington himself but Coventry declined the offer.

Although a subscription to the Parr & Wisden Cricket Club ensured that '… all kit was provided', it is reasonable to suspect that many of the gentlemen cricketers from the Tennis Court Club would have preferred to have their own. JW would have been happy to have supplied them, possibly drawing stock from the Lillywhite emporium in London.[11] Although this may have been the first commercial activity of JW personally, John Wisden & Co was not formed until 1858, following the dissolution of the Lillywhite & Wisden partnership he shared with Fred Lillywhite.

In the autumn of 1863, with JW having retired from playing and George Parr on his way to Australia with a touring team, the partnership relinquished its lease on the ground. However, the venue continued to be known as The Parr & Wisden Ground and continued as a cricket centre for both the town and the wider region. JW occasionally returned to the town to support the local teams, including, on one occasion in

---

[11] At this time JW was using the Lillywhite family's home and business premises as a 'pied à terre'.

1864, travelling with an Army team called Knickerbockers to France for a match where he was to act as umpire.

From 1864 the Gentlemen of Warwickshire side transferred their matches back to the Hampton Road site in Warwick but when in the early 1880s plans were being made to establish a Warwickshire County Cricket Club it was envisaged that the playing ground would be in Leamington and the initial meeting was held at the *Regent Hotel* in the town centre. However, by now, the great population centre and thus the source of paying spectators was Birmingham and that was where the county club was born in 1882.

The original site at Leamington was larger than the needs of a single cricket ground, so when the section nearest the town centre was taken for housing cricket simply moved across the site and it continued to be used as a cricket ground until the present century when the owners and local authority, Warwick District Council, ceased to maintain any of its parks cricket pitches. The site, now known as Victoria Park, remains a place for physical recreation with tennis courts, a jogging track etc. maintained by the council. The town's major cricket ground and the home of the present Leamington Cricket Club is now on Arlington Avenue to the north of the town centre. It was established on a site that was originally set aside for a place of worship. During the Edwardian years this ground staged first-class cricket. When it was opened in 1899, coincidentally, the town's Member of Parliament was again a sometime president of MCC. Hon Alfred Lyttelton still holds the best Test match bowling figures for a wicket-keeper. He was also the national real tennis champion and was making use of the Bedford Street premises of the Leamington Tennis Court Club established by Lord Heneage Guernsey who had also simultaneously been the town's member of parliament and President of MCC.

The Parr & Wisden partnership had introduced lawn bowls to this part of the town and that activity has survived and thrived with the greens becoming firstly a national and then an international venue. When the Commonwealth Games were staged in Birmingham in 2022 the bowls competitions took place in Leamington. The competitors were able to look across Archery Road to the wall of *The Cricketers* public house where they could see the plaque commemorating John Wisden, George Parr and the ground that the partners established. When bowls tournaments took place the old cricket pitch was used as a car park with the smart, two-storey, 20th century pavilion majestically rising above the competitors' cars and camper vans.

5

MORE THAN JUST A CRICKETER

Unlike previous seasons JW did not go up to Cambridge in the spring of 1849 but was in Leamington negotiating and working with George Parr to establish their newly leased ground. The season ahead was to be a demanding one for as well as playing for AEE, Sussex and nationally selected elevens he was active in promoting the new ground, frequently returning to play in key matches to boost its appeal.

He began his playing season with the All England Eleven in a sequence of northern matches. He took 16 wickets in the win over Durham XXII (Hillyer took all the rest) as AEE won by 42 runs but had an indifferent match when AEE beat Scotland by 161 runs in Edinburgh. On the way back south the tourists played against Bedale in North Yorkshire and JW had an altogether better match. Batting at No 8 he scored 14* and 29 and then he and Hillyer bowled unchanged throughout both of their opponent's innings. JW had figures of 33-22-20-11 and 25.3-14-16-6 (again, such detail suggests the presence of Fred Lillywhite). Perhaps on the strength of his runs at Bedale JW opened the AEE innings at Rugby but scored only 11 and 4. His first innings bowling figures of 34.2-13-32-6 give an economy rate of around 1 run for every 4 balls.

Between the middle of May and mid-August JW played in just a single match for AEE but then, in the late summer, he re-joined the group to play at Atherstone in Warwickshire against twenty-two local players. For the second Atherstone innings he is given figures of 44-11-18-11[12] bowling throughout the innings. After the North v South match on the Parr & Wisden Ground at Leamington the AEE players returned to where their inaugural match had been played. Sheffield were now allowed only 15 players in an acknowledgement of their strength and it appears that this was about the right balance as AEE won by just 10 runs, JW taking 5/24 from 25 overs in Sheffield's second innings.

---

[12] These figures are incorrect. They are the ones given in *Scores & Biographies*. The match report in *Bell's Life* did not include bowling figures. *Cricket Archive* does not specify the number of maidens.

From there the group moved to Manchester to face a team of twenty-two local players. JW had second innings figures of 31-?-39-11 (leaving Clarke, Hillyer and Martingell to share out another 9 wickets) to set up a four wickets win. An injury in the next match at Leamington brought his playing season to an end.[13]

Between his two spells with AEE and around his efforts to launch the new ground JW played in much of the county cricket programme of 1849. But before any of these matches he appeared in two rather artificial ones. Continuing the format started at Hambledon, MCC was established as a gentleman's club which sought to stage cricket, in part as a form of entertainment for its members. An objective was to have a match staged at Lord's starting each Monday morning from May through to the beginning of August when the programme would end with the school matches between Eton, Harrow and Winchester. At this point many of MCC's members would depart for the moors of Scotland. At this time there was a growing clamour, particularly in newspapers such as *Bell's Life*, for higher skilled and more competitive matches to be staged. To fill in gaps some artificial divisions between the available cricketers were made to create matches. Thus, JW found himself playing for the Fast against the Slow Bowlers and then for the Single men versus the Married ones. He was on the winning side each time.

With his all-round cricket skills and his general athleticism JW had become a highly successful exponent of single-wicket cricket. By 1849 many were judging him to be the best in the land with some suggesting he was unbeatable. Rather in the manner of 'taking on the fastest gun in the west' several strong players were keen to challenge him to a match. Thomas Hunt from Sheffield was particularly persistent and so on 17th June JW had a short letter published in *Bell's Life*:

> Wisden and Hunt: Mr Editor, In answer to Hunt's challenge of Sheffield, to play me at single wicket, I beg to say that I decline playing any single wicket match. Your humble servant, John Wisden. Leamington, June 14.

What might be seen as the county programme had been steadily expanding. Now the sides representing Kent, Surrey, Sussex, MCC and England (MCC selected) essentially all played each other home

---

[13] See chapter 4

and away and then had additional fixtures against counties such as Nottinghamshire. The home matches for MCC and England were part of the Lord's programme. JW's next appearance at Lord's was on 18th June 1849 when he was a member of the England team that beat Surrey by two wickets. Generally in matches at this level JW was more successful as a bowler than as a batsman but here his 26 in the second innings, batting at No 3, set up the win. The strong England attack comprised JW, William Clarke, William Lillywhite and James Dean – JW took seven wickets in the match. In the second half of the week the same quartet bowled for an alternative 'England' team raised by William Clarke, on behalf of AEE, in a match against Kent at Gravesend. JW took half of the wickets. On the following Monday, back at Lord's, JW was in the Sussex team that lost to MCC by 9 wickets. The team then crossed the Thames to take on Surrey during the second half of the same week. Sussex were without several key players and lost by 15 runs, JW taking 9 wickets in the match.

After a week away playing for Leamington JW was back in London on Monday 9th July to be one of the England team to play Kent at Lord's. He bowled throughout both innings taking five wickets and three wickets to set up a convincing seven wickets win. Opening the bowling with him was his long time mentor William Lillywhite who was reported to have 'bowled beautifully'. The veteran had celebrated his 57th birthday the previous month. The Kent and Sussex players then made their way to Hove where they were to meet on the new Gausden's or Royal Brunswick Ground. Kent won the match by 116 runs, perhaps because JW managed only five wickets. He did, though, score 35 in Sussex's first innings. This was a relatively high scoring match (nearly 700 runs in the four innings) and perhaps a sign of an emerging trend on this ground. The mighty Alfred Mynn scored 92 and Thomas Adams 78 in Kent's first innings.

Sunday was, notionally, a day of rest before it was back to Lord's for Monday morning and the start of the first of the season's two North v South matches. The North had a crushing win by 243 runs and the four Leamington players JW (4 and 38), Parr (47 and 16), Guernsey (2 and 28*) and Armitage (0 and 48) all contributed good runs. JW bowled throughout both South innings capturing a total of seven wickets. The South's innings was opened by Arthur Haygarth who, in his notes to the scorecard in *Scores & Biographies*, suggests that the South's heavy defeat was due to the fact that JW was allowed to play for the North and not his native South.

As the match at Lord's was a two-day fixture JW had a spare day to make his way to Petworth for the Sussex v Surrey match. Lord Egremont and his family living at Petworth House had been great supporters of the county's cricket and played a key role in founding a county club. Sadly, MCC saw fit not to release JW's friend James Dean to play in this match at a venue close to his home at Duncton. Sussex won by an innings with JW claiming six first innings wickets. He took only three wickets in the second innings which was half of those available as four batsmen were run out.

When the young JW joined William Clarke's All England Eleven, Mynn and Felix were the 'elder statesmen' of the group. Although their best playing years were behind them, they remained a great attraction for the public and, thus, a commercial benefit to Clarke.

The early finish to the match at Petworth gave JW a whole weekend free before reporting back to Lord's to be part of the Players' team for the fixture with the Gentlemen. It looks as though the extra day off did him little good as he had a poor match and the Players crashed to a very rare defeat by an innings and 40 runs. William Lillywhite was the oldest player to have appeared in the fixture and brought the match to a close when he declined to bat (at No 11) in the second innings. He had been hurt batting in the first innings when struck on the wrist by a delivery from Harvey Fellows.

At the end of July 1849 JW left London and after a disastrous, in playing terms, trip to Newark for an AEE match and a fortnight with Leamington, he made his way to the south coast for a sequence of matches involving Sussex and neighbours Kent. In the three weeks following his last appearance at Lord's he played only seven days of cricket. In this instance the time to rest from the usual hectic schedule seems to have been beneficial. Playing in three first-class matches he took 13, 11 and 12 wickets, though he achieved little with the bat. In MCC's second innings in their match with Sussex JW dismissed 'bowled' seven of the batsmen and trapped an eighth 'lbw'; an illustration of his consistent accuracy of line and length. This left Sussex to score just five runs for a ten wickets win and earned his side a valuable extra free day before they travelled to Tunbridge Wells to play Kent. Here JW's wickets were not enough to give Sussex a win as they lost by 18 runs in a low scoring match (126 and 54 v 54 and 108). The following Monday (20th August) he moved to Canterbury to be part of an England team. A strong bowling attack could not make up for an appalling batting display and Kent won by 206 runs. In the England first innings no player scored double figures and in the second JW's 18 was England's second highest score of the match.

That match completed JW's county programme for the year. The following day he arrived in Atherstone for an AEE fixture in which he took 18 wickets. He then remained in Warwickshire for the North v South and Leamington & District v AEE matches[14] before an injury brought his playing season to a premature end.

While JW was busy setting-up the new ground in Leamington an initiative was launched in London, the consequences of which were to provide challenges for him for the rest of his working life. On 6th May 1849 *Bell's Life* ran an article:

[14] See chapter 4

THE UNITED ENGLAND ELEVEN

In consequence of the increasing popularity of cricket and the many applications from all parts of the country to make matches, it has been suggested, and the suggestion is approved of by some influential gentlemen of the Marylebone Club, that another eleven should be formed, as it is totally impossible for the present "All England Eleven" to comply with *all* the requests made to them to play matches in the course of the season. The veteran Lillywhite, of Lord's Ground, has been appointed secretary, and the following are the names the "United Eleven" will be selected from:

Lord Burghley	Sampson	John Lillywhite	Parr
Hon R Grimston	Dean	G Picknell	Wisden
Hon F Ponsonby	Royston	Bushby	Chester
Sir F Bathurst	Diver	Hammond	Bodle
Adams	Lillywhite	Day	Hodson
Chatterton			

Reading between the lines it would appear that MCC were alive to the increasing potential influence of William Clarke's peripatetic squad. The expansion of Clarke's operation would increase the opportunities that the professional players would have to generate their own income and so reduce their dependence on gentry-led activity. It would also provide a core around which the professionals could coalesce and so increase their influence on the game. This in turn would bring them into opposition with MCC. On the other hand once Clarke no longer held the monopoly on 'touring Elevens' his commercial strength and thus his influence would be weakened. That would have been the theory but the enthusiasm with which the Hon Robert Grimston faced the prospect of trailing up north to face Twenty-Two of … (some northern industrial city), can only be surmised.

It would seem that the project had been under-planned and it took only seven days for it to generate dissent. Writing to *Bell's Life* from Edinburgh, where he was with AEE, George Parr said that he and JW were not consulted about the proposal or the inclusion of their names and further said that they did not wish to play. A few weeks later JW amended his position saying that he would be willing to play if other commitments allowed.

Interestingly, JW's letter to *Bell's Life* carried an address in Leamington. Even at the time there was much uncertainty as to whether JW was ever fully resident in Leamington; his supposed lack of residency was part of a case made to object to his inclusion in teams representing the north. It was claimed that his birth place of Brighton should be the critical deciding factor and that he should play for the South. However, both JW and George Parr were recorded in local directories of the time as living in Guy Street, Leamington. Although no number was given for the house, it seems likely that the pair had rooms in one of several lodging houses in the street. The surviving records suggest that JW's former Brighton home broke up on the death of his father in 1847 and he would be foot loose and fancy free as a young bachelor and able to rest his head where his work took him. At various times in the following ten years evidence, such as the letter declining Hunt's challenge, suggests that JW had at times at least temporary residence in Leamington.

Richard Daft, the Nottinghamshire and AEE batsman, who lived in the same village as George Parr, recorded in his book[15] that in 1849 JW became engaged to Annie Parr, George's younger sister. Later evidence casts doubt on the continuing strength of their relationship.

In its list of fixtures on 11th August 1849 *Bell's Life* announced two fixtures for 'The Eleven of England', one at Norwich and one at Gravesend. Despite the impression given by this chosen name for the team these were not fixtures for William Clarke's eleven and it took him just two days to write to *Bell's Life* and tell them so; he objected strongly about the use of any team name that might be confused with his AEE. A first match was played on 23rd-25th August, when the hosts were Twenty of Norwich and District and the visitors described as 'Eleven of England' (still) by *Bell's Life* but, with the benefit of hindsight, as 'An England (John Lillywhite's) Eleven' by *Scores & Biographies* (1863). The veteran William Lillywhite played briefly for the visitors before he was taken ill. Son James played alongside him but son John Lillywhite played for the hosts. Eight of the players who appeared for the Eleven in this match had appeared on the MCC list published in early May (above). JW was not available for this match as he was playing for Clarke's Eleven at Atherstone.

---

[15] *Kings of Cricket*

The second fixture, at Gravesend, did not take place as the hosts were unable to raise a side. However, a seed had been sown. William Clarke had suggested in his letter of protest that United England was a good and worthy name for a touring eleven and so it would prove to be. Six of those who were on the MCC list went on to sign 'The Adelphi Declaration'[16] three years later at the launch of the JW-led and longer-lasting United Eleven of England.

Earlier in the 1849 season *Bell's Life* had published a United Islington Amateur Club (UIA) scorecard with the names Wisden and Lillywhite well to the fore. However, neither of these was John, a James or a William. It was George Wisden, JW's elder brother and Fred, the younger of the Lillywhite brothers, who had played. George's wicket-keeping and Fred's bowling were picked out in the report for particular praise. Both scored runs in a very low-scoring match but still ended up on the losing side. George, who was working in the City of London for an import-export company, made frequent appearances in UIA match reports over the next few years. UIA was a newly formed club worthy of a match against the powerful Islington Albion's second eleven. George's performances frequently attracted favourable comment. In some matches he was joined by John Lillywhite. When Islington Albion staged an internal match for the benefit of Edwin Paul, George was included in the 'Middlesex' team that played 'Surrey'.

It had been a long, hard season and one suspects that there were benefits for JW in being injured and missing the last few matches. Each season had seen an enhancement of his standing within the game, nationally. By the end of 1849 he was clearly one of the best bowlers in the land and had become a young gun challenging Clarke's status as the premier bowler in England. The older man was to find this increasingly difficult to deal with. JW was also developing into a competent lower-middle order batsman and had always been an athletic and skilful fielder. In most of his opponents' innings he took at least one catch. All he now needed to do was to address his propensity to get run out.

The season's cricket coverage in *Bell's Life* ended on a slightly bizarre note when a letter had to be published to confirm that 'Tom Box is not dead!' Tom Box had been a colleague, mentor and friend of JW since the days when the young man first started playing in Brighton.

---

[16] A statement of principle at the time of the formation of UEE in 1852.

This image of the 22-year-old Wisden bowling round-arm,
by Charles Basébé, was published in 1849.

6

ZENITH

1850 was to be not only JW's most successful season but it was also to be his busiest to date. In fact there are indications that he found it to be physically over-demanding. The matches in which he played were divided into three distinct phases. From late April to the middle of June he played in All England Eleven fixtures. From then until mid-August he played in what might be loosely considered the county cricket programme. In each of these two phases he also played in some other fixtures. However, from 20th August until 2nd October he played exclusively on the treadmill that was now the All England Eleven match programme.

The AEE season had begun on the last day of April when they met Twenty-Two of Carlisle (JW 11/26 from 44.2 overs in their first innings). They then progressed to Edinburgh where they played Scotland (22 players) before returning via Manchester (18) and Huddersfield (18) to Oxfordshire (18) and Rugby (22). From these opening six fixtures of the AEE season JW took no fewer than 64 wickets with a best match return of 15/105 at Manchester. For these matches William Clarke seems to have employed an early version of 'squad rotation'. As well as JW and Clarke there were also Hillyer and Martingell to share the bowling; probably as good an attack as could be assembled in England at that time. The chore of working their way through the long lists of local batsmen, many of limited ability, was shared amongst the four. Often one or two of the bowlers were given 'an innings off' – on some occasions even Clarke, who was ever eager to bowl as many overs as possible, had a rest. JW put in more than his share of the overs and generally took between one-third and a half of the wickets that fell. His nagging accuracy can be seen in the high number of maidens he bowled and his general economy rate of less than 1½ runs per [four ball] over.

AEE generally had the better of these matches – the team would have lost some of its commercial attractiveness if it had lost too often. However there were two exceptions. Against Oxfordshire they allowed the opposition to field eighteen players, who turned out to be young and athletic. On a small, well-kept ground a high scoring match saw the locals win by 187 runs. At Rugby the hosts were allocated a fairly standard twenty-two players, but these included John Lillywhite and Frank and Cris Tinley. Also, for the '& District' element the Rugby net had been cast very wide to include, for instance, Thomas Rose from Warwick and Rev. Edward Elmhirst from Leicester. The Tinleys took most of the wickets and John Lillywhite made 52*. When time was called on the final day Clarke would have been relieved because his team, having trailed by 61 on first innings, were then just 128-5. John Lillywhite was in the Rugby team because he was now coach at the school. The school's boot maker at this time was one William Gilbert who also made the balls that the school used for their unique version of football.[17] Thus a contact was made that would be of future commercial benefit to both John Lillywhite and Gilbert, as well as JW. Towards the end of the 20th century both the names 'Wisden' and 'Gilbert' were trademarks of a company led by the Gray family, descendants of another highly skilled Victorian sportsman. One of the shops that sold their products was called 'Lillywhites', in Piccadilly, London having been started by John's family.

Fred Lillywhite's Printing Tent. This printing tent accompanied the England cricketers' tour to the United States and Canada in 1859.

[17] See *The Gilbert Story* by James Gilbert

66

In June 1850 JW began with a couple of one-off matches which were then followed by a week comprising two distinctly different types of AEE matches. On the morning of Monday 10th they were at Hyde Park, Sheffield to play a side representing Yorkshire whose developing strength was such that they were now allowed only 14 players. Both JW and business partner George Parr were in the AEE team with their Leamington professional George Armitage in the Yorkshire team. The pitch was difficult and the match short and low scoring. AEE batted first and Armitage's excellent bowling (5/28) was the main reason why they were dismissed for 107. Yorkshire (118) did little better but then bowled out the visitors for 38 (Armitage 4/16) and lost only two wickets in winning the match. Teams drawn from whole counties were now ready to consider playing AEE at eleven-a-side. This match was retrospectively classified as 'first-class'.[18]

The early finish gave the touring team an extra day to lick their wounds and make their way to St Ives (Hunts.) to play twenty-two from the town. JW enjoyed himself there. When AEE batted first he opened the innings scoring 41 before being run out (again). With most of the team chipping in AEE totalled 248, at that time their best ever total against a twenty-two. JW was not called on to bowl in their first innings as St Ives were skittled out for 44 but when the hosts followed-on he took 13 wickets, twelve of them bowled, for AEE to win by an innings and 154 runs.

At the start of the following week JW was back in familiar territory as part of the Sussex team to play Kent; the first match of his county cricket programme. By now JW had raised his player status to critical team member. At the end of the previous season Sussex had lost by an innings and 45 runs to AEE and the size of the loss had been put down to JW's absence through injury from the Sussex team. In AEE's only innings wicket-keeper Tom Box took 5/45 bowling slow lobs. He had been Sussex's seventh choice bowler. In 1850 JW's bowling was generally more crucial than his batting.

In the Kent match JW took five first innings wickets and three of the five that fell in the second innings – Sussex losing by five wickets. A week later Sussex had a better match versus MCC, winning by seven wickets;

---

[18] The Association of Cricket Statisticians act as advisors to both MCC and ICC on the status of matches and have retrospectively classified some matches as first-class.

JW took 13 wickets in the match. For the second half of that week Sussex crossed the Thames and were soundly beaten by Surrey, losing by an innings and 77 runs. JW took four wickets in Surrey's only innings and he also took two catches. He was an agile close to the wicket fielder and more often than not held at least one catch in any innings.

At this time he seemed to be playing against Kent on a regular basis and on 8th July he was a member of the England team to play them at Lord's, this time being on the winning side. He took four wickets in each innings having bowled unchanged in the second to set up a six wickets win. Bowling through an entire innings was becoming a more frequent and no doubt physically more demanding occurrence.

During this run of matches JW was gaining a more settled place in the batting order coming in at either six or seven. His scores were acceptable but little more being 16, 9, 10, 14, 1 & 8. However, there was one notable exception. On Thursday 4th July Sussex were in Tunbridge Wells ready to start the return fixture with Kent but rain prevented any play on the first day. When the match began the following day Sussex batted first with JW promoted to number five and scoring a creditable 21 out of a team total of 99. When Kent batted JW took four wickets as they were bowled out for 153. JW was now promoted again, this time to open the Sussex second innings and he scored 100, his maiden first-class century. This was to be only the first of his monumental achievements during the season. *Scores & Biographies* recorded that he 'ran 189 runs', because 189 were scored while he was at the wicket. In general there being no boundary 4s & 6s and all runs had to be run out, the main exception being when the ball was deemed 'lost', when six runs were given. JW's innings included three sixes. Sussex's innings closed at 289 but the loss of the first day meant that there was not sufficient time to complete the match.

On the morning of Monday 15th July 1850 JW reported to Lord's where he was to be one of the North XI to play the South XI. His presence in the North side remained controversial; long-standing friends and team-mates such as John Lillywhite, Jemmy Dean and Tom Box were all appearing in the South team. His place in the North team was said to be due to his continuing residency at Leamington, although there was something of a pragmatic counter-argument that JW playing for the North balanced up the sides. If ever there was a match to be described as Wisden's Match this must be it.

South batted first and *Bell's Life* reported that the betting at the start of play was 6 to 4 on the North. JW and William Clarke opened the bowling for the North and in just 70 minutes the innings was completed. Bowling unchanged the pair dismissed the South for just 36 – JW took three wickets, Clarke six. No batsman reached double figures. At this time Lord's was a notoriously difficult ground for batsmen and the North struggled to do better. When Lord Guernsey walked out to join JW at the wicket the score stood at 53-8. The Leamington pair then created a partnership that doubled the score and after Mynn bowled JW for 22 Clarke joined his lordship and they pushed the score up to 131 before Clarke was dismissed. This left Lord Guernsey undefeated on 27 and with George Parr having earlier made 17 this Leamington trio had the three top scores.

So quickly had the wickets fallen that there was still time on the first day for South to start their second innings. As it turned out there was also time for them to finish it. All ten of the wickets to fall were bowled by Wisden – only Mynn escaped the fate, being undefeated on 17. Of JW's bowling *Scores & Biographies*[19] noted: 'His performance is more wonderful as the batsmen opposed to him were nearly all first rate'. And then: 'Without exaggeration his balls turned in a yard from the off, he delivering from the Pavilion'. It also goes on to note: 'It is a pity no [bowling] analysis was preserved'. Where was Fred Lillywhite when he was needed? The South were dismissed for 76, thus losing by an innings and 19 runs in a day.

Whenever a bowler so dominates a passage of play, questions are asked about 'Who was at the other end?' JW bowled throughout the innings with Clarke bowling at the other end for all but the few overs bowled by Richard Skelton. At this time Clarke was becoming increasingly aware of JW's challenge to his jealously guarded position as the leading bowler in the land. He would have done everything within his power to restrict the scope of JW's achievement. It is also worth noting that in terms of playing strength this was the foremost match of the season with as strong a collection of batsmen as anywhere mustered. JW had stepped onto the premier cricket ground in the land and performed an outstanding feat in the strongest possible company. It remains a unique performance in first-class cricket.

[19] *Scores & Biographies Vol. IV*, p. 158

At Lord's, July 15, 1850.

THE SOUTH.	1st Inn.		2nd Inn.
J. Dean, b Wisden	3	— b Wisden	0
J. M. Lee, Esq., b Clarke	5	— b Wisden	6
W. Caffyn, b Clarke	9	— b Wisden	24
T. Box, b Wisden	3	— b Wisden	1
N. Felix, Esq., st Chatterton, b Clarke	3	— b Wisden	0
J. Chester, b Clarke	8	— b Wisden	17
R. Kynaston, Esq., b Clarke	0	— b Wisden	0
A. Mynn, Esq., c Burghley, b Wisden	2	— not out	17
John Lillywhite, not out	0	— b Wisden	0
T. Sherman, run out	0	— b Wisden	2
Sir F. Bathurst, b Clarke	0	— b Wisden	4
Byes 2, leg bye 1	3	Byes 3, leg bye 1, noes 1	5
	36		76

BOWLERS { Wisden. { Clarke.

BOWLERS { 1. Wisden (all the innings). { 2. Skelton (a few overs). { 3. Clarke.

THE NORTH.	1st Inn.
T. Hunt, b Sherman	7
R. B. Smythies, Esq., b Sherman	4
J. Guy, b Sherman	4
G. Parr, b Bathurst	17
R. T. King, Esq., b Sherman	13
Lord Burghley, run out	2
G. Chatterton, run out	0
R. F. Skelton, Esq., b Sherman	0
J. Wisden, b Mynn	22
Lord Guernsey, not out	27
W. Clarke, b Sherman	13
Byes 14, leg byes 5, wides 3	22
	131

BOWLERS { 1. Bathurst. { 2. Sherman. { 3. Mynn. { 4. Chester. { 5. Dean.

The North winning in one innings and 19 runs.

North v South scorecard when Wisden uniquely bowled all ten wickets

Coming only nine days after he had scored his maiden first-class century (the only one of the season) this success marked out JW as an outstanding all-round cricketer with few, if any, equals anywhere in the land and thus the world.

Before his spectacular performance against the South, JW had also had a successful visit to Lord's the previous week. This was Lord Guernsey's year as President of MCC and he had promised to bring big matches to the North to assist in launching the new ground at Leamington. Another match to raise the profile of the Parr & Wisden operation was the first ever visit of a Leamington side to Lord's. The visitors batted first and when JW accompanied George Armitage to the wicket to open the Leamington innings he found himself facing some very familiar bowling. Opening the attack for MCC were the now 58-year-old William Lillywhite and JW's life-long friend Jemmy Dean. Armitage went for 7 but JW scored 16, George Parr 49 and Lord Guernsey 2 as Leamington totalled a very creditable 186. JW then took five wickets to earn a 42 runs lead. A second innings of 112 set MCC 155 to win but their hopes were quickly set back when JW and Armitage reduced them to 8-5. Jemmy Dean (52*) led a rally but another five wickets haul for JW saw Leamington home by 11 runs. A notable scalp for the newly created club.

In mid-August while JW was in Leamington scoring 82* and taking nine wickets for the Gentlemen of Warwickshire v I Zingari,[20] Sussex were playing MCC and being beaten by an innings and 40 runs. It was again noted that Sussex struggled when JW was not playing. AEE also missed him when, at the beginning of the month, he had missed the match at Derby so that he could play for Leamington versus MCC. After the locals scored 150 in their second innings AEE were struggling to save the match with four wickets down. His inclusion as a bowler was now critical to all the teams for which he played.

For JW the match at Leamington had been his second of the season against I Zingari. On 22nd June 1850 JW played in an interesting one day match in Westminster. Five years earlier I Zingari had been formed as the first of the gentlemen's elevens, almost the counter-point to the touring professional squads. In this match on the historic Vincent Square ground, situated in the heart of Westminster, IZ played the newest of these occasional, amateur teams, then known as Houses of Lords and Commons (later abbreviated to Lords & Commons) in their first match. On the evening before the match Lord Ward pulled out of the parliamentarians' team and JW was recruited to make up the team. He was close-at-hand and his general demeanour meant that he would fit easily into this social grouping. Although *Scores & Biographies*[21] lists the match as '… with Wisden' he was not playing as a given man but simply a late substitute, a fact made clear in the match report in *Bell's Life*. There would have been no need to have given men to boost one side or the other, both teams comprising a full set of experienced and capable amateur cricketers. However, despite being a guest, JW was to dominate a low-scoring match. Lords & Commons batted first and JW opened the batting with Lord Burghley, their scores of 13 and 15 respectively being the highest of the innings. When IZ batted JW dismissed them virtually unaided. Seven batsmen were dismissed 'b. Wisden'. The two top scorers, Spencer Ponsonby (26) and Morse (22) were dismissed 'c & b. Wisden'. Mostyn escaped by getting himself run out, leaving Hon E Bligh undefeated on

[20] See Chapter 4
[21] *Scores & Biographies Vol. IV*, p. 133

19. I Zingari led by 22 on first innings and the parliamentarians' second innings totalled 132 but in a one day match there was not time for the fourth innings. By 21st August JW had fulfilled all of his commitments to both Leamington and Sussex and was making his way to Southampton where he re-joined AEE. As was by now becoming common when the touring eleven played a team drawn from, or representing, a whole county their opponents were restricted to fourteen players and seldom allowed any given men. More teams representative of the whole of their counties were beginning to emerge. JW shared the wickets with Clarke and Hillyer as Hampshire were bowled out for 74 and 57. As AEE scored 131 in their first innings the scores were now level. Clarke chose to open the second AEE innings taking with him the amateur John Walker. No doubt to Clarke's total displeasure Sir Frederick Bathurst dismissed him first ball. This brought JW to the wicket and he cut the first ball that he received for the one run required to win the match. This little two-ball scenario would, no doubt, have not gone down well with Clarke and was another nail in the coffin for JW's relationship with his AEE captain.

By the 1850s England had a greatly expanding network of railways linking the major towns. However, it did not reach all the locations to which Clarke wished to introduce professional cricket, leaving the players with some hair-raising, often overnight journeys. Here they have lost their way on Holbeach Moor in the dark. In the days before cameras it was good to have such a skilled artist as Felix to record the adventures.

From Southampton AEE made their way to Peterborough where they were well beaten by a team comprising twenty locals with the additional assistance of William Buttress and Frank Tinley, losing by 13 wickets. They then moved to Manchester who were still permitted eighteen players including the veteran William Lillywhite. JW opened the batting and scored 22 before being run out and then he and Clarke bowled all through the first innings and all but five overs in the second innings despite having Hillyer in the team (obviously this was one of his resting matches). JW took six of the seventeen wickets in each innings as AEE won by 94 runs.

One of the positive features of the development of the AEE programme was that it took the best cricketers in the land to some places off cricket's most beaten tracks. This not only raised the profile of the game in these localities but also identified able local players who could be encouraged to play at a higher level. This concept has been at times described as 'missionary'. In amongst these fixtures a new type of contest was developing and a new function emerging. The beginning of September found JW, with AEE, ready to play Sheffield who had been the very first fixture in 1846. Sheffield had, also, long been opponents of Clarke's Nottingham teams. For their first match against The Eleven of England (as AEE had initially been known) they had been allowed twenty players. However, as their sides became stronger and they continued to win the annual matches their advantage was steadily reduced and in 1850 it was only fifteen players from Sheffield (just one more than Yorkshire had been allowed) who faced the eleven of AEE. Comment made at the time noted that efforts to make the local team more competitive led to players being drawn from an ever wider area. A similar situation pertained at Leeds and other Yorkshire towns such as Bradford. There was a particular Yorkshire element in this. It was recognised that there needed to be a county team but there was no agreement about where this team should be based. So as well as each team competing against the visitors they were also, in effect, competing against each other to be the town to host the county team when it was formed. Eventually a county club was formed in 1863.

A similar development occurred further south where AEE's initial visit to play against the city of Hereford set in train the process that created Herefordshire County Cricket Club. Thus the visits of the touring sides would start to draw together the best players in any county and would become a spur to expanding the county cricket programme that eventually was to largely replace the touring elevens as the principal programme of professional cricketers.

JW had a quiet match at Sheffield taking six wickets across the two innings and scoring a creditable 19 when opening AEE's first innings. He also opened the batting in the next match at Darlington without success but took 13 wickets in the match. After the brief trip to County Durham, the group returned for a further week in Yorkshire. The sequencing of the fixtures suggests that they were arranged for the convenience of the local promoters rather than for ease of travel. After Peterborough the tour had gone: Manchester – Sheffield – Darlington – Bradford – Langton Wold (midway between York and Scarborough) which was not the most efficient order for travel. JW had another quiet week in Yorkshire; the scorecards and match reports seeming to indicate that he was losing a little of his edge at the end of a long season; it was, by then, mid-September. Although he opened the bowling at Bradford he took only one wicket in the first innings and appears not to have bowled in the second (no bowling figures are recorded). At Langton Wold he took just three wickets. Having one innings in each match he scored 15 and 8. Both matches ended as a draw.

The chore of travelling continued and by Monday morning the Eleven were on the south coast at Hove ready to begin a slightly bizarre fixture with a team from Sussex. It seems that the full county team felt that they were too weak to play AEE but this fixture was made against a team of 16 amateurs. In the end the Sussex side also included a number of professionals but it soon transpired that the team was out of their depth. On a good pitch they were bowled out for 115 and 99 to lose by an innings and 104 runs. JW seems to have played only a minor part in the match, perhaps enjoying an undemanding game, taking a single wicket and scoring a modest 13. Match reports suggest that the sun shone, the ground was in excellent condition and the local supporters greatly enjoyed the match, even at this late stage of the season.

In the final three weeks of the season the AEE only played a match in the first half of each week. JW appears to have benefited from the easing of the pace, giving him the opportunity to restore some of his energy. In the match at Louth (Lincolnshire) he took 14 wickets in the first innings to dismiss the local side for 107, leaving Clarke and Hillyer to bowl them out in their second innings for 69. George Parr scored another 90 runs to add to his 118 at Hove.

The final match of the season started on the Edgbaston Reservoir Ground on Monday 30th September and in many ways proved to be a fixture too far. This was to be the final match played on the ground before it was taken over for house building. Recent heavy rain had left the ground wet and 'dead' in its play and frequent showers during the first two days added to the difficulties for the players. One of the skills that William Clarke, and later JW, needed was accurately assessing the strength of the opposition so as to calculate fair odds in terms of players for the match. Here allowing Birmingham twenty-two players including George Armitage and Frank Tinley turned out to be a little too generous. At the end of the first day's play AEE had 'staggered' to 72-8 which became 75 all out on the following morning. When the hosts batted they fared only a little better. JW had figures of 37-14-48-9, sharing the bowling with Clarke (56 overs) and Hillyer (19 overs), as they dismissed Birmingham for 94, a lead of 19. As AEE scored only 40 in their second innings Birmingham needed only 22 to win. After JW and Clarke had bowled seven overs the score had crept to 3-1. At this point AEE conceded the match. It was time for everyone to go home.

It was a messy end to a long and arduous season. But for JW it was one which had been highly successful, in playing terms probably the zenith of his career. He was now firmly established as one of the most able, if not the most able, cricketer in England. Also, he had risen to the top without alienating too many of his fellow cricketers.

William Clarke heralded from Nottingham and was the creator of the first enclosed Trent Bridge Ground. He believed that the professional cricketers should create their own opportunities to earn a living from their skills and not be beholden to the gentry to arrange matches. His creation of the All England Eleven can be seen as the first step towards turning cricket into a national, professional sport.

7

ENOUGH IS ENOUGH

The 1851 season opened with JW at the height of his cricketing powers. He was undoubtedly one of the best two or three cricketers in the land and almost certainly the best all-rounder. He was certainly viewed as being pre-eminent in single-wicket cricket, although this status was becoming something of a nuisance. JW did not need the additional cricketing activity that single-wicket matches created.

As can be seen from the accompanying chart [Appendix A] his diary was full. After he had begun the season at the end of April in a warm-up match with the local players of the Parr & Wisden Club in Leamington, his national programme began on Monday 5th May at Lord's where he played for AEE against an MCC & Metropolitan Clubs XV. Unusually for AEE this was a two-day match but the playing arrangements may well have been dictated by MCC. The free day on the Wednesday would be welcome as it was to be one of the few that he was to get until mid-autumn.

Pressure created by Clarke's All England Eleven operation seems to have led to the season being divided up into two slots of three days each week: Monday to Wednesday and then Thursday to Saturday. No cricket was played on Sundays – that was for travelling. Between 5th May and 8th October JW had two free slots and half-a-dozen free-days when, for instance, matches at Lord's were still set for two-days or rain and early finishes freed-up a day. With the adjustments of starting matches on Saturdays and Wednesdays and finishing the competitive season at the beginning of September this was to become the summer routine for professional cricketers for more than the next 100 years.

For JW the season finished on 16th October. The match AEE v Sixteen of Sussex on CH Gausden's ground had stretched into a fourth day after rain had prevented play on 15th. In this match JW opened the AEE first innings with Grundy and scored 25 (out of 146). By contrast in AEE's previous fixture these two players had bowled unchanged throughout the match in which Clarke had not played. Now, coming on as second change in the Sussex innings Wisden ended with figures of 22-12-20-8. His final wicket was Frederick Lillywhite b. Wisden 0.

Fred's rare appearance at this level is an illustration of the weakness of the Sussex team. While Dean, Gausden and Brown joined Fred Lillywhite in the Sussex team, Box and JW played for AEE. In *Scores & Biographies*[22] Haygarth was moved to note:

> The last match between England and Sussex was in 1849. Sussex, however, in this instance was merely a "scratch" team.

And then adding:

> Box and Wisden both appeared this season in forty-three matches, which is a larger number than has yet been played in by any cricketer in *one* year. Indeed, some of the *great* cricketers of former days have not *recorded* to their names even that number in their *whole* career.

1851 and 1852 were to prove to be something of a high-water mark in extending the fixture lists of the touring professional elevens. As 1851 was also a pivotal season in the career of JW and some other professional cricketers it is worth looking at in some detail. The record of the season will serve as an illustration of the summer life-style of the emerging band of professional cricketers for whom cricket was now their principal, not subsidiary, occupation. As well as being a full season for JW it was also a highly successful one.

In that first AEE match at Lord's v MCC & Metropolitan Clubs JW opened the innings with William Clarke and was then involved in an unusual incident. Haygarth, who played in the match, recorded in *Scores & Biographies*.[23]

> Wisden in his first innings was run out and given out by Bayley, the umpire. His decision, however, was over-ruled, and he was allowed to return to the wicket, as Mr. Rogers had accidentally knocked his (Wisden's) bat out of his hand, thus causing him to be out of his ground. He was, however, run out again shortly after.

This is a good illustration of JW's propensity to get himself dismissed 'run out' which seems to have been a weakness in his batting throughout his career. AEE's innings totals of 30 and 47 failed to match the XV's first innings total of 95 and so the match was over in two days. This left AEE a

[22] *Scores & Biographies Vol. IV*, p. 333
[23] *Scores & Biographies Vol. IV*, p. 220

free day to make their way to St Ives (Huntingdonshire) to play against a team of 20 local players plus the two given professionals, Charles Arnold and William Buttress, and so the weekly pattern for much of the rest of the season was launched.

In St Ives' first innings JW and William Clarke bowled unchanged (JW 14 wickets) to dismiss them for 55. However, Arnold and Buttress then dismissed AEE for 36 – no batsman made double figures with JW's 8 being the top score. The local team managed 75 in their second innings and AEE went on to lose the match by 30 runs.

Blisworth Station 1852, by Felix
Most professional cricketers have found transporting their kit an onerous task. Alfred Mynn was already in his late 40s when he began travelling around the country with the All England Eleven and so his luggage would be an additional burden. On more than one rail journey Mynn became parted from his luggage.

Over the weekend 10th/11th May AEE travelled to Yorkshire for the start of their first northern tour of the season. On Monday they met a Yorkshire XIV at Sheffield. The hosts batted first and were dismissed for 183 (JW 10/58). Skelton and Armitage then dismissed AEE for 47, only George Parr (16) making double figures. AEE followed-on and were then dismissed for 83 to lose by an innings and 53. Sheffield had been the venue of the very first AEE match in 1846 when they played against 20 local players and lost by 5 wickets. Over the years AEE had only limited success against Yorkshire based teams.

Played three lost three! Clarke would not have been happy and someone was going to suffer. He was keen to develop the brand (modern terminology) and this required his all-star team to be successful in its matches. That someone turned out to be Stockton-on-Tees who were beaten by 104 runs. Although all 22 Stockton players batted there was an agreement that only 15 should field. This may have been part of the reason why AEE managed to score nearly 300 runs in the match. *Scores & Biographies* noted that 'Several of the best playing for Stockton came from other villages'. One of the positive contributions of the AEE operation was the drawing together of the best players in a district.

The tour continued to Newcastle (AEE had much the better of the draw with Northumberland XXII) and then the group started to make their way south. The first stop was Thirsk (birthplace of Thomas Lord) where they beat XXII of Thirsk and District by just 9 runs. Amongst the several players who played in this match and who had also turned out for Stockton was the exotically named Prince Stockdale. JW took 9 out of the 21 wickets in the first innings and 14 in the second. AEE continued their way south calling at Gainsborough (won by 8 wickets), Manchester (won by 21 runs), Wisbech (won by 61 runs) and Oxford (unfinished – rain). They were now back in London ready to take on MCC at Lord's on Monday 9th June. It had been a month since they had set out for St Ives as the first stage on their journey north.

The MCC match began an eight-week period when AEE matches were interspersed with county and representative fixtures. For the players one of the advantages of these few weeks was that they could have some sort of base in London as most of the matches were either in the capital or the surrounding towns. For each of the first seven weeks at least one of the two matches was played in London. In terms of accommodation, it is probable that JW was still able to make use of the Lillywhites' base in Caledonian Road, just to the north of King's Cross railway station.

However, William Clarke was not beyond filling in any spare slots with a quick dash off to a country ground. Many of the matches at Lord's were scheduled for just Monday and Tuesday which made Wednesday available to travel to, say, Ross-on-Wye with Sunday for the journey back. A similar trip to Sleaford allowed AEE to call in at Derby on the way back as the South v North game at the Oval was scheduled for the second half of the week.

During this phase the reduction in travelling coincided with an improved standard of cricket. At least the batsmen would have to contend with only eleven fielders. JW's form became a little variable. In the two

Players v Gentlemen matches he took only three wickets in three innings and when batting had scores of 22 and 8. Despite a pair for Sussex versus Surrey his batting seems to have held up better than his bowling. In the first South v North match he took only one wicket but had scores of 32 and 10. A quiet performance in one of the first-class matches was for England against Kent with scores of 14 and 11* and no wickets in the first innings and not being required to bowl in the second

However, despite these varied fortunes when the occasion arose JW displayed the capacity to take over and dominate a match for the benefit of his team. A good example of this was the season's second North v South match played at Lord's on 14th-16th July. For 1851 he switched sides again and was back playing for the South. This called into question his allocation to the North team in 1850 on the basis of residence, although in March the 1851 census recorded him as lodging in a bakery in Abbots Street, Leamington. Correspondence in the national press showed that he was still using a residential base in Leamington but he was re-allocated to the South for this fixture.[24]

The match had many interesting features and merits a more detailed look while in other aspects it was typical of many matches at this level. North won the toss and elected to bat with Wisden and Hillyer opening the bowling for the South. Mainly thanks to Hillyer the North were reduced to 37-7 before Chatterton and Dakin staged a recovery. The innings closed at 4.10pm when the North were finally all out for 95; Hillyer took eight wickets, JW the other two. In their turn the South fared no better. As Grundy tore through the top order there were four ducks from the first six batsmen. JW, coming in at No 9, and Julius Caesar who had opened the innings, began to repair the damage. However after Caesar (39) and JW (11) were dismissed the innings quickly closed for 61; a deficit of 34. Grundy matched Hillyer by taking eight wickets.

By 6.45pm on the first day the North had begun their second innings though this time Dakin opened the innings with Guy instead of Grundy who may have had his feet up after his successful bowling stint. Forty-five minutes later Dakin was run out for 7 to bring an eventful day to a close. The following morning, after Parr went for 8, Guy and Vernon took the North's score to 108-2 before JW bowled Vernon for the innings top-score of 45. As the match began to drift away from the South, JW then bowled out (literally) the rest of the northern side with the sole exception

[24] See also Chapter 4

of Anderson who fell to Day, to finish with eight wickets. The innings closed at 4.30pm for 166 – a lead of 200. The last man out was Lord Guernsey, bowled by JW for 4. So in this innings JW had dismissed both his business partner and his patron.

The South's second innings had a better start than in the first innings and when on the following morning Haygarth was dismissed after a three-hour innings for 41 they were 79-3. At this point Grundy started to work his way through the batting again and the innings slumped firstly to 104-6 and then 123-8. Now the betting odds were very much on the North. Whereas the ebb and flow of a 21st century match might be illustrated by the changes to Duckworth-Lewis targets, in 1851 it was the betting odds which measured the advantage. These were much quoted in match reports to measure and illustrate the changes in prospects. The fall of the eighth wicket brought Hillyer to the crease to join JW. JW now took charge of the innings, managing the support from his bowling partner as they added 45 priceless runs. *Bell's Life's* match report reads as if it were Paul Collingwood organising the England tail in another highly focused rear-guard action to save an Ashes match. JW was reported as '… scoring off almost every ball', while Hillyer was '…remarkably well and steady'. But eventually Clarke had Hillyer caught by Grundy and last man Day came to the wicket with 33 still needed. But all was not lost. JW continued in 'making every run possible' and 'cleverly stealing two'. Day remained undefeated and the pair got to within 13 runs of their target when Grundy got a ball to pop at JW and he was caught at mid-wicket. His innings of 52 was the highest of the match, having earlier been one of the few players to reach double figures in either team's first innings. He had also taken ten wickets in the match. He had dominated the second half of the match, dragging the South back into the game with his bowling and had so nearly organised a dramatic win with his batting. For the North, Grundy took 14 wickets – a match-winning performance.

Bell's Life concluded its match report with:

His [JW's] batting was really beautiful, and elicited repeated demonstrations of applause from all parts of the ground, and at the close of his lengthened innings he was called up to the pavilion, when the Hon F Cavendish, in the name of the Marylebone Club, presented him with a new ball as a testimonial, not only for his fine play upon this occasion, but for his general good conduct as a professional player. Mr Cavendish afterwards made a present to Grundy for his excellent bowling in the match.

A fortnight later the Lord's season came to a close when from 30th July to 5th August the schools of Eton, Harrow and Winchester played their annual series of matches. Harrow lost both of their matches – a situation that was to be remedied in future seasons following another significant development in JW's career. He became the professional cricket coach at the school implementing significant improvements in the coaching arrangements.

The sequence of county matches for the 1851 season was drawing to a close with England v Kent, as part of the Canterbury Week, which began on 10th August. Many of the AEE group were involved on one side or the other of this match that finished at 1.00pm on the third day (Wednesday) and *Bell's Life* noted that the AEE players then made an early start on their journey to Huntingdon. This next match marked the beginning of the second concentrated sequence of fixtures for AEE which was to last until the end of the season. This sequence of fixtures was based on the original part of their annual programme and had more geographical coherence to it; moving from the south, through the Midlands to Yorkshire before spending a week in Scotland. After Huntingdon AEE moved to Sherborne to play Dorsetshire (18th-20th August). JW, along with Tom Box, was granted leave of absence from this match to play for Sussex against MCC. Sussex won handsomely in two days with JW taking 10 wickets in the match. This gave the pair plenty of time to catch up with the rest of the AEE party for the match at Worcester. AEE then moved via Trentham Park and Ilkeston to Sheffield to start, on 1st September, a fortnight in Yorkshire. Sheffield were beaten by an innings and 24 runs mainly thanks to a strong batting display in which all the AEE players reached double figures except for Clarke, who was undefeated on 0; George Parr was run out for 78 in a total of 263. JW and Clarke did most of the bowling but Clarke took the lion's share of the wickets.

Although it was George Parr who instigated the development of the new ground at Leamington, JW seems to have given more support to the teams that played there, even returning after his first-class career had finished when he was concentrating very much more on his business activities in London. On 4th & 5th September he again took leave of absence from AEE in Yorkshire to join nine Gentlemen of Warwickshire and Berry in taking on I Zingari on the Parr & Wisden Ground. Parr was originally listed to join him but then declared himself to be full of aches and pains and persuaded John Berry, who had played for Sheffrield, to travel to Leamington in his place. This may be the first recorded incidence of the syndrome sometimes referred to as 'Abbeydale Back'.[25] The two professionals were very much needed. JW (48) and Berry (26) made three-quarters of Warwickshire's first innings total of 96 and had two of the three double figure innings in the second. They also shared all of the wickets as IZ went on to win by 21 runs. George Parr played in neither this match nor the AEE match played on the same days but both he and JW were back on duty in Yorkshire on the following Monday when AEE had a close-fought match versus Twenty of Bradford.

AEE's fortnight in Yorkshire was completed with a match against Twenty-two of Newburgh Park on 11th-13th September. The local team included George Armitage, the match professional from the Parr & Wisden ground, in their number. JW scored 28 in the first AEE innings with Armitage taking eight wickets. Then JW and Clarke bowled throughout the Newburgh Park innings, sharing the wickets between them. JW also bowled throughout the second innings, taking 9-20 and leading AEE to win by just 11 runs.

Over the weekend (13th-14th September) the group was back on the road again and made its way to central Scotland, apparently leaving Clarke behind. They presumably took George Armitage with them as he played for the local teams in each of the next two fixtures. JW scored only 2, 0, 0* & 7 but bowled unchanged through the two innings of Edinburgh XXII (AEE won by 20 runs) and all but five overs in the draw with Glasgow. His wicket hauls were, 6, 11, 11 & 10. Martingell had similar returns from an almost equal workload. This heavy workload was necessary in Clarke's absence.

On their return journey to the south coast AEE played in Birmingham (draw), Hereford (draw), Teignbridge, Devon (lost by an innings) and Southampton (draw) before arriving at Brighton for the final match. In each of these matches JW did almost half of the bowling.

[25] There was a spell when Yorkshire CCC played home matches at Abbeydale Park, Sheffield. The pitch was seen as lively, and it was noted that a number of senior batsmen incurred back strains in the days leading up to fixtures on the ground, making them unavailable for selection.

Arthur Haygarth, who was born at Hastings and educated at Harrow played 3 first-class matches for Sussex between 1848 and 1860. A defensive right-hand batsman his lasting memorial is the set of 15 'Cricket Scores and Biographies' volumes, the first four published by Fred Lillywhite and the remainder by MCC. The publication of later volumes has in recent years been continued by Roger Heavens.

In a November review, published in *Bell's Life*, the AEE 'publicity officer' Nicholas Felix wrote of the final match:

> The last of the England matches took place on Monday, Oct 13, 1851, at Gausden's Ground, Brighton, but owing to the lateness of the season, and the inclemency of the weather, it was rather a dull affair to witness, a tiresome match to play in, and as heavy a subject to treat of in the way of a report. To detail its proceedings would be to imitate the expression of the poet, "Montes parturiunt ridiculus mus;" for we are sorry to say, spite of all energies to show good sport, there was indeed a "ridiculous mus"ter. Four days, broken by the weather, were occupied in bringing the match to a drawn game.

At the end of a long grinding season this was clearly one match too far.

Haygarth, in a footnote[26] to the *Scores & Biographies* scorecard for this final match, commented on the 43 matches that JW and Tom Box had played during the season. In November *Bell's Life* published its Cricket Averages for 1851. These showed that they were only a short step ahead of many of their AEE team mates. William Caffyn (41 matches), Nicholas Felix (40), Joseph Guy (39), William Martingell (42) and George Parr (41) followed them. William Clarke, himself, played in 35 matches.

[26] *Scores & Biographies IV*, p. 333

Amongst these Martingell and JW stood out as they put in prodigious stints as bowlers. Sadly, as bowling statistics were only partially kept in those days it is not possible to give any indication as to the number of overs that they bowled in total as a measure of the amount of work that they put in. However, JW's total of 445 [27] wickets taken in the season was an outstanding achievement. Clarke was nearest to him in total with 343. Of the rest only Grundy (223) and Hillyer (211) were close to half as many.

JW also scored 728 runs, a total only exceeded by George Parr (1016), William Caffyn (916) and Nicholas Felix (831). These three all played a similar number of matches but all played as specialist batsmen.[28] Given the unrelenting grind of this highly compacted programme not having to contribute both as a batsman and a bowler must have been a huge advantage. Not so for JW whose achievements of 1851 were truly outstanding.

He had made an unequalled contribution to AEE's 1851 match programme, making the rejection that he experienced during the close season even more bizarre. His achievements during 1851 made him the leading cricketer in the land.

---

[27] This figure is taken from the end of season averages published by *Bell's Life* in November 1851. The basis for the newspaper's calculations are those matches that had been reported in the paper during the season. Other calculations exist.

[28] It was later that William Caffyn became an all-rounder.

8

THE UNITED ENGLAND ELEVEN

It is doubtful that he would have been aware of it at the outset but 1852 was to be a career-changing season for JW and indeed for professional cricketers as a group. In his play *Twelfth Night*, William Shakespeare gives Malvolio the lines:

But be not afraid of greatness,
Some men are born great,
Some achieve greatness,
And some have greatness thrust upon them.

In the context of the play 'greatness' can be interpreted as 'leadership'. JW seems not to have been afraid of greatness/leadership though it is doubtful that he was born to it. Whether he achieved his greatness or had it thrust upon him we cannot tell; I suspect that over a couple of seasons it was a mixture of the two. He certainly retained a leadership role within the community of professional cricketers for the rest of his life.

1851 had been a long, hard season, especially for those professional cricketers who comprised William Clarke's AEE. The season had clearly generated some resentment and grievances within the team and also some criticism from outside. It had been in September 1846 that Clarke had first assembled his troupe of professional cricketers and set off for Sheffield to begin an eight-day match programme. It was a success and the following year the programme covered 30 days from mid-August onwards, and in 1848 45 days (JW had joined AEE late in 1847 for the match versus Sixteen of Yorkshire). No doubt these events had being monitored at Lord's where some would have seen the development of the 'workers' (professionals) organising and controlling their own employment as unacceptable.

On 6th May 1849 *Bell's Life* had published an announcement that indicated MCC intended to promote and sponsor a travelling eleven to be known as 'The United England Eleven' under the leadership of William Lillywhite.[29] William Clarke had responded by saying that it would be a

[29] See Chapter 5

good name for such a team. The team played just one match that season and none after that. However the idea was dormant not dead. It was in that same year that the start of the annual AEE match programme had moved from August to May.

Meanwhile AEE had marched on. The table below shows the season by season increase in the number of 'fixture' days for each season as a measure of the programme. 'Playing' days might be slightly less due to rain and early finishes.

The Gradual Expansion of the All England Eleven match programme

	Apr	May	Jun	Jul	Aug	Sep	Oct	Total
1846						8		8
1847				11	16	3		30
1848				21	24			45
1849		14	5	8	12	21		60
1850	1	16	7	3	19	19	2	67
1851		23	19	2	15	26	9	94
1852		16	26	3	22	17		84
1853		4	20	9 (+6*)	20	12		65 (+6)

* in-house matches between two teams drawn from AEE ranks.

The nine days of cricket which JW played in October 1851 were to be his last for AEE. The sequencing of elements of JW's move from AEE to Harrow School is clouded in mystery and more so the reasons for the move. JW's final match for AEE is reported in *Bell's Life* but without comment about his future. However, in the *Brighton Gazette* of 23rd October at the end of another report on that final match, it is reported that Clarke had engaged Bickley as a replacement for JW as the latter had accepted a lucrative engagement at Harrow. As such arrangements are not completed in a few days it must be assumed that JW had for the past few weeks been working out his notice while playing for AEE. No further explanation is given at this time (October/November 1851), and there is no further comment until the following April when it was noted that when AEE began the 1852 season they would have to do without Wisden.

While AEE's 1852 programme was slightly shorter than in 1851 the tensions within and around the squad and its operation were still there. It was after another summer's cricket that some of these stresses and strains exploded onto the pages of *Bell's Life* at the beginning of December 1852. Claims and counter-claims raged on until January 1853 when the paper's editor decided enough had been said and refused to publish any more contributions. Much of the comment had been unedifying but it did at least offer some information about JW's parting from Clarke and AEE. One outcome of the publication of so much comment was the news that JW had been expelled from AEE by Clarke. No reason for the expulsion was explicitly given. As Clarke challenged any comment about him that he thought to be inaccurate we must assume that JW's expulsion claim was accurate. He said that Clarke had 'sent him away' and their differences 'were not about money'. Given JW's workload and achievements during the 1851 season the reasons could hardly be about cricket performance. If, then, consideration is made of the characters of the two men and in the light of future events, a reasonable assumption is that Clarke had identified JW as a focus around which dissatisfaction was beginning to coalesce. Clarke seemed always to want to be the single focus and to be a strong lead within the group.

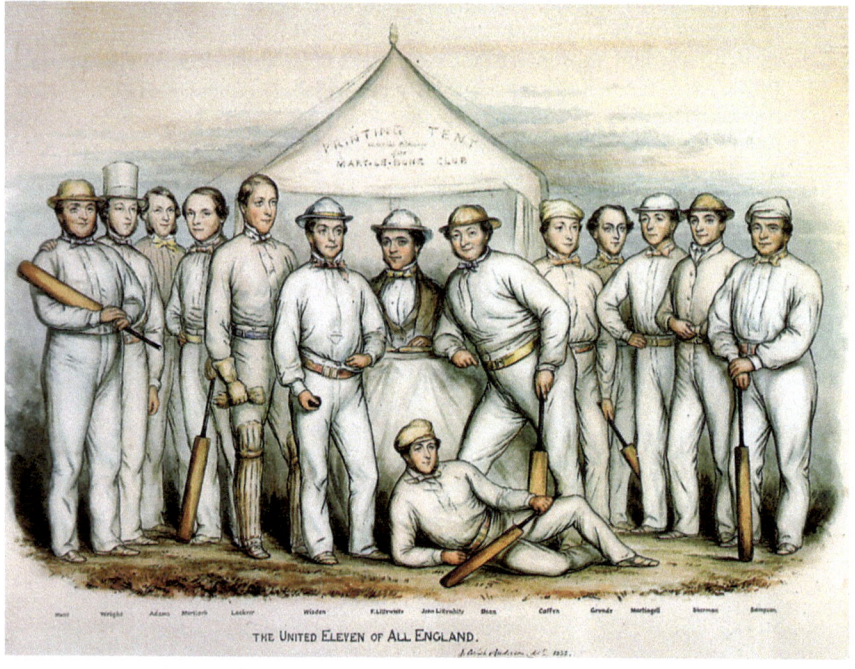

Fred Lillywhite became the attached scorer for UEE and where he went his scoring and printing tent went with him. When UEE were presented with a team flag they attached it to Fred's tent.

JW 'went away' and by mid-April he had already taken up his post as the new coach at Harrow School. As AEE were about to embark upon a match programme almost as daunting as that of 1851 Felix felt obliged to use the pages of *Bell's Life* to issue a 'call to arms' to his team-mates, expressed in the style of the words that Shakespeare had given to King Henry V on the night before the Battle of Agincourt. So his team-mates stiffened-up their sinews and left their neighbours still abed before setting off for Scotland. Thus the season progressed and while JW was having a noticeable, and much approved-of, impact at Harrow he was released at times from his duties to play for Sussex, etc. On these days he would no doubt be updated by colleagues about events within the AEE group. It would seem likely that other conversations had also taken place.

Without apparent previous warning, on 8th August 1852 the following made a first appearance in the fixtures column of *Bell's Life* (complete with compositor's slip):

THE UNITED ELEVEN OF DNGLAND.

This Eleven have made the following matches, viz:—

Aug 19, at Salisbury—Against Twenty-two of the South Wilts Club.
Aug 23, at Brighton—Sussex against Surrey.
Aug 26, at Ipswich—Against Twenty of Ipswich (with Two Bowlers given).
Aug 30, at Newmarket—Against Twenty of Newmarket (with Two Bowlers given).
Sept 2, at Gravesend—Against Eighteen of Gravesend and District.
Sept 6, at Sheffield—Against Fifteen of Sheffield.

Other matches are in progress, but the days are not fixed. The Eleven will be chosen from the following list:—Adams, G. Brown, Chatterton, Dean, Dakin, Grundy, Hunt, John Lillywhite, Lockyer, Nixon, Sampson, Shearman, Wisden, and Wright.—All communications respecting matches must be addressed to Messrs Dean and Wisden, Lord's Cricket Ground, Marylebone, London.

It is interesting to note the inclusion of the Sussex against Surrey fixture in the list. This is an early indication of the UEE's intention to arrange their matches so as to avoid clashes with county matches. Presumably MCC were content for correspondence about UEE to be delivered to Lord's. They may have been pleased to see some challenge to the dominance of Clarke's AEE operation being set up.

Whatever was known up to that point this announcement made public the intention to organise an alternative to William Clarke's AEE. No doubt many more conversations had been held.

The following run of fixtures gave ample opportunity for the exchange of views about this new initiative:

There is no clearly discernible evidence as to what motivated Clarke to apparently abandon his team at Ilkeston and travel to Newmarket to berate the emergent UEE squad. If he had objected to the concept of UEE he could have tackled JW and Dean at Northampton, although, as they had not fulfilled the published fixture with South Wilts, he perhaps thought (hoped?) that this UEE would go the same way as the Lillywhite UEE. Whatever his motives he clearly upset the UEE squad members with the extraordinary outburst at Newmarket of which few reliable details are available.

An important development was what might be titled the 'Adelphi Declaration'. This is recorded in *Scores & Biographies* at the foot of the record of the match Fifteen of Sheffield v The United England Eleven, played on 6th-8th September. It read:

> At a meeting held at the Adelphi Hotel, Sheffield, this 7th day of September, 1852, by the members of the United Eleven of England, it was unanimously resolved, – That neither the members of the above Eleven shall at any time play in any match of cricket, for or against, wherein William Clarke may have the management or control (county matches excepted), in consequence of the treatment they have received from him at Newmarket and elsewhere.

Throughout the early Victorian years the Adelphi Hotel was a meeting place for cricketers in Sheffield. It was here that a group of players in the newly formed UEE met to agree their relationship with William Clarke and AEE. In later years Sheffield Wednesday cricketers, who used the Adelphi Hotel as a base, launched a football team.

This was signed by:

John Wisden	George Picknell
James Dean	Samuel Dakin
Thomas Adams	George Chatterton
Thomas Hunt	Thomas Lockyer
George Grainger Brown	James Grundy
John Lillywhite	Thomas Sherman
Thomas Nixon	Henry Wright

What exactly was 'the treatment received from him at Newmarket'? As the events of these few weeks were to greatly influence JW's life-long commitment to professional cricketers and their welfare, it is worth examining them in some detail.

Fulfilling an annual match programme as demanding as those for AEE in 1851 and 1852 would require a leader with outstanding man management skills. While William Clarke had the vision and drive to take forward the AEE project, his management of his players fell short of the demands of the match programme. Several of the leading professionals of the time, such as Caffyn and Daft, have autobiographies recalling anecdotes about their experience of Clarke and about playing for his team. Clarke was variously characterised as acerbic, grasping, mean and self-focused. He was a generation older than most of the players who joined United and had had a harder life than many of them. His second marriage was failing and he was living away from his Nottingham base, in London. A touring eleven was not only his idea and his project, it could also become his pension fund. This meant that he had to maximise the commercial opportunities around each match and to pack in as many fixtures as possible in the season, which only increased the travel burden. It had all become very intense.

By contrast JW came from a large, well established and increasingly prosperous family. He had served an apprenticeship to enable him to take his place within that family's construction businesses. He was not dependent upon his cricket skills for his livelihood. He could, literally, afford to be more generous and more relaxed.

In creating the United England Eleven, the players were seeking a more relaxed format where the cricket could have a greater precedence over the necessary commercial arrangements. There was little comment on the subject of fees for UEE matches, so it must be assumed that the players found them acceptable. As can be seen from the 1854 programme (Appendix B) there were few days when there was a clash between a UEE fixture and a match in the national programme. There were also plenty of free days for travelling, although the overnight trips from Nottingham to Dublin and then in another year Dublin to Rochdale were challenging exceptions.

JW had a reputation for generosity and it became a fault on occasions when setting the match terms; UEE were badly beaten in a number of matches where it would seem that their opponents were given an over-generous allowance in terms of the number of players and additional professionals. For JW and UEE showing cricket to its best advantage was of more importance than winning every match.

UEE is too often portrayed as having been set up *against* Clarke's AEE. In the ensuing years the evidence would come to suggest otherwise. One of the consequences of AEE's early travels was the discovery of a significant number of cricketers able to play as professionals. Now there were enough able cricketers to support two travelling elevens, although by giving local promoters a choice as to which of the two elevens to invite to their town they weakened Clarke's commercial bargaining power. UEE were in *addition* to AEE and very much an *alternative* to it. As can be seen from the fixture lists for 1854 and 1857 (Appendix C) UEE also had a different selection of opponents, playing more existing institutions and fewer sides raised by, say, civic groups in market towns. Over time there would also be something of a geographical divide with AEE drifting northwards and UEE coming south. By the mid-1860s this would move to a more marked divide and then to a damaging schism. By 1857 UEE's fixture list looked more like one for I Zingari than for AEE.

The initial core of UEE was the fourteen players who signed what might be called The Adelphi Declaration. With a few exceptions they tended to be much younger (Clarke was born in 1798), southern based and with other occupations that might fit around a less all-demanding match programme. They might be involved in industries that still used home-completed piece work which occupied the whole family with output varying according to the cricketer's playing commitments.

The Adelphi Fourteen			
John Wisden	Brighton	1826	Cricket Coach
James Dean	Duncton, Sussex	1816	Farm worker
Thomas Adams	Gravesend	1813	Ordnance worker
Thomas Hunt	Chesterfield	1819	Coach builder
George Brown	Brighton	1825	Decorator
John Lillywhite	Hove	1826	Cricket outfitter & coach
Thomas Nixon	Nottingham	1815	Lace maker
George Picknell	Chalvington, Sussex	1813	Farmer
Samuel Dakin	Sileby, Leicestershire	1808	Lace weaver
George Chatterton	Sheffield	1821	Servant at Wentworth House
Thomas Lockyer	Croydon	1828	Bricklayer
James Grundy	New Radford, Notts	1824	Lace worker & grocer
Thomas Sherman	Mitcham	1827	Block cutter (has shop)
Henry Wright	Sheffield	1822	Groundsman

One of the changes that JW and James Dean made from the AEE model when setting up the UEE was greater inclusion of amateur or *gentlemen* players, usually on an *ad hoc* basis, although Mr FP Miller became something of a regular who on occasions captained the side. Clarke had played Mynn because his personal popularity helped to enhance the crowds and Felix who provided a softer more cultured face to AEE's public relations.

On Sunday 19th September 1852 the following appeared in *Bell's Life*:

THE UNITED ENGLAND ELEVEN.—Mr Editor : We wish through the medium of your widely circulated paper, to state, in answer to numerous letters and inquiries, that it is the intention of the above Eleven to play matches during the months of May, August, and September. The months of June and July will be devoted to the Marylebone Club, where most of the members of that eleven are engaged. There is, now and then, a Thursday in June when the United can play, as the Marylebone Club have seldom a great match at Lord's on those days ; and it is also the intention of the above Eleven, wherever they go, to be on the ground by eleven o'clock (railway or coach delays excepted), so that all matches might be played out, thereby giving satisfaction to the public and proprietors of grounds generally. We wish to return thanks to many gentlemen for the kind wishes they have expressed towards the United.—Yours, &c, JAMES DEAN and JOHN WISDEN. London, Thursday, Sept 16.

This was both a statement of good intent, using their different style of operation, and also a side-swipe at Clarke. From the time that AEE annual fixture lists began to start before August there were conflicting demands on professional players; there had been instances of players declining to leave an AEE tour in the north to travel south to play in a county match. AEE had also developed the habit of ensuring that all their matches continued into the third day, so maximising commercial opportunities for their promoters. This led to late starts, early 'stumps' and other various time-wasting manoeuvres during the day.

The caveat about rail and coach delays was an important one. Although the rapidly expanding rail network greatly assisted the expansion of cricket into a truly national sport, in its infancy it was not without its operational challenges. Also the autobiographies of leading players of the time include many yarns of adventures encountered on overnight stage coach journeys. Getting lost in fog-shrouded marsh lands and having a loaded blunderbuss pointed at their heads were just two of the more picturesque tales.

JW, with Jemmy Dean as his faithful assistant, would lead UEE through the next two decades, until it faded away in the era of an emerging county championship which it had done much to create. Also at this time the differences between northern based professionals and cricketers and clubs in the south was becoming increasingly acrimonious. In 1865 many UEE players transferred to the newly formed United South of England Eleven.

9

OFF TO SCHOOL

The issue of *Bell's Life* for 9th May heralded the start of the 1852 season proper. It reported on the MCC Anniversary Dinner (effectively the AGM) and announced the club's early fixtures. Nicholas Felix, the public relations officer for AEE contributed a piece to the paper which was a 'call to arms' for members of the eleven. Its militaristic tone resonates with Henry V's, Shakespeare drafted, speech to his troops before the Battle of Agincourt. Several commentators had observed that AEE's programme of matches would be harder work without JW playing for them.

Even before his former team-mates had had the opportunity to heed Felix's call to leave their firesides, stiffen up their sinews and head north, JW had reported to Harrow School and begun his work with the boys. He was clearly keen to get involved. Before the first set-piece match on Saturday 1st May he had played for a School team v A to L, for Marillier's XI v Curteis's XI and again for School against a combined team drawn from the Sixth, Upper Fifth and 2nd Fifth forms. The set-piece match, of sufficient status to be reported in *Bell's Life*, featured Wisden's XI v Royston's XI; Henry Royston being a locally based professional. Despite being his team's top-scorer in both innings and taking 9 out of 15 wickets, JW's eleven lost by five wickets.

The defining contribution for Royston's XI was by AH Walker (one of the famous Southgate cricketing Walkers). In Wisden's XI's first innings he kept wicket (two victims) and then made 42 when his side batted, easily the top score in the match, before becoming a bowler in his opponents' second innings taking five wickets, including that of his brother VE (bowled for 0).

JW and AH did battle again when JW played for the School and AH for the Fifth form. JW's first innings score of 31* was more than matched by AH's 46. JW only scored 1 in his second knock and the Fifth Form needed only 17 to win the match which they reached for the loss of three wickets. JW took eight wickets in the match to AH's six. There were clearly some able cricketers at the school. JW was to establish a long-term and beneficial relationship with the whole Walker family.

It is claimed that the playing fields at Eton facilitated victory at the Battle of Waterloo. In their turn the playing fields at Harrow School certainly made a major contribution to the development of cricket, association football and, thus, rugby football, into international sports. Being at the foot of a hill the grounds were notoriously wet and 'soft'.

Throughout May the ablest cricketers within the school were regularly divided up in various ways to create practice matches. In today's terminology they might be labelled 'sixth form games'. JW played in most of these games, the last of the sequence being when he augmented a second XI to play what was now emerging as the first XI.

At the end of the month JW spent some days playing cricket away from Harrow. In one of the matches he and Sam Dakin bolstered a Manchester side at Lord's where they lost to MCC by three wickets. JW bowled throughout both MCC innings taking seven wickets in the first and four of the seven to fall in the second. The following Monday he was back at Lord's as part of a combined Sussex & Surrey team to play an MCC-selected England XI. JW scored 29* in the counties' second innings to set up a 51 runs win. Again he bowled unchanged throughout both innings, returning figures of 26-10-27-4 and 34-17-37-2. Clearly the weeks of coaching had done nothing to take the edge off his own skills.

On 5th June[30] the School XI entertained an Old Harrovians XI and had the better of a match that was left unfinished because of time lost during the day. The match report in *Bell's Life* noted that JW 'could be proud of the improvement in the School XI's bowling'. During an interval in the match Hon Robert Grimston made a presentation to the long-serving Old Dick (Pipes) Chad who had been JW's predecessor as coach at the school. In *Haygarth at Harrow*, Roger Heavens notes that Richard Chad was born in the town in 1787. He had been a long-time servant of the school as coach, groundsman, pavilion keeper, umpire and occasional player and was described at the time as an 'honest, simple minded man of character'. At this time JW was only 25 years old and so at an age where he was able to establish an entirely different style of relationship with the boys.

Having used May to clarify the best eleven the nature of the matches in June and July took a different form as the School XI played against a succession of external sides. Old Harrovians, Quidnuncs, Harlequins, Harrow Town, I Zingari and MCC came in turn up the hill to Harrow School. IZ had a chastening experience as the School side amassed a total of 330. It was recorded in the IZ-penned match report in *Bell's Life* that this formidable score was due to 'steady play'. Clearly, another indication that JW was having an impact; in today's phraseology he would have been said to have 'tightened their game'. The School's win over the Town had been its first in 10 years. News of the run-feast in the IZ match clearly reached Lord's and when MCC visited the school a fortnight later they brought the professionals Grundy and Nixon with them. The pair bowled out the School XII for 36 and 75 to win a one-day match by 68 runs. This was the final match of the series and the following week the boys set off to Lord's to face Eton and Winchester.

Unlike today the coach did not necessarily accompany the boys to matches. So as the now settled School XI played the series of matches through June and July, JW could be released to play in his own programme of matches. On Monday 14th June he reported to Lord's to join the Sussex team that were to play MCC. Despite JW taking 9 wickets in the match Sussex were badly beaten by 148 runs.

On 1st July JW played in a somewhat unusual match at the Oval. A team selected by the Surrey committee comprised eight of their players plus Box, Mynn and JW to take on a North side selected not by MCC

---

[30] *Scores & Biographies* gives this date as 8th June.

but by William Clarke. Despite JW's efforts (49-24-48-4) his side lost by an innings. In *Bell's Life's* list of fixtures this fixture was described as North v South – Mr Houghton's match. Surprisingly, given the ability of the players, this match was not reported in the newspaper. *Scores & Biographies* lists the match as being one under Clarke's control; the dismissive tone in *Scores & Biographies* added to the absence from *Bell's Life* may indicate the lack of approval of Clarke's activities. However, if JW was prepared to play in the match it must be assumed that he thought that it was being arranged by either Surrey CCC or Mr Houghton, the club's proprietor.

Over the next two weeks at Lord's MCC selected England sides to play firstly against Kent and then against Surrey. JW did not play in either match but his absence was deemed worthy of comment. He was not missed in the Kent match as England romped home by seven wickets but a match report on the Surrey game said 'Wisden did not play and was much missed'. His status as a player was now such that even his absences were noteworthy.

By mid-July, with the Harrow boys well through their preparations, JW was able to return to his county side. In the first match, at the Oval, he helped Sussex to an impressive 10 wickets win over Surrey. His bowling performances of 49-27-60-6 and 41-24-27-6 were either side of an innings of 30. With the Georges Brown (86) and Picknell (50) both scoring heavily Sussex were left to score just 28 to win. JW was sent out with his great friend Jemmy Dean to safely accomplish this. Both of the Georges were to join JW and Dean in the early UEE sides.

The following Monday saw the Gentlemen v Players fixture which the Players won by a comfortable five wickets. JW had a quiet match, opening the batting but scoring only 6 and 2 (run out) and taking just two wickets. Could it be that he was saving himself for the second half of the week when he joined the Sussex team for a match with Kent at Hove? Batting at No 6 where he seems generally to have been more comfortable, he scored 20* and 14 and then recorded match figures of 10/57 as he and Dean bowled unchanged throughout the match and Sussex won by 6 wickets. A week later the teams met at the Common, Tunbridge Wells, the scene of JW's great innings two years earlier. In this return match Sussex completed the double winning by 53 runs. JW again bowled unchanged through both Kent innings for match figures of 12/68 and scoring 23 and 6 in his two innings. He had taken 22 first-class wickets in a week at an average of 5.68.

Fred Ponsonby was a contemporary of Arthur Haygarth at Harrow in the early 1840s. During the 1850s he visited the school to act as the Eleven's batting coach, while JW focused on the team's bowling and 'out-cricket'. Ponsonby also worked, to great effect, on JW's batting.

While JW was doing battle for Sussex his 'boys' were at Lord's for their two key fixtures of the year. The first was against Winchester College who were coached by JW's former mentor William Lillywhite. Despite taking a first innings lead Harrow lost a high scoring match by 68 runs. No sooner than they had finished one match they were back out for the second to face a rested Eton. This time they were to be successful, winning another high scoring match by 71 runs. The impact of JW's coaching was the crucial difference. He had worked to 'tighten' the boys' game and in the first innings the last two wickets battled out 52 runs and in the second the last pair added 41, a total greater than the margin of victory. This win was to be the start of a long winning sequence for Harrow. The final day (Monday) of the match was umpired by James Dean and John Lillywhite who travelled to London from Kent after playing for the victorious Sussex team. Whether or not JW travelled with them seems not to have been recorded.

It was becoming clear and being commented upon in the press that JW was having a marked and positive impact on the Harrow side. While Fred Ponsonby continued to act as a batting coach JW focused on the other aspects of the game which were traditionally less attractive to gentlemen cricketers. The boys' approach to matches was viewed as more thoughtful and the bowling and fielding much improved.

The following Sunday *Bell's Life* included the United England Eleven in its list of forthcoming fixtures for the first time.[31]

After ten days' rest, and with news of UEE out in the open, JW began the sequence of matches leading up to UEE's first match. He joined James Dean and George Berry as one of the three professionals 'given' to a local Northampton side for their match with AEE. Whatever the distractions

[31] See Chapter 8

that the UEE announcement may have caused on the sidelines, JW 'put in the overs' returning figures of 69.2-42-47-4 in AEE's first innings. He only had to bowl eight overs in AEE's second innings as they romped home by nine wickets. With just a single day off for travelling, JW, Dean and many of the AEE players made their way to Canterbury where they formed the bulk of the England team to play Kent. Who travelled with whom is not known but there would have been scope for some interesting conversations about the future of professional elevens. In JW's case the journey was hardly worthwhile in playing terms. He bowled just 8 overs in Kent's first innings and none in the second. He opened the batting in England's only innings but scored just one run. The England bowling was dominated by Clarke and Grundy.

No longer being driven by the concentrated AEE match programme JW had several days off before becoming part of the Sussex team to play Surrey at Hove. With fine weather and a very well prepared ground batsmen dominated the match. JW opened the batting for Sussex and scored 52 out of a massive total of 288. It was well into the second day when Surrey began their innings and they spent over a day amassing 210 in reply thus ensuring a drawn match. JW had bowling figures of 60-24-89-2, thus conceding a run every three deliveries as opposed to his normal one every four. The higher run rate would be a coming feature of matches played on this ground.

History was made the following day (26th August) at Portsmouth when in front of a good crowd JW led out UEE for the first match of this newly formed team against Twenty Gentlemen of Hampshire with Day. Daniel Day was the manager of the ground on which the match was played. JW led from the front in his new team, bowling throughout both Hampshire's innings, taking ten wickets in each. UEE won their first fixture in a very low scoring match by eight wickets. And so to Newmarket for a match listed as against Twenty-two of Newmarket with Arnold and F Tinley. It was here that William Clarke, forsaking his responsibilities with AEE, arrived to berate the UEE players but any unpleasantness off the field did not distract UEE on it. However, his visit may have been the reason that the game did not get underway until 12.30pm. Again JW led from the front, bowling throughout both the Twenty-two's innings and taking 20 wickets. Bowlers dominated a low-scoring match, Arnold and Tinley bowling the bulk of the hosts' overs and taking all but four of the wickets. UEE went on to win by 95 runs.

Gravesend had clearly been assessed as providing stiffer opposition as they were only permitted eighteen players. The assessment proved accurate; the local team included the local rising star Edgar Willsher. When UEE could muster only 38 in a first innings reply to Gravesend's 142 they were required to follow-on. JW's undefeated innings of 30, 'steadily and carefully made'[32] was enough to help the tail wag and set the hosts 66 to win which they were unable to reach by stumps and so the match was left drawn.

As the Gravesend match had finished on a Saturday UEE had a free day to make the long trip to Sheffield. Sheffield were known to be a strong side from their encounters with AEE so the match was made at 11 v 15. JW and Dean were reported to have brought their strongest possible side to Yorkshire and at the start of the match the betting odds were 5 to 4 on UEE. It turned out to be a dour game not helped by some torrential rain. JW returned figures of 37-24-29-2 as the hosts gained a first innings lead of six runs. However, in their second innings JW (19-6-23-5) and Jem Grundy shot them out for 37 and JW then scored a quick 23 to lead UEE to an eight wickets win.

On the second evening of the Sheffield match the UEE players met and agreed the Adelphi Declaration in opposition to William Clarke.[33]

As would become the norm UEE proved themselves to be pleasant guests and at the end of the match Lord Milton invited the team to spend the rest of the week at his Wentworth home enjoying a combination of cricket and shooting (which would have pleased JW). It was also announced that UEE would visit Sheffield twice in 1853.

JW skipped his lordship's hospitality to hurry back to Leamington where he and George Parr were included in a Gentlemen of Warwickshire side to play I Zingari at Parr & Wisden's ground. IZ were the guests of Lord Guernsey at his Offchurch Bury home,[34] half a dozen miles from the ground. It was a classic IZ trip with lavish hospitality and the *Bell's Life* match report (signed J.L.B. [35]) gave as much space to evening theatricals as it did to the cricket. The two professionals made their presence felt, Parr

[32] *Bell's Life*, 12th September 1852

[33] See Chapter 8

[34] Offchurch Bury was a former manor house a few miles east of Leamington. It had a well recorded history dating back to the 12th century. There is evidence of earlier occupation of the site with supposition that the 'Off' element of the name of the house and village comes from occupancy of the Mercian King Offa.

[35] Presumably J.L.B. is John Loraine Baldwin, one of the three founders of I Zingari.

scoring 53 and 19 and JW 33 and 1. JW also bowled throughout both IZ innings and returned figures of 2/28 and 7/26 as the Warwickshire side won by 164 runs. The Gentlemen's team included Mr Thomas Rose who had been a highly successful local cricketer for a number of years. His old-fashioned, fast underhand style of bowling must have caught IZ unawares as he took 7/34 in the first innings. His involvement locally helped to strengthen the group of cricketers who would sustain Parr & Wisden's ground in future years.

With the county cricket programme completed and no longer being committed to the AEE's autumn schedule, JW's playing season was completed by 11th September and he returned to his London base with the Lillywhite family. Although no longer tied to the six days per week drudge of playing for AEE JW still had a formidable workload. He had responsibility for a cricket ground in Leamington and was leading coach/professional at a major public school. He was an essential member of Sussex county teams as well as various representative ones. He had now added to this his duties with UEE where he was secretary, with James Dean's assistance, manager and captain as well as being the best player.

Back at Harrow the boys had returned from their 'long vac' and JW had time to play in three internal games before the School's cricket season ended with a second match against Harrow Town (won by five wickets). Most of the 1852 eleven had left school and JW and new captain Kenelm Digby would have to make an early start to putting together the 1853 eleven. Over the next three seasons JW was to develop a good and highly successful partnership with Digby.

A line drawing by GF Watts showing a batsman playing the draw shot.

JW's early reputation was founded on his bowling skills. However, he was also a very good batsman. His all-round skills made him a formidable single wicket opponent.

For the most part of their careers JW and William Caffyn played in similar, or the same, matches. In his autobiography *Seventy-One Not Out*, Caffyn gives this description of JW's batting:

> As a batsman he was first-rate. He played with a beautifully straight bat, which he appeared to hold very lightly, but nevertheless he could hit hard and clean. In 1849 he scored exactly 100 in the Sussex and Kent match, and in 1855 his score of 148 for Sussex v. Yorkshire was much talked about. There is no doubt that if Wisden had had less bowling to do he would have been still more famous as a batsman. He was clever at making the old-fashioned "draw" between the right leg and the wicket.

The '100 in the Sussex and Kent match' was actually scored in 1850; it was the only century scored that season. He, also, took four wickets in Kent's only innings of that match. Also, in 1848 he made the season's highest score, 92, at Trent Bridge having taken 4/53 in Nottinghamshire's only innings of the match.

Having begun his career as a school-based coach and also launched a new high profile team, 1852 had been a demanding season for JW and he, no doubt, was looking forward to a quiet, recuperative winter. At the beginning of December any such hopes were dashed – at least in the short term. On 5th December *Bell's Life* published an extraordinarily long article titled 'Notes on Cricket' or 'Doings of the Past Season'. The article was signed by A Lover of Cricket, and generally accepted as the work of a Cambridge-based barrister called Merrywether. He stated 'My object will be to touch upon the principal events and enlighten your cricketing readers upon the doings of the game, as played of late'.

It is true that there was an account of, and comment upon, the matches played in the past season. However, within it there was a significant attack on William Clarke and his management of the All England Eleven. Much of the piece reiterated well-rehearsed grievances about Clarke – his autocratic manner, his miserliness and the team's poor match time keeping, amongst others. Clarke was to admit that he had been advised by friends and senior MCC members to let the matter go but that was not in his nature. If he felt that he had been unfairly represented his character required him to challenge the writer. His initial reply was published in another newspaper, *The Era* [36], but then all and sundry waded into a debate that rumbled on throughout the January issues of *Bell's Life*. In hindsight it was an unedifying spectacle but one which revealed some useful information.

On 2nd January 1853 *Bell's Life* published a copy of Clarke's response that had appeared in *The Era*, and on the same pages JW's response to that Clarke piece. Clarke's response can at best be described as a rambling stream of consciousness. A less kindly description might be that it was a verbose diatribe. Amongst other matters he addresses the nature of justice, the declining commercial value of 'Old Dean' and 'Old Lilly' and the many hours spent and journeys he had undertaken during the winter months arranging the AEE match programme. One informative statement was: 'Wisden and I did not part on money matters, but quite a different subject.'

In much of Merrywether's original case JW and UEE had been presented as the good guys, so Clarke attacked JW, no doubt seeing him as a leader of the opposition. JW expressed a reluctance to get involved but felt that as a figure with a public profile he needed to defend 'my character as a cricketer'. His response made a number of challenging assertions about his relationship with Clarke. Clarke had already conceded that he always had a wish to challenge any and every inaccurate statement about himself. Therefore, as he did not challenge any of JW's assertions we must assume that they were accurate. Clarke had quoted a very selective and self-promoting set of match statistics in an apparent attempt to demonstrate how much more effective and successful he was as a cricketer than JW.

From his performances during the 1850 and 1851 seasons JW had a very strong claim to be both the hardest working and the most successful player in the AEE squad. It was generally acknowledged that AEE were significantly weakened by his non-appearance in 1852. Within his reply JW stated:

- Mr Clarke has tried for the last two years to do me all the injury that he could but for what reason I am at a loss to imagine
- ... how often does he keep on bowling when he ought to go off
- I have played in great matches for him and have always done my very best
- ... for the last three years ... I have done considerably more towards winning them [great matches] than he has
- So what can his motive be in trying to run me down? I should perhaps not have left him [AEE] had he treated me as a cricketer

[36] *The Era*, 26th December 1852

JW quoted some more summative statistics, those for the four matches in 1849 and 1850 in which both he and Clarke played for North versus South. The total number of wickets that the pair had taken between them in the four matches was: 16, 19, 19 & 19. The share of the total was 39 to 34 in Clarke's favour. However, JW pointed out that he also contributed with the bat and in this aspect it was 113 to 22 in his favour.

JW summed up with:

> I should not have said so much had not Mr Clarke made the attack. I hoped he had done with me, but it would be wrong if I did not make some reply as a public man, but with no ill will to Mr Clarke if he had not so maliciously pointed out circumstances which are in fact quite the chances of cricket. Respecting the United Eleven signing their names [to the Adelphi Declaration], I maintain we were perfectly justified in so doing. At the same time I beg to say it was not out of disrespect to the other players, but this plainly shows that Mr Clarke is not much liked by the majority of players or the "signing" would not have taken place.

And ends with:

> In conclusion I, on behalf of the United Eleven, will thank Mr Clarke not to interfere with our match making, and we shall not trouble ourselves with him. – Yours &c,
> Warwickshire, Dec 31st   John Wisden

The debate ground on into January 1853 with players and followers making claims, justifications and counter-claims. While most of the players signed their contributions, many of the followers hid behind pseudonyms or initials. Eventually, in their 23rd January edition *Bell's Life* called a halt to this debate by refusing to publish any more contributions. However, many of the issues continued to exist over the coming seasons.

Although nothing was explicitly stated there was a cultural difference between Clarke and JW. As well as being a generation older, Clarke had had a harder life, originally combining his work as a bricklayer and/or publican with his cricket. JW came from a much more assured background with his grandfather, father and uncle all engaged in a prosperous business and being leaders within their civic community. William Clarke's financial security was now bound up in the operation and success of AEE. JW had been apprenticed as a carpenter and would have the fall back of a place within his family's construction business if things went wrong with his cricket. Other skills that he had acquired within the family business meant that he would never again have to pick up his carpenter's tools.

Cricket in the major public schools began early each year and before March 1853 was out Rugby had played their first matches. JW had been invited to play in one of the matches but had been unable to accept. Grundy took his place, joining Martingell and John Lillywhite (the resident professional/ coach). The boys did not want for expert guidance.

The early cricket at Harrow followed the same pattern as it had in 1852. Of the 1853 group only the new captain, Kenelm Digby, had been in the 1852 eleven and so he and JW had some work to do putting together a new team. During April and May there was a sequence of thirteen 'internal' matches played, JW taking part in most of them. On more than one occasion James Dean made the journey to Harrow on a day when he was free from his MCC duties to play in the matches and assist in the development of the new team. JW seems to have been able to call on other leading professional players as Thomas Nixon and Henry Royston made appearances along with such gentlemen alumni as Fred Ponsonby, Arthur Haygarth and Robert Grimston. The last of this sequence of matches saw a School XI (including JW) play the exotically named Harrow Philathletic Club. JW's eleven wickets and 9* led the School XI to a six wickets win.

The matches against 'external' teams began with a 45 runs loss to Harrow Town. From this point the improving performance of the School XI can be judged by the outcome of the matches against Quidnuncs (drawn), Harlequins (won by 9 wickets), MCC & Ground (won by 1 wicket) and I Zingari (drawn). The final match on 23rd July brought the only other defeat when the School were beaten by an Old Harrovian side boosted by Henry Royston.

Up until the end of May JW played in just one first-class match when he was in the England side at Lord's to play Nottinghamshire. William Clarke opened the Nottinghamshire innings and was run out on both occasions – were the years catching up on him and was he no longer quite as quick between the wickets as he had been? JW had figures of 34-18-25-4 and 44.3-22-50-3 to leave England to chase just 76 to win. They did not make it being bowled out for only 48. This match was under MCC's control so although Clarke was prominent in the Nottinghamshire side JW felt able to play, as did Dean, Hunt and Chatterton. However, when AEE met Sixteen of Sussex at Chichester at the end of June all the Adelphi men were absent, abiding by their Declaration. They also declined to play in a North v South match promoted by Clarke.

As the main Harrow school matches settled into a pattern of regular Saturday fixtures JW started each week by playing either for UEE or in first-class cricket. On Sunday 5th June 1853 he was part of the UEE that travelled to Sheffield to take on Yorkshire. The Yorkshire team had yet to be beaten by either AEE or UEE and so the match was now made at 11 v 14. As a result of having arrived the evening before UEE honoured their commitment to be on the ground and ready to play by eleven o'clock. But when they reached the ground they found it in poor condition, apparently lacking the application of a roller. Yorkshire batted first and were twice bowled out cheaply, their two innings not totalling 100. JW and Grundy bowled unchanged through both innings, JW's figures being 21.3-13-27-9 and 30-22-19-8 (conceding less than 1 run per 10 deliveries in the second innings). In their only innings UEE had totalled 130 so won by an innings and 36 runs. Yorkshire had lost their unbeaten record and UEE had posted notice that they were not going to be any pale imitation of AEE.

The following Monday JW was joined by James Dean and John Lillywhite in playing for UEE against Sussex at Hove.[37] The extent to which this mis-matched the two sides is shown by the fact that the county team were allowed 18 players and still had very much the worse of the drawn match. JW, however, had a good match with innings of 33 and 15* and 11 wickets in the county's first innings. A week later the trio reverted to their county side for its fixture with MCC at Lord's. A high-scoring match led to MCC being set 115 to win and at 75-4 looked set for victory. JW was always inspired by a tight match situation and he led the way to a Sussex win by 33 runs as the last seven wickets fell for four runs, numbers 8, 9 and 11 all being 'b. Wisden' for just two runs between them.

The next Monday's match at Lord's was England v Kent but did not include JW as he was back at Harrow playing in the match School v

---

[37] Both *Bell's Life* and *Scores & Biographies* recorded this match as being played at Brighton. In fact the match was played at the Royal Brunswick Ground which was across the boundary in Hove. It was not only the house building of the Wisden family, and others, that was moving the conurbation slowly westward. The principal cricket ground was moving in the same direction and still had one more move to make.

Fifth, his 38 runs and 11 wickets being a crucial contribution to the School's win. Clearly there was a need to continuously strike a balance between playing in first-class cricket and his duties at school as cricket coach. He had earlier played in a match First XI v Second XI when he helped the Second XI to win. In this match the winning team also included a Lillywhite but in the cursory way in which the professionals were recorded in scorebooks it did not say which one. As William was at Winchester and James at Marlborough it must have been either John or Fred. Although Fred was a competent club cricketer it was more likely to have been John. Because Rugby School traditionally had an early summer vacation John may have been released from his coaching duties and able to help out at Harrow. The likelihood is that after the MCC v Sussex match John L followed JW up the hill, showing that releasing JW to play county matches had advantages for both school and player.

On Friday 1st July UEE were in Maidenhead to play a local side of eighteen. The match is a good example of the variable circumstances in which such matches took place. It was unusual for such a match to start on a Friday as it restricted play to two days, but to accommodate the local promoters JW and Dean agreed to do so and a further agreement was made that there would be a prompt start and good use made of the available playing time. Punctually as promised at a quarter to eleven JW led UEE out onto a pitch that might be described as a little rough and ready. When the local side's second innings closed they had a lead of 120. While the match was in progress Tom Adams had been exploring the far corners of the ground and discovered a five-ton roller. In the absence of a horse Adams recruited a gang of 30 or so people to pull the roller. Within a minute of the close of the Maidenhead innings Adams's Gang was seen pushing the roller out to the pitch – much to the amusement of the spectators. Adams was of the opinion that the use of the roller was the only way to give UEE a chance of winning the match. However accommodating UEE might have been in setting the arrangements for the match, they were now determined to try to win it. Dean had batted at No 11 in the first innings but now, in a rearranged batting order, he opened with Adams (no doubt eager to score runs before the effects of his rolling wore off). Dean batted with such determined caution that his innings of 19 filled five hours and he had taken the score up to 30-4 when JW, who had pushed himself up the order, came out to join him. The team principals were now to become the team leaders and eased the score up to 78 before Dean's long vigil came to an end. This now became another of the sort of situations in which JW revelled. With variable support from essentially the tail he had inched the score up to 109 when the last man Wright came out to join him. Sadly, Wright's innings lasted just one ball leaving UEE to lose by 11 runs and JW on 44*. The hosts reported themselves well pleased with UEE's performance and expressed the wish to play them again next year.

UEE's boycott of matches under the control of William Clarke meant that JW played a limited amount of cricket in July. He did not play for either Sussex or Kent & Sussex in their matches against AEE, nor did he play in the Clarke-sponsored North v South match. Also he was not one of the eleven Players who lost to the Gentlemen by 60 runs; a rare reverse. It may be that he was limiting his time away from school. He did, though, play for an England side that lost to MCC by 70 runs at Lord's on 11th & 12th July 1853. JW bowled unchanged through both innings for figures of 50-31-43-5 and 31.2-16-29-7 but the England batting was weak with totals of 43 and 64. During the match Thomas Adams scored a six by hitting a ball into the cellar of the Tavern.

A fortnight later JW was no doubt pleased to play at Lord's again this time in a Farewell Benefit Match for his former tutor and mentor William Lillywhite, now aged 61 years but still playing. The match was appropriately England v Sussex with George Parr added to the Sussex team. In honour of the 'Nonpareil', Mr CG Taylor (as he was listed) made his first appearance in a Sussex team since 1846. Despite putting in two long stints of bowling JW had an indifferent match although on a personal level he would have been pleased to be part of the tribute to the man who had taught him so much in their days back home in Brighton and on those annual trips to Cambridge. England overwhelmed the county side, winning by 197 runs.

No sooner had his Sussex colleagues vacated the pitch than JW's Harrow boys were coming out to take on Winchester; there was clearly a need for MCC to keep the action going so as to entertain their membership. In a low-scoring match Harrow were comfortable winners by 70 runs. The following day they began a tighter match against Eton and won by three wickets with none of the innings totals reaching 100. It was noted by the press that in the Harrow team only the captain, Digby, had played the previous year and there was much favourable comment both on the ground and in the newspapers about the way that he and JW had created such a well organised and successful team. This was to be the start of a long run of Harrow success.

The following Monday was 1st August 1853 and saw JW begin on the by now familiar round of matches towards the end of the season but this year with UEE rather than AEE. First call was at Stowmarket where the town side were allowed twenty-two players including Edgar Willsher and Thomas Sherman. The two professionals scored a significant part of the first innings total of 127 and then bowled out UEE for 87. Edgar Willsher was beginning to have a regular and noticeable impact on matches at this level. His eight first innings wickets was the match winning performance. JW and Jem Grundy then dismissed the hosts for 68 leaving UEE 109 to win. By stumps on the second evening UEE were 15-4. When Thomas Adams walked out the following morning to resume his innings he was accompanied by JW who had pushed himself up the order. For the next hour and a half these two eased the total upwards until with the score at 53 Adams was out for 18. John Lillywhite came and went quickly and at dinner the score was 64-6. The betting odds which were constantly fluctuating were a good measure of the changing balance of the game. On the resumption of play the score inched upwards until at 75 Lockyer executed a 'Yes – No – Whoops – Sorry' on JW who was run out for 27 after a battling innings lasting nearly three hours. This effectively brought the run-chase to an end and the visitors lost by 22 runs. They had probably been over-generous in the odds agreed for the match. Their hosts were delighted to have won and gratified by the 5,000 plus people who had paid to see the match. Not surprisingly they expressed the hope that UEE would be back next season.

Having observed the usual social pleasantries at Stowmarket UEE set off for Rotherham where they were due to play next day. Despite the rapidly expanding network of railways part of this journey had to be completed by (stage) coach and the team travelled through the night. They arrived just in time to meet their 11.00am deadline. As *Bell's Life* noted their journey left them in no fit state to face the poorly prepared 'bumping' pitch and they were shot out for 32. Six of the wickets were taken by James Lillywhite who was in Yorkshire to act as private coach to Lord Milton; his lordship was also in the Rotherham side. JW and Jem Grundy shared all but one of the wickets as Rotherham could manage only 64. When UEE batted again they scored 43 leaving the home team to score 12 to win. As a measure of the difficulties of the pitch, JW and

Grundy took nine wickets while they did so. One consolation for playing on such a poor ground was that UEE now had a rest day. To fill this time Lord Milton invited UEE to Wentworth Wood House (the home of Lord Fitzwilliam). Whilst enjoying lavish hospitality UEE players mixed with locals to play a one day, one innings match. The event was much enjoyed by all. During the day Lord Milton spoke to JW and James Dean about taking a side to Dublin. He was later to become a valuable friend of UEE.

The following day, Sunday, was a rest day and the team had only the comparatively short journey to make to York where the lavish hospitality was set to continue. On Wednesday morning before the third day's play the UEE players were entertained to breakfast by none other than the Archbishop of York. His Grace seems to have been a generous host as the match report described the players spending much of the rest of the day consuming the fruit that they had brought away with them. Clearly, being well-mannered and courteous tourists brought its advantages. They needed to ensure themselves 'replete' as several, including JW, had to be on the field in Horsham before noon the following day. This meant a tiring overnight journey.

The match at York had been made against Twenty-two of York & District.[38] Allowing 22 players was generally agreed on the basis that they were to be drawn from the locality. Such was the drive to put up a good show against a visiting eleven that the organisers had stretched the 'district' as far west as Bradford and as far north as Bedale. In other locations this desire led to teams being drawn from and being largely representative of a whole county. This was proving problematic in Yorkshire which had several locations wishing to be the centre of the county's cricket. UEE did well to finish the match with a draw.

Following the conflicts of the previous autumn and winter JW spent much of the 1853 season avoiding William Clarke; opting out of matches where Clarke was either in control or had an input. However, 1853 was to be the season when Sussex re-commenced fixtures with Nottinghamshire, which had not been played since 1848. JW and Clarke were the 'champions' of their respective teams so something of a head-to-head contest was unavoidable.

---

[38] The *Bell's Life* match report called the team York & District. However, in *Scores & Biographies* the home team is called Yorkshire. It may be that Haygarth thought that the county name was a better descriptor of the team. He had previously made similar points about expansion of the 'district' element in team names.

The first match was at Hove starting on 29th August. JW had an ineffective match which may have been the reason that Sussex were swept to defeat by an innings in just two days. His 19* in the first innings was one of the few double figure innings for Sussex. Just a week later Sussex travelled to Nottingham for the return fixture at Trent Bridge. The home team batted first and JW bowled throughout the innings to return figures of 46.3-33-31-6 as the hosts were bowled out for exactly 100. His wickets included those of business partner George Parr (36 – top score) and William Clarke. Sussex in turn were dismissed for 98 despite the dogged resistance of James Dean who was left undefeated on 22. The third day began with Nottinghamshire at 52-5 but with the ever dangerous Parr still there with 23. The betting odds had moved to evens. Then JW turned the match taking a brilliant catch at point to dismiss Parr for 28. Little resistance followed and the innings closed for 69 when Clarke was run out for 0. JW followed his catch by mopping-up the tail for figures of 20-8-36-5 to give him match figures of 11/67 from 66.3 overs. Aided by the overnight rest he and Hodson had bowled unchanged throughout the innings. The bookmakers now made the odds 5 to 4 on Sussex who were set 72 to win.

The Sussex reply got off to a poor start when Brown was dismissed second ball for 0. Pushed-up the order, out walked JW to bat at three. This could become another of the dogged fights that he relished. However, when the score had reached 13 Dean, who had opened the innings, was bowled by Frank Tinley. John Lillywhite now came out to join JW and the pair began to build up the innings and moved the score to 43 when Lillywhite was dismissed in bizarre circumstances. He sent a fierce drive crashing through the stumps at the bowler's end but then lost track of the ball. He had started to run before he realised the ball was being returned to the wicket-keeper. As he turned to make his ground he slipped, fell and was run out while lying in the middle of the pitch. 43-3, needing 29 to win, as the players went in for dinner (lunch). After dinner Sussex inched forward until JW was dismissed for 35 with the score at 52. The score had reached 61-7 when Hodson came out to join Carpenter and the pair slowly ground their way to reach the target without further loss of wickets. From the moment his catch had dismissed George Parr JW had been the dominant player in this match.

The match finished at 4.15pm amid great celebration by the Sussex players. JW and Jemmy Dean were grateful for the early finish as they had to be on the ground in Phoenix Park, Dublin by 11.00 the following morning.

The Dublin match was an instance where enterprise overwhelmed cricket capacity. *Bell's Life* reported that 'This match … was arranged entirely by telegraphic dispatch'. It went on to explain that on it being known that they [UEE] were disengaged on the 8th, a telegraphic dispatch was sent from Lord Milton in Dublin to Dean and Wisden at Nottingham … to bring eight of the United Eleven, which with his lordship, Mr Fenn and James Lillywhite was to have comprised the eleven who were to play against a very powerful Twenty-two of the Phoenix Park Club. This was always going to be a significant challenge and after travelling through the night seven UEE men arrived on the ground just before 10.00am. Amongst those not included in the seven were Sampson, Lockyer, Chatterton, John Lillywhite, Grundy and Martingell. Not surprisingly UEE were badly beaten, losing by an innings with no batsman getting to double figures.

To make matters worse JW injured himself. Attempting a sharp return chance he took the ball on the top of the thumb 'straining the sinews'. He had to leave the field and later batted with one hand. These injuries began to accumulate and contributed to the arthritis that would probably hasten the end his cricket career.

The match finished in two days which meant that the Saturday could be added to the Sunday for travelling back to England; UEE had a fixture at Hove starting on Monday. In the match report of Fourteen Gentlemen of England v UEE *Bell's Life* described JW's thumb as 'crippled'. It was his left hand that was injured so he was still able to do 40% of the bowling in each of the Gentlemen's innings. Coming in at No 11 in the first innings he batted for a few balls before Dean got himself out and as UEE won by seven wickets he was not required to bat again. At this point discretion seems to have overcome valour and JW did not play in the last three matches of the season.

With his contributions to Harrow School, Sussex CC and UEE, JW had had a demanding season. In 1851 he simply had to play, now he was also needed as a coach, administrator and leader – both on and off the field. All in all 1853 had been another successful season.

10

STAYING ON AT SCHOOL

By the spring of 1854, after the upheavals of the previous two seasons, JW's cricket season was settling into something of a pattern. Early spring would see the beginning of internal matches at Harrow School as preparation for establishing 'The Eleven' for the summer. From the beginning of May JW often spent the first half of the week (Monday-Wednesday) playing for Sussex, UEE or some other team. The second half of the week would see him back at Harrow. One of the benefits for the school of this arrangement seems to be that he often brought another highly skilled cricketer back with him. From the beginning of June onwards the focus of the school's preparations moved from mid-week, internal matches to their Saturday fixtures against external sides. As coaches were not expected to be with their teams on match days, this gave JW even more time to follow his own match programme. For the school team the summer season culminated in the matches at Lord's, soon only to be between Harrow and Eton when the (Head) Master at Winchester decided to stop releasing his men (= boys) for a week in London. There would be some further cricket at school in September when the boys returned from the Long Vacation.

In 1854 preparation at Harrow started as early as 13th March, two of the earliest matches being between Wisden's XI and Lillywhite's XI. In the scorebook Lillywhite is clearly labelled as 'Jas'. The two professionals seem to have taken a back seat during the first match, each batting at No 11 and most of the wickets being taken by Brockwell and Walker (VE). Judging by the scorecard, in the second match the two Sussex players took a more active part. James Lillywhite frequently appeared in the internal matches in April and May and at times was joined by Arthur Haygarth (Harrow School, 1839-1842) who was another Sussex county cricketer. The boys did not want for expert support, guidance and the opportunity to test their developing skills against players from the highest level.

UEE's match programme began on 1st May against, probably, their strongest opponents. Sheffield had been one of the opponents in AEE's first tour and had been regular hosts to both touring teams ever since.

They were also one of the strongest of the town teams (they would probably claim to be *the* strongest); in their first match with AEE they were allowed 20 players but this advantage had been steadily reduced and UEE's 1854 match was with Sheffield XV. The match was played on the recently opened Newhall Ground which had been created out of a former country house and park. The recently laid pitch had yet to settle and as a result although UEE totalled only 120, they won by an innings. JW bowled throughout both innings and took 14 wickets in the match.

UEE's next four fixtures were of a different kind to both their earliest fixtures against town-based teams and also the AEE fixture list. Their opponents were Rugby Club and School (22 players), Cambridge University (13 + 2 professionals), Oxford University (14) and then a combined Cambridge & Oxford University side (15). The great (public) schools and these two universities played an essential role in the development of cricketers at this time. From them came a steady stream of amateur players, the best of whom becoming important members of the emerging county cricket clubs. Also, these were the people who would be able to provide the commercial and administrative leadership for those emerging clubs and also in some cases the established clubs. The majority of these gifted players would make their names as amateur batsmen and playing against UEE would give them the opportunity to test and hone their skills against the best professional bowlers in the land in much the way the Harrow boys were given that opportunity. This wider purpose was very much part of JW's aspirations for the team that he led both on and off the field.

The match at Rugby was one of those where UEE (or JW) was proved to have been rather too generous in the agreed terms for the match. Despite JW taking 14 wickets during two long bowling stints, Rugby won by 83 runs. Conversely at Cambridge the students perhaps needed more players, UEE winning by eight wickets. In the students' first innings JW had figures of 40-23-37-8 with only 10 (of 13) wickets falling to the bowlers. As ever his accuracy was such that he conceded on average about one run per over. For the next in this series of matches UEE went to Christ Church Ground at the end of June to play 14 undergraduates of Oxford University (no given professionals) and would have been pleased to escape with a draw. Having dismissed the students for 86 in the first innings, UEE sportingly bowled on through appalling wet conditions in the second allowing them to total 270 as the bowlers struggled to hold the ball. JW did not play in this match but clearly the sporting ethos had been set within the group. There is the suspicion that AEE might have been off the field in such conditions.

The last of this series of matches was played at Lord's against a combined Cambridge & Oxford Universities XV on 10th July. The match had been eagerly anticipated, probably because it was one of a restricted number of competitive matches involving the most skilful players. For the first time the UEE team included Arthur Haygarth, a Lord's based amateur and someone with whom JW had worked at Harrow. The start of the match was delayed by rain and the wet conditions were to spoil the match with none of the innings reaching three figures. In failing light on the first evening UEE were shot out for just 47 leaving them 17 behind on first innings. As ever, JW rose to the challenge of a tight match situation and followed his first innings 6/38 with 28.1-?-19-9, leaving UEE with a target of 75 to win the match. His 14 runs proved to be a valuable contribution towards reaching the target for the loss of eight wickets.

Throughout the months of May, June and July 1854 JW played in a new match starting each Monday. Some of the matches were at Lord's but he also played in matches elsewhere. In these matches he played for a variety of teams: England, MCC, Sussex and UEE. On two successive Mondays, 12th and 19th June, JW played for Sussex, leading them to two wins. The first of these was at Hove[39], a seven wickets win over Kent, the report on which said 'Wisden's bowling was very wonderful'. His match figures of 34-23-22-6 and 38-27-14-5 show that not only did he take a high proportion of the wickets but he was also very economical in terms of runs conceded even on one of the most batsman friendly pitches in the country. In the second innings of this match it was less than one run per two overs. As usual, he bowled virtually throughout both innings, as he did the following Monday when Sussex visited Lord's to play MCC. JW took five wickets in each innings as Sussex won by four wickets. In MCC's first innings the five wickets that JW did not claim fell to James Dean, four of which were to catches by JW.

JW was often called 'The Little Wonder', the name of the horse that had won the Derby in 1840, because of his small stature at 5ft 4ins and 7 stones; although a good number of the leading cricketers of the time were no more than an inch taller. The MCC match featured a player who was even shorter when the Sussex side included George ('Tiny') Wells who stood 5ft 2½ ins – although he was reported to weigh 9 stones.

Sussex's return match with Kent was not played in the first half of the week but JW seems to have been 'let out of school' nevertheless and he played a leading role in another win for his county team. He bowled throughout both Kent innings taking 12 wickets and holding three catches. In their second innings he dismissed, bowled, seven batsmen and held catches to dismiss two more. Only Kent's No 11 batsman escaped him. This match was played on the Gravesend ground with none of the innings totals reaching 100 in marked contrast to the match played on Sussex's home ground. The other Sussex match in this phase was at the Brunswick Ground in Hove, one of the emerging group of grounds where pitches were improving and runs becoming more plentiful, thus making bowling more demanding work. The frequency of just a pair of bowlers operating throughout an innings was beginning to decrease. In this match Surrey used five bowlers in Sussex's first innings and six in the second. Sussex used five and then four. However, JW still did the lion's share of the work, bowling 94 overs to take three wickets in the first innings and four of the five to fall in the incomplete second innings. Sussex totalled 146 and 199 to Surrey's 196 and 95-5. The match ended as a high-scoring draw.

From the earliest days JW and Dean had a stated aim[40] of ensuring that UEE fixtures fitted in around the national programme of county matches (including MCC fixtures) (see Appendix B). Not so William Clarke and AEE, so when the Gentlemen v Players match was staged at Lord's on 17th & 18th July AEE were busy playing Eighteen of Maidstone and their players were not available for selection. The Players' XI which took the field looked very like a UEE XI. As ever, JW played his full part (nine wickets) in the match and the Players had a comfortable nine wickets win despite the absentees. This added to the growing clamour in the sporting press and elsewhere for a greater number of competitive matches featuring the most able cricketers. One strong and oft-repeated suggestion was for the two touring elevens to play each other. However, while William Clarke led AEE his antagonism towards UEE and its Wisden-Dean leadership ensured that this was never going to happen.

---

[39] Since 1848 Sussex's home matches were being staged at the Brunswick Ground. Its exact location seems to have remained a mystery for those compiling contemporary match reports. In this instance *Scores & Biographies* locates it in 'Hove, Brighton'.

The following Monday 24th July 1854 JW and Dean were unusually absent from the UEE team playing at Northampton; both were busy at Harrow preparing the boys for the critical end-of-season matches. During June and July the boys had played their familiar sequence of Saturday matches against IZ, MCC, Harrow Town, etc. However, unlike previous years this phase of the programme was significantly supplemented by internal matches involving some of the country's leading players. In the run-up to the Lord's matches, for instance, the School XI took on Wisden & Dean's XI which also included Arthur Haygarth. Haygarth had made several appearances at school earlier in the summer and the boys had played in a match A Haygarth's XI v F Ponsonby's XI (Ponsonby being another alumnus) a few weeks earlier. When the prestigious Lord's matches were played Harrow had two convincing victories and the value of the preparation was noted in the *Bell's Life* report of the victories which asked:

How is it that Harrow gets such fine players?

And then offered the simple answer:

In the first place they could not possibly secure a better man as their professional tutor; his talents as bowler need no remark from us. Again, he is never out of temper, persevering and determined – which is the man for a public school.

It concluded with:

The Eleven, in consequence, was brought to Lord's in perfection – good at every point, and, we understand, the best "team" ever assembled. Wisden was highly complimented for his exertions, and will have, next season, but to bring forward three fresh ones, ...

This highly professional preparation was in contrast to the style of services offered by 'Pipes' Chad, groundsman and pavilion keeper for many years and who was of the faithful school servant model. JW had introduced a new structure and level of expertise to the preparation of the team. This included not only his own involvement in coaching and playing but also arranging the retention of the coaching services of such alumni and amateur players as Fred Ponsonby and Arthur Haygarth.

Harrow beat Winchester by 117 runs and Eton by 98 runs; two convincing wins.

[40] *Bell's Life*, 19th September 1852, see Chapter 8

JW was at this time attracting critical acclaim not only as one of the best players in the land but also as the captain, manager and, critically, very much the leader of the UEE. He was now also being recognised as an innovative and highly successful coach.

While Eton, Harrow and Winchester were playing in the traditional end of the Lord's match programme, JW joined the UEE group as they travelled to Shaftesbury to take on Eighteen of Dorsetshire. JW was clearly unwell and did not play in the match as UEE won a low scoring match by 20 runs. Over the weekend the group made the short trip to Southampton to play Eighteen of South Hants. UEE came into existence two years earlier when JW led them onto the field at Portsmouth to play a Hampshire side and the fixture had been repeated in 1853. Now *Bell's Life* reported that meetings had been held with a view to forming a Hampshire County Cricket Club so as to have a permanent representative side to play in these and other fixtures. Despite the day's rest JW's health had not improved. Although he opened the bowling in the local side's first innings he bowled only nine overs, taking a single wicket. Later in the match he seems to have made a recovery for in the second innings he bowled 25 overs and took 5/21 (and, as ever, held a catch).

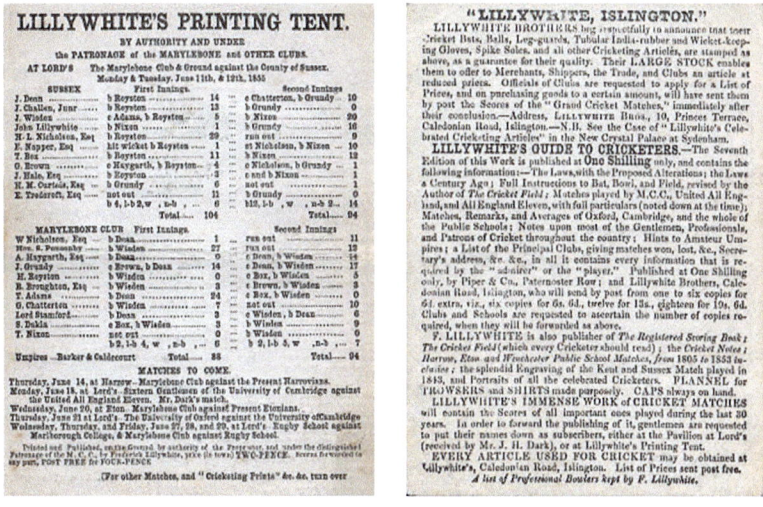

From Southampton JW along with James Dean, John Lillywhite and others made their way across the South Downs to Horsham. Here they joined a group of professional cricketers who spent the next two and a half weeks moving around, mainly, the south of England playing in a series of county matches. County matches involved teams such as MCC and an England side who, in 21st century terminology, might have been called 'Rest of England'. At this time Nottinghamshire were playing more matches and the three original counties were playing each other, home and away, more regularly. However, sides were of varying strength and professionals from other counties were often added to make a more even match. This only partly addressed the wide-spread appeals for there to be more frequent and more competitive matches at the highest level. The professionals were increasingly dominating the Gentlemen v Players fixtures and the North v South matches seemed to have petered out. This was a group of the best professional players enhancing a series of matches.

The first match was Sussex v MCC at Horsham with both sides having an approximately equal mix of amateurs and professionals. The match illustrated how important it was for JW and Dean to ensure that UEE matches avoided clashing with Sussex fixtures. The pair, along with John Lillywhite, were much needed by the county side. In UEE matches there was some element of squad rotation amongst the bowlers within any match. Not so here, JW and Dean did the bulk of the bowling for Sussex and took the bulk of the wickets but were unable to prevent a six wickets defeat. Happily JW appeared to be feeling better but perhaps another long season was beginning to take its toll; it was now the middle of August and he had been playing cricket in one form or another since the middle of March.

From Horsham the group moved to Canterbury for the Kent v England fixture with the Kent side including Bickley, Parr and Clarke (all from Nottinghamshire) as well as JW. Dean and John Lillywhite were included in the England side. Kent also had Edgar Willsher to bowl but they were unable to prevent England totalling 231 in their first innings and easing to a seven wickets win. For once JW and James Dean were on opposing sides. JW dismissed Dean in both innings and Dean took JW's wicket in his first innings. However, the pair managed a collective total of only 13 runs across their four innings.

The Kent match finished in two days which gave the group Wednesday free to move to Hove where the next engagement was Sussex v England.[41] JW, Dean and John Lillywhite played for the county side where they were joined by Parr and Clarke. Clarke and JW did the bowling for Sussex with

---

[41] The fact that *Scores & Biographies* lists this match as being played 'On G Knight's Ground, Brighton' illustrates the variability of the Victorian records. The venue might be better described as the Royal Brunswick Ground, Hove, its more usual name.

just a little help from Dean. JW had the outstanding figures of 45.2-27-41-8 and 32.3-20-27-6 (Clarke took the other wickets) leading Sussex to a 68 runs win. Despite their differences over commercial and organisational arrangements for the touring elevens, clearly JW and William Clarke could still combine to create a considerable force on the field.

The 'caravan' now set off northwards using Sunday to travel to Nottingham. They seem to have 'dropped-off' some of the southern based players en-route and picked up some others for the rest of the journey north. In a re-mix of the personnel Clarke and Parr naturally moved to the Nottinghamshire team while JW, Dean and Lillywhite re-joined the England side. JW seemed now to be back to full fitness putting in two good bowling spells and taking five wickets in the match as England won by an innings. Most of the group then returned to the south where Nottinghamshire played Surrey at Godalming and UEE travelled to Gravesend to start a normal end-of-season block of fixtures.

The match at Gravesend began on 24th August 1854 and was against Fifteen Young Players of Kent. It had a number of interesting features. Kent batted first and after having bowled 34 overs and taken two wickets and two catches JW finished the innings by keeping wicket claiming a victim when he stumped No 14, Captain Brenchley off Chatterton's bowling.[42] JW top-scored with 16 but UEE were shot out for only 70. With a lead of 51 the youngsters started to pile on the runs. Jemmy Dean was off the field, unwell, and UEE used nine bowlers as Kent set UEE 278 to win in the fourth innings. Although records are sparse it is thought that no side had ever successfully chased such a large fourth innings total. A recovered, and possibly rested, Dean opened the innings and while scoring 99 runs he featured in partnerships totalling 233 runs to set up a record breaking victory. JW (8*) was at the wicket with Henry Royston as UEE won by two wickets – another of the sort of tight finishes in which he so often prospered. The fixture had been created to give some of Kent's up and coming young talent a chance to develop their skills by playing against some of the best cricketers in the land. It was the kind of initiative that UEE were happy to be involved in.

The UEE fixture list continued with a return trip to Dublin. As the match at Gravesend had finished on a Saturday the players could spend Sunday making their way across to the west coast and then by ship to Dublin, unlike their hurried crossing the previous year. They docked at

[42] It is assumed that the 'st.' in *Scores & Biographies* is not a typographical error.

10am and immediately made their way to Phoenix Park where a team of 22 of the club which was based in the park awaited them. Despite the long overnight journey a prompt start was made. Fortunately for the jaded travellers their hosts won the toss and elected to bat.[43] Unlike the previous year UEE had arrived with a complete team, including Lord Milton and Mr Fenn, and so bowling shifts could be rotated. Although diligently maintained the pitch proved difficult; JW had figures of 42-23-28-5 thus conceding one run every six deliveries as compared to the more usual one-in-four. In early evening UEE began their reply and quickly ran into trouble exacerbated by the fatigue of the journey and the gathering gloom. The UEE players were by instinct front-foot batsmen and this was to be their downfall. Six players made 0, none reached double figures and the side were dismissed for a miserable 25. The Irish side played almost exclusively on the back foot in a style atuned to the pitches on which they commonly played. When Phoenix Park batted again they scored a further 116, leaving UEE 188 behind. They never got near to that total and lost by 135 runs.

Fred Lillywhite had travelled to Dublin with the team and umpired the match on behalf of UEE. It is reasonable to suppose that he provided the match report that appeared in *Bell's Life*. When published the report was headlined 'England v Ireland', which at first glance seemed a little over the top. However, it would appear that as much as UEE were representative of England the Phoenix Park Club were representative of Ireland, both drawing players from a wide geographical range. At the end of a long season JW would, no doubt, have been disappointed that such an arduous journey had ended in such a crushing defeat. But he would have written off the defeat as a contribution to the development of cricket. JW set the tone of UEE arrangements, both in terms of the fixtures made and the manner in which they were played. This was one of the essential differences between AEE and UEE. While Clarke's operation was happy to travel the land, spread the word and pocket the cash, UEE were much more focused on encouraging the development of the game, raising standards and sustaining enough first-class cricket to enable professionals to engage in full-time careers. It was thought that if UEE came back to Ireland in 1855 it would be to play against only 18.

[43] There is evidence that UEE had come to the conclusion that they were better placed working-off the effects of travel while fielding. In this way they avoided being dismissed for a low score in their first innings and having to try to make good later in the match.

The match in Dublin finished early on Wednesday morning. This enabled the visitors to hurry back to the docks and catch a mid-day ferry across to Lancashire where they were due in Rochdale on Thursday morning. They had been sufficiently impressed with the performance of JN Coddington Esq that JW recruited him for UEE and he joined them for the match at Rochdale.

After having again travelled through the night UEE were ready to make a prompt start at noon against a Rochdale team well supplemented with given professionals. Excellent preparations had been made but the match was still very low scoring: 95 and 107 v 81 and 60, to give UEE a 61 runs win. The match report said that JW gave an exhibition of his excellent batting style before he was run out for 19. The (professional) bowlers dominated the match, JW putting on a particularly good display with twelve wickets in the second innings.

After the match UEE were the guests at the customary dinner during which they were presented with a team flag in the colours of red, white and blue with their name in gold lettering. The plan was that the flag would be displayed on Fred Lillywhite's printing tent wherever UEE played. Fred had been at the match and he was responsible for the complete scorecard and a copious match report. The players eventually managed to get away at 11pm on Saturday evening to make their way to Manchester as the first phase of their journey to Lewes where they were scheduled to play Sixteen of Sussex on Monday.

The Sussex side were a rather strong team to be allowed 16 players but this may have been some compensation for the fact that JW and Dean played against them and the Lillywhite brothers were absent altogether. JW bowled as tightly as ever as he and Dean took 18 of the 27 wickets to fall to the bowlers and UEE won by eight wickets – a good result against a strong team in a match later deemed first-class.

Such was the bizarre planning of the fixture list that after having travelled from central Lancashire for the match at Lewes, UEE now turned around and headed back north to complete the season's list of fixtures with two matches in Scotland. In the Edinburgh match they won by an innings and 20 runs and in Glasgow by nine wickets. JW had a noticeably limp match at Glasgow; perhaps the long hard season had now caught up with him. Intriguingly, two players who were listed in the press to play for UEE in Scotland were Lord Garlies and Hon R Stewart, both boys having been in the highly successful Harrow Eleven of that summer. In the event neither boy was able to get to the match but JW clearly intended to help his former pupils to the next stage of their playing careers.

Once they had returned from Scotland UEE had completed their programme for the season. However, JW had one more match to go. The Oval was closed for matches during 1854 so the return Surrey v Sussex match was also staged at Hove on 28th & 29th September. JW was not at his best and so was not able to lift the Sussex side as they slumped to a 10 wickets defeat – in fact Surrey's second innings needed only two balls.

Towards the end of August JW experienced some personal sadness. August saw a virulent outbreak of cholera in London and one of its many victims was William Lillywhite. The Nonpareil had been JW's first coach when he was still a schoolboy and was then his mentor in his early days as a cricketer. He passed on coaching skills during those April trips to Cambridge University which JW was now using to good effect at Harrow.

JW was a family friend of the Lillywhites. At this time William and sons James, John and Fred were living at Princes Terrace, on Caledonian Road close to the modern King's Cross railway station, and JW frequently lodged with the family. In *Bell's Life* of 7th January 1855 readers were informed that they could contact Wisden at Lillywhite's Emporium on Caledonian Road. Thus it is likely that JW was lodging with the Lillywhite family at this time.

As an indication of out-of-season activity for professional cricketers, the 11th February 1855 issue of *Bell's Life* reported that 'James Dean (of cricketing celebrity)' had recently been engaged in a shooting competition with Mr Boxall at Petworth. The report said that 'The Hero of Duncton' had won the match, and £5, by five birds to three. It further reported that the following week Dean would be partnered by JW in another match against Boxall and his partner. JW was an enthusiastic and capable marksman.

On 18th February *Bell's Life* gave details of plans for a memorial to the late William Lillywhite. At the same time his son Fred announced that he was taking on his father's project to publish a great work of cricket scores (the project that was to become the series of books known as *Scores & Biographies*). This work would involve JW during the years of the Lillywhite & Wisden partnership (1855-58) and later when his own Almanack become one of the annual cricket handbooks.

By mid-March 1855 *Bell's Life* was turning its attention to preparations for the coming season and produced a column detailing the arrangements that had been made for the appointment of coaches/professionals at the leading public schools. The paper reported that Martingell was to be the new appointment at Eton and that Caffyn was to become coach at Winchester in succession to William Lillywhite. Both of these players had moved from AEE to join JW's UEE which already included the Lillywhite brothers. John was to continue at Rugby and discussions were in hand which it was hoped would lead to James starting at Cheltenham College.[44] Jemmy Dean would 'officiate' at Marlborough until he was required at Lord's. This all seems to support the developmental ethos within UEE and its players.

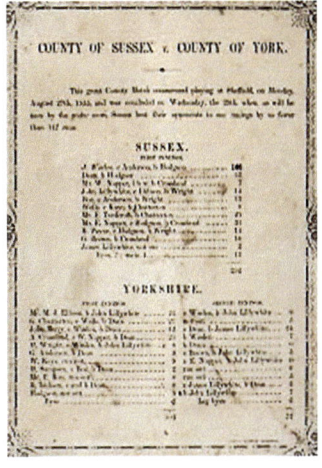

When the new Bramall Lane ground was to be formally opened, Sussex were invited to travel north to play a team representing Yorkshire (who had yet to have a formal county team/club). JW's century was the only one scored in first-class cricket that year. Bramall Lane became another of cricket's bequests to association football – it remains the only venue to have staged both a Test Match and a Premier League football match.
Reproduced by kind permission of Nicholas Sharp.

The column also reported that half the 1854 Harrow XI would not be available for the 1855 season. This would be an improvement on 1853 when almost the whole team needed to be replaced and further encouragement came from the fact that Kenelm Digby would be captain for the third consecutive year. *Bell's Life* seemed assured that JW and Digby were well up to the task of creating and developing a new eleven.

Preparations for the 1855 Harrow season began a little later than in the previous year when on 26th April Digby's XI played Wisden's XI. JW's side won by five runs. The established pattern of internal matches continued through May. In one of these JW bowled (out) all ten of his opponents, just as he had done at Lord's in 1850 while playing for North in their match against South. A developing feature of these games was

---

[44] In the end James Lillywhite did not start at Cheltenham till 1st March 1856.

the inclusion of external, highly skilled players. For instance, when the Fast Bowlers played the Slow Bowlers JW and Dean were included in the Fast Bowlers' team. Their opponents included Hon Robert Grimston and Arthur Haygarth and the professionals Thomas Nixon and Henry Royston (both UEE men). When the school second eleven needed strengthening to face the first eleven they were given JW, Haygarth and two Grimston brothers.

This, the first phase of the preparation, culminated in the annual match against Harrow Town, won by the school by five wickets. As usual, the Eleven were left in the captain's capable hands leaving JW free to play in the North v South fixture at Lord's. He showed himself to be as good as ever, taking 6/37 in the first innings and 5/44 in the second, bowling through most of both innings. JW bowled a wide, an event that was considered sufficiently unusual to be included in the match report. When South could muster only 52 in their second innings they lost by 18 runs, largely due to the skilful bowling of the 56-year-old William Clarke, in what was to prove to be one of his last noteworthy performances.

From this point in the record, *Scores & Biographies* decided to stop recording maiden overs, deeming them to be superfluous. However, *Bell's Life* recorded that JW bowled 28 maidens within his 53.3 overs in the match. Clearly there was still work to do for the future Lillywhite and Wisden partnership by way of improving and standardising the recording of matches. Some of this would be achieved through the design and publication of enhanced scorebooks.

The Surrey v England match that began a couple of days later was one that had been arranged by Clarke, so JW, along with James Dean, John Lillywhite and others from UEE, who might have been in the England side did not play. On 11th June JW was in the Sussex team to play MCC at Lord's. His figures of 5/45 and 7/47 showed how essential he was to the Sussex team as they beat their hosts by 16 runs. As per the now established routine, later that week JW returned to Harrow to umpire the school's match with MCC & Ground. At the end of the match he presented Mr Lang with a bat for his outstanding innings of 50 in a very low scoring match. The fact that the professional/coach might make such an award to one of the boys illustrates JW's enhanced standing within the school and its cricket.

At this stage of the season the school eleven's preparation was a mixture of internal, practice matches and more formal fixtures with outside opponents. JW was able to continue with the previously established pattern of spending the first part of the week playing national level cricket and then going back to school for the second half. On three successive Mondays following the MCC v Sussex match he played for UEE v Cambridge University (Past and Present), for Sussex v Surrey at Hove and then UEE v Oxford University (Undergraduates). Both of the matches against university sides were at Lord's with the students fielding 16 players allowing Oxford to win by six wickets and Cambridge by 13 runs. In all these matches JW emphasised his place as a key member of the side, typically bowling economically through much or all of the innings and taking half the wickets to fall. In the Sussex v Surrey match he scored 23 in the first innings and followed that with 45* in the second. Having taken 6/33 in the first innings JW had a noticeably reduced bowling stint in the final innings of the match as Sussex bowled out Surrey to win by 2 runs. Sussex's task had been made easier by the absence of Caesar and Stephenson from the Surrey side. The two professionals were on strike in a dispute over match fees and expenses; part of the growing unrest amongst professional players and an example of the type of dispute that would give JW some headaches in the years to come. A mounted ball from this match is in a private collection.

Rackets was a popular sport at Harrow School, with many courts available to the pupils. Several of the best rackets players also appeared in The Eleven (cricket).

UEE's loss to Oxford University was in part due to the generous odds that UEE had given their opponents. Haygarth, in *Scores & Biographies*[45] was of the opinion that the students' team was one of the strongest to have been put out against UEE. Because the match was at Lord's the UEE side included three amateurs, two of whom – Frederick Miller and William Nicholson – were more than just able players. Miller was a highly effective captain of Surrey who later guaranteed the funding for the publication of *Scores & Biographies III & IV* – a commitment he was later to regret.[46] Nicholson was an old Harrovian who had been captain of the eleven in 1843. *Scores & Biographies* said of him '… 1843, when, by his strict management and fine play, he helped much to win both against Winchester and Eton'.[47] Nicholson would go on to become an important personality both in the world of commerce and in the administration of cricket at a national level, including his role in saving Lord's from building development. JW was starting to assemble an extensive network of influential contacts.

Sometime captain and committee member for Surrey CCC, Fred Miller was an influential man and a very capable cricketer. Whereas, Wm Clarke's All England XI was very much organised for professional players, JW's United England XI was more about developing the game and embracing all-comers. Mr Miller was an amateur who not only played for UEE in many matches but also captained the team on several occasions.

F. F. MILLER ESQ.

The second Surrey match at the Oval was played on what normally would have been a 'school day' for JW. [Possibly, as some form of *quid pro quo*, JW did not play for England against a combined Kent and Surrey team and neither did he travel with UEE to Coventry.] As a supplement to the school Eleven's programme of matches against external opponents there was a series of matches where the 1st XI

[45] *Scores & Biographies V*, p. 49
[46] See *Sketches at Lord's*, p. 102
[47] *Scores & Biographies III*, p. 39

played a 2nd XI augmented by JW and various other able players. The extra input worked wonders and when the Eleven went to Lord's at the beginning of August they beat Eton by an innings and 66 runs – a most convincing win. This year there was no match against Winchester as their head master had decided not to let his men (= pupils) loose in London. JW was not at Lord's to witness the final, emphatic, victory of his tenure but both on the ground and in the press there was much praise for his skills and his achievement in raising Harrow to this level. There was also recognition of the effective partnership that he had created with Digby. For his part Sir Kenelm Digby wrote his personal recollections of JW in *Wisden* 1913.

The teams that JW had coached at Harrow had included several of the Walker brothers, a family with whom he would maintain contact in the years to come. Probably the best cricketer of the brothers was Teddy (VE) Walker. In the book *Old English Cricketers* by the Yorkshire journalist 'Old Ebor', Teddy Walker recounted:

> Recalling my Harrow days brings to mind the memory of old John Wisden. Wisden was at Harrow in my time for two or three years. He was the most excellent, civil, obliging and painstaking fellow you could possibly meet. I suppose I may say he was as accurate a bowler, with as pretty a delivery, as any man ever saw. At that time he would be termed a fast round-arm bowler, though he was not as fast as Jackson, who was the bowler of England for a few years. Yes, Wisden was a good deal faster than Attewell, but not so fast as Lockwood. In appearance he was a funny little mite of a fellow.

For his own cricket 1855 was developing into a good season with the bat. When Sussex achieved their seventh successive win over Kent, JW had innings of 6 and 58 (as well as eight wickets) and he scored 23* as the Players easily beat the Gentlemen by seven wickets. The 'county matches' part of the season continued to the end of August and occasionally beyond that – possibly to the relief of Scotland-based grouse. At the end of August JW joined his Sussex team mates for the trip to Sheffield where, as part of a first season on the new Bramall Lane ground, Sussex were to play Yorkshire. Sussex batted first and JW opened the batting. His innings of 148 (= 400+ in current values) was his highest ever score as he energetically plundered some ineffective bowling. JW's century was the only one scored in 1855 in those matches that *Bell's* Life classified as important. Sussex totalled 292 and then bowled out their hosts for 103 and 72. Winning by an innings and 117 runs certainly poured rain on the Yorkshire parade.

Prior to the trip to Sheffield JW had been part of the Sussex team that beat MCC by an innings and 68 runs at Horsham and then a member of the England team that narrowly lost to a combined Kent & Surrey side at Canterbury. In this match JW had figures of 33-?-22-1 and 41-?-19-2, which *Scores & Biographies* observed were excellent figures for so few wickets. The other match before the trip to Sheffield was at Hove when Kent were the visitors and the winners by 62 runs; their first win over Sussex since 1850. This was a match when the old men did well. Mynn (48 years) scored 38 and 21 while Box (47 years), who had come in to bat at No 8, joined James Lillywhite (33) in a last wicket stand of 49 to give Sussex a small first innings lead.

The remainder of JW's season was played out in UEE matches. As July turned into August they were at Stourbridge to play Earl of Stamford's team. Allowing the hosts 22 players including a good selection of able professionals proved to be, yet again, rather too generous and the Eleven were lucky to escape with a draw – despite JW's 14 wickets and two catches. The following day UEE started a match against Langton Wold (Yorkshire). JW took 11 wickets for barely 20 runs in each innings but having been allowed to include six professionals the hosts won by 37 runs. JW picked up another 20 wickets from a match at Chichester against Twenty-two of the Priory Park Club which included a number of able guests. A low scoring match saw Priory Park set 88 to win. They scored 65 of them with eight wickets still to fall. JW, ever 'up for a scrap' and aided by Jemmy Dean, took those last eight wickets for no additional runs, to win by 22 runs.

In mid-August UEE promoted a South v North match at Tunbridge Wells. The match turned out to be a public relations disaster.[48] The preponderance within the UEE ranks of players based in the south had made assembling a competitive North side difficult. The situation was exacerbated when players who had previously agreed to be part of the North team withdrew at a late stage and went and played for AEE in Cardiff. In the end the North XI was completed by George Wells of Sussex. Having scored 57* in South's only innings JW did not bowl in

---

[48] Surprisingly this 'scruffy' match has been given first-class status, presumably because of the status and ability of the players involved.

the match. The spectating public were not pleased when the teams who took the field were so different from those announced in the advance publicity. The match did little to enhance the reputation and status of professional cricketers as a whole and again pointed to the need for a co-ordinated season long programme of first-class cricket.

JW clearly set the lead in UEE affairs. Although announcements were often made in the names of 'Wisden & Dean' Jemmy himself was ever ready to admit that he was very much just JW's assistant. As mentioned above a feature of the year had been the introduction of new recruits to UEE, especially gentlemen amateurs. This not only broadened the base and potential appeal of the team but also helped to further develop JW's network of contacts – men of influence who might (and would be) useful in years to come. When UEE played at Small Heath, Birmingham, their batting line-up included F Burbidge, the Surrey batsman and future captain. Three days later for the match with Twenty-two of Bedfordshire UEE included Hon Edward Chandos Leigh as well as Mr Burbidge; Edward Chandos Leigh became President of MCC in 1887. In this match UEE's innings lasted 248 (4-ball) overs thought to be the longest ever innings to date.[49] JW completed a good season for batting with 80 out of a total 334.

UEE finished the season with return visits to three northern venues. In the week beginning 17th September they beat Rotherham by one wicket after Chatterton (24*) and Bell (4*) had put on 27 for the final wicket. JW had helped set up the win by returning bowling figures of 27-?-20-12 in the Twenty-two's second innings. In the latter half of the week they moved on to Bradford where UEE beat a team of twenty players by one wicket, JW making only modest contributions to the win. Over the weekend the Eleven travelled to Edinburgh to lose to Twenty-two of Scotland[50] by 37 runs. Batting at No 4, JW acquired a pair and bowled only eight overs in the first innings. He made a greater contribution in the second innings with figures of 42-?-50-11.

Thus ended a long, arduous season but one that was successful on several fronts. Harrow were now the pre-eminent public school in cricket terms, UEE were a well-established part of professional cricket and in their end-of-season averages *Bell's Life* rated JW as the second most successful batsman (behind George Parr) and one of the best bowlers. However, autumn would bring no rest as JW was about to start on an entirely new venture.

---

[49] See *Scores & Biographies V*, p. 129
[50] The team were reduced to 21 players by the absence of C Lawrence.

11

BECOMING A BUSINESSMAN

Evidently traffic congestion in London was not a 20th century 'invention'. The capital city had a problem as early as the 1840s with one solution being the construction of an extension to Coventry Street, taking it into the north-west corner of Leicester Square. This short extension meant that Haymarket and Piccadilly Circus were now connected to Leicester Square and then through Cranbourn Street to Long Acre. This was an area dominated by high-class shops and no doubt the carriage-trade was at least in part responsible for the congestion. The extension was to be called 'New Coventry-street'.

As early as April 1852 an advertisement by Lillywhite Brothers, placed in *Bell's Life*, included the announcement:

> CRICKET – LILLYWHITE BROTHERS & CO ...
> West End Agent: W. J. Keed (late Fownes and Keed), glover to the Queen, shirt maker, hosier, &c., 6 Coventry–street, Piccadilly, where an assortment of their goods may be inspected.

A month later this agency was absorbed as just a second address for Lillywhite Brothers in their weekly advertisement, which continued to be run until 30th April 1854. At this point it was announced that the agent had opened a second shop at nearby 2 New Coventry Street, Leicester-square.

Clearly the reference to being glover to the Queen was intended to signify quality. In 1852 Keed had occupied 2 New Coventry Street as a hatter. Next door at number 3 was Edwin Law, a confectioner, and the other side of Law was Miss Hannah King, a milliner. Also in the street were the offices of Catholic Law and General Life, presumably an insurance company. This seems to clearly indicate a shopping street above the ordinary. The Lillywhite advertisement in *Bell's Life* stated that the selection to be viewed at Keed's premises was of the *best* articles.

Up until this time the centre of the Lillywhites' cricket outfitting business had been their Cricket Warehouse in Princes Terrace on Caledonian Road, Islington. Here, father William had overseen the

The area around Leicester Square became a centre for cricket and cricketers. Cricketers frequently gathered in Wisden's shop. Gregory's Hotel, in Rupert Street, was used for meetings of the Cricketers' Fund Friendly Society. In 1872 JW moved his shop across the square from New Coventry Street to Cranbourn Street. Later, Tom Box took over a public house in Bear Street, which may have been useful for a 'pub lunch' or a 'swift half' at the close of business.

2 New Coventry Street was one of a row of fashionable shops along a newly created link road between Leicester Square and Regent Street. The header board shows the 1862 name of the company.

commercial activities with his sons James, John and Fred. As well as cricket equipment they also sold cigars, with James listed in a street directory as a cigar retailer at that address. In the summer of 1854 London had suffered a vicious outbreak of cholera and one of its victims was William Lillywhite whose death was to trigger the fragmentation of the Lillywhite Brothers' commercial activities. In March, 1856 James made his way to Cheltenham where he was to establish one of the many operations of the Lillywhites as sports outfitters.

In the issue of 21st October 1855 *Bell's Life* contained two pieces announcing the new partnership of F Lillywhite and Wisden:

A LOUNGE FOR CRICKETERS – We have much pleasure in complying with Messrs F. Lillywhite and Wisden's request of calling our readers' notice to the opening of their Cricketing and Cigar Depot, No. 2 New Coventry-street, Leicester-square, where, we trust, they will meet with the patronage they deserve. Their advertisement will be found in another part of our impression.

The advertisement was:

LILLYWHITE and WISDEN'S CRICKETING and CIGAR DEPOT, Leicester-square.—L. and W. beg most respectfully to inform noblemen and gentlemen that they have OPENED the PREMISES of No. 2, Coventry-street, Leicester-square, where they have a large STOCK of the finest FOREIGN CIGARS, superior tobaccos, and snuffs, as well as an extensive assortment of meerschaum pipes, and other fancy articles. Every article connected with cricket, of the best manufacture, may also be obtained at this establishment, where they hope to merit the patronage of the above. N.B.—Parcels carefully packed and sent to any part of the country. Proprietors: Frederick Lillywhite and John Wisden.

The wording gives a clear idea of the target clientele and the manner in which the new partners planned to conduct their business. The editorial piece mentioned a lounge and the advertisement concentrated on smokers' requirements. There was also a clear indication that noblemen and gentlemen were welcome to call in for a chat, sample a cigar before buying a box and possibly look over the range of cricket bats that was available with thought to buying one for next season. Clearly there was an intention to be of service and to provide quality goods.

As ever, *Bell's Life* was supportive of a John Wisden initiative and of course Fred Lillywhite was already one of their correspondents.

Both men had assets to bring to the new partnership. As well as being one of the leading cricketers in the land JW had built up a good set of contacts. His equable temperament and his general demeanour had made him a favourite not only at Lord's and in Brighton but on all the grounds on which he had played. His time at Harrow had allowed him to make the acquaintance of gentlemen cricketers, fathers and sons, who would become good customers for both cricket bats and cigars.

Back in his Brighton days Fred had been apprenticed as a printer and he was already applying his knowledge of that craft to cricket. He had devised, designed and published sheets for both scoring matches and for sending the scorecards and results to *Bell's Life*. Fred was already publishing his annual *Lillywhite's Guide*, which was the first of cricket's regular annual handbooks. He had also set up and run a subscription results service, making good use of the penny post. All this helped to make him well known and well connected as a businessman within cricket.

Fortunately those wishing to sell goods to the general public, or at least some part of it, needed to advertise their goods and services. We are thus able to track the progress of the new enterprise through advertisements within *Bell's Life* and similar publications. The L&W partnership's advertisement of 2nd December 1855 listed what they had to offer beyond playing equipment and, of course, cigars.

The following week *Bell's Life* contained a block of advertisements which announced a step change in the supply of cricket equipment (and smokers' supplies). For several years the firm of Lillywhite Brothers had been a major presence amongst cricket outfitters. However, since mid-summer 1854, they had experienced a number of changes. Now that Fred had moved to New Coventry Street and James was thinking of a move to Cheltenham, John was left on his own at the Caledonian Road warehouse. On 9th December an advertisement appeared announcing that John Lillywhite had 'resigned from his position at Rugby [school] and taken over the Caledonian Road operation'. Lillywhite Brothers would now be known as Lillywhite's Cricket Warehouse. The warehouse and the L&W shop were to become major players in the provision of all forms of cricket equipment (and football when it got itself organised). It was also the beginning of the weekly repeated blocks of many advertisements detailing the two companies' many offerings that were at times to fill as much as one-third of a column in *Bell's Life*.

The two advertisements shown below John Lillywhite's 9th December announcement in a *Bell's Life* column were both from Lillywhite & Wisden.

The first introduced the new lines, mainly in what might be collectively referred to as stationery. Scoring books were offered – no doubt of Fred's design – and also copies of the laws of the game. The other new line was portraits of celebrated cricketers. In *Sketches at Lord's*[51] Fred is listed as the publisher of many of the lithographs of John Corbet Anderson's excellent portraits. In an age before photographs were commonly available these lithographs provided the definitive visual images of the famous players. His sketch of JW is probably the most common image of him to this day. Fred firstly (1851) published the portraits jointly with Anderson then in partnership with JW and finally (from 1859) on his own.

The first book in which JW had a role in publishing was not his eponymous *Almanack* but the 1856 edition of Fred's *Lillywhite's Guide* which was published by Lillywhite & Wisden. At the end of January 1856 the weekly L&W advertisement in *Bell's Life* announced the availability of the Circular of Information which club secretaries and others were asked to complete and return to provide some of the copy for *Lillywhite's Guide to Cricketers* (to give its full title). At about this time the concept of the shop at 2 New Coventry Street as a focal point for all matters relating to cricket and cricketers was developed with L&W's offer to help obtain positions for professionals at clubs, schools, etc. By April another service was being offered to the cricketing community when L&W acted as a collection point for charitable donations. This was a function in which the shop was to play a leading part for several years to come.

Towards the end of January 1856 John Lillywhite was also offering to act as agent for both clubs and professionals, helping to arrange the placements of bowlers. By February he was offering to assist in the collection of data for his brother's Guide. For many years the two companies appeared to exist and prosper in harmonious parallel.

Over the coming years the style of advertisements seemed to reflect the various advertisers' approach to business. John Lillywhite had an all embracing stance no doubt drawing upon the considerable stock built up over several years in the family's warehouse. When on his own Fred favoured a scattergun approach making sure that every element and avenue was covered. JW seemed to have been a restraint on the Lillywhite & Wisden advertisements where there was always an emphasis

---

[51] *Sketches at Lord's* by Michael Down and Derek West is the definitive publication on the cricket work of John Corbet Anderson.

on guaranteed quality. He seemed to be keen to make good use of the reputation that he had built up amongst the noblemen and gentlemen who not only dominated the running of the game but also had the deepest pockets.

The Lillywhite & Wisden advertisement in *Bell's Life* for 6th April 1856 was the first to indicate supplies for sports other than cricket when it included 'Racket bats, balls, foot-balls and all articles used for British sports'. The inclusion of rackets is ominous in the light of the role the game was to play in bringing JW's playing career to an end. The emphasis on quality was reinforced later in the year when residents were advised: 'Racket bats and balls (of the first make only, and selected by george erwood) and foot-balls (Gilbert's make) may be obtained.' George Erwood was one of two brothers who were the leading rackets professionals at the time. Gilbert was William Gilbert, the boot and shoe maker at Rugby School who, it is believed, made the ball which William Ellis 'took up and ran', thus instigating the Rugby version of 'foot-ball'.[52] At this time the versions of football were still many and various, and often local, although initiatives were taking place at Cambridge University to create a common set of rules. When eventually (1863) The Football Association was formed, the community of cricket outfitters would do much to help the newly organised game establish itself with the publication of sets of rules and the manufacture and supply of playing kits for both teams and individual players.

During the time that he was the contracted coach/professional at Harrow JW developed the use of visitors to be involved in preparatory matches. They, no doubt, provided a stern test for the members of what became a succession of very strong school teams. The visitors generally fell into two groups. One group was of Old Harrovians amongst whom was Arthur Haygarth, Hon Robert Grimston, and future leaders such as William Nicholson. Another group was JW's professional cricket colleagues. James Dean and both James and John Lillywhite made increasingly regular appearances, all three having experience of coaching at this level in other schools. In 1856 JW, no longer the contracted coach/ professional, joined the group of visitors. The press happily reported that he would be visiting Harrow once a week but the school's scorebooks suggest that it was at times more than that.

[52] Many years later, in the 1920s, John Wisden & Co published *Wisden's Rugby Almanack*. See *The Little Wonder*, p. 140ff.

JW was clearly a man of great energy. As well as playing for Sussex, where he was an essential member of the county team, he also had UEE to arrange, organise and lead on the field. In London he had both a shop to run as well as his involvement at Harrow. He was a bachelor engaged to Annie Parr[53], although the state of their relationship at this time is not known. It is assumed that she was still living in Radcliffe-on-Trent and occupied as a dressmaker.

At the same time that he was busy developing the new business venture JW needed to keep his own cricket career on track; his successes, and thus prestige, as a cricketer were an important attribute for the shop. JW's 1856 season had a gentle start. He made his weekly visits to Harrow School, often on a Tuesday, where he took part in the matches organised to identify the eleven for the season. On Thursday 22nd May he was part of the UEE team to play Fifteen Undergraduates of Oxford on the Magdalen Ground. He scored 35* and 12* and, despite bowling 30 overs, he took just 1/29. UEE had much the better of the match but as only two days were allocated the match ended in the inevitable draw.

There were seven weeks in June and July when JW started with a new match. The first of these was MCC v Sussex. Sussex were badly beaten totalling only 75 in their first innings and 23 in the second; MCC winning by nine wickets. JW scored 14* and 1 (run out) and took 3/15 and 1/4 in the MCC innings.

The following week, beginning 9th June, UEE played a team of sixteen from Cambridge University, the team comprising ten current undergraduates [54] and six 'old Cambridge men' (as they were described). JW opened the batting but scored only 5 and 15. He failed to take any wickets in the first innings but his 8/23 was instrumental in ensuring that the university side never got anywhere near their 195 runs target and lost by 94 runs. There was no match on the 16th with the University Match being played over the following two days. The undergraduates of Oxford were back at Lord's on 23rd when a team of sixteen played UEE. JW had a generally successful match taking 6/45 and 9/26 and scoring 12 and 15 in his two innings. However it was not enough to prevent the students from winning by 35 runs.

[53] Although listed as Ann Parr in both the 1851 census and on her death certificate she was often also listed as Annie.

[54] Amongst the undergraduates were RA Fitzgerald who later became secretary of MCC and AB Trollope who went on the take holy orders but did not write books about Barchester.

These matches against teams of higher social standing were becoming an increasing part of UEE's early season match programme. Evidence elsewhere suggests MCC had engaged UEE to play matches within the programme of Monday matches as an element of their response to the complaints from members and elsewhere about the poor quality of the cricket being played in these matches in previous seasons.

Not having an engagement on 16th was convenient for JW as he needed to mix his own cricket with his commitment to pay a weekly visit to Harrow. Later in the week he went to Hove to be part of the Sussex team to play Surrey. Fred Lillywhite went with him and acted as Sussex's scorer. Sussex were again beaten by nine wickets. He returned figures of 41-21-37-3 [55] in Surrey's first innings a commendable achievement on an increasingly batsman-friendly ground. His 23* in Sussex's second innings was not enough to set Surrey a challenging target. Sussex then suffered a third nine wickets defeat when they travelled to Gravesend for a match starting on Thursday 3rd July. JW had a poor match, Sussex did not score anywhere near enough runs and lost easily after having had to follow-on.

Back at Lord's on Monday 7th July JW had played in a match between more evenly matched teams. A combined Kent & Sussex team lost to England by just four runs. JW's bowling figures of 6/47 and 5/53 show a significant contribution. The match was completed in two days, Monday and Wednesday, with all of Tuesday being lost to rain; it was to be a wet season.

In this part of the season there was one more Thursday start for JW and one more comprehensive defeat for Sussex. The return Surrey v Sussex fixture was at the Oval and the hosts won by a massive 240 runs. While JW's 6/33 helped Sussex to restrict Surrey's first innings to 106, they scored 297 in the second innings. Like the Royal Brunswick Ground, the Oval was becoming an increasingly batsman-friendly pitch although Sussex still only managed innings totals of 78 and 85.

Prior to playing for Kent & Sussex JW had taken part in the first of the representative matches for the season. He played a major part in South's six wickets victory over North, scoring 21 in his only innings and having bowling figures of 32-15-39-5 and 25-6-47-3. Edgar Willsher took all but one of the remaining wickets. In playing strength this was probably the toughest fixture of the year so these

---

[55] Full bowling figures are a testimony to Fred Lillywhite's presence.

were commendable performances. The next representative match was Gentlemen v Players, another of the Lord's fixtures, this one starting on 21st July. Once more JW was on the winning side and his bowling figures of 4/25 and 4/57 were a major contribution to the win. Edgar Willsher took nine wickets in the match; the pair of bowlers were forming an effective partnership.

JW's final match at Lord's for the season began on 28th July when he was part of an England team to play an MCC team bolstered by William Caffyn and Tom Lockyer. JW (5/46) and Willsher (4/43) combined to restrict MCC to 140 and thus a first innings lead of 10 runs. In their second innings England scored a massive, for Lord's, total of 298, of which JW contributed 39. MCC wilted in the face of the target and the combined bowling of JW (2/19) and Willsher (6/33).

For the two central months of the cricket season, June and July, JW's match programme had a strong pattern. On Monday he would travel to Lord's and join one of the several teams for which he played. Later in the week, usually with a Thursday start, he would play in some other match for Sussex, UEE, etc. May had been largely given over to his days at Harrow and August and September would be mainly UEE fixtures with a few first-class matches added in.

This pattern to his season had been emerging over the previous few years, in fact since he had parted company with AEE. It had also worked well during the years that he had worked with Kenelm Digby to turn Harrow into the powerhouse of schools' cricket. However, this pattern seems to have escaped the attention of those in charge of the Harrow Eleven now that neither JW nor Digby was there. In mid-May the non-playing (ill) captain of Harrow wrote to Sussex CC to complain about the number of days that JW would be away from school because he was playing for Sussex. However, the complaint does not stand up to scrutiny. JW's commitment to Harrow was for one day per week. His appearances in the school's match book suggested that he did at least that, and that the chosen day varied according to the school's needs. During June and July there was only one week when JW played on all six days, so there was plenty of scope for him to visit for a day working around his other commitments. Sussex's reply to Harrow's complaint was robust. JW played in all of Sussex's county matches for 1856. In future years he only helped at Harrow during May.

Sir,

Hearing that you purpose fixing another county match in July, I think it right to tell you that Wisden cannot be absent from Harrow for so many matches. His services are required for 4 or 5 first rate matches at Lords; and should he be absent for 4 or five county matches besides, he will be away from Harrow for nearly half of the days in June & July. The school have always done all they can in giving leave even at times when it caused great inconvenience and I feel that I shall not be justified in allowing him to be absent as much this year unless the Sussex Cricket Club can provide during his absence, a suitable substitute which Mr Dark always does when he is absent at Lords.

> I remain Sir yrs
> W. S. Church
> Captain of the Harrow Eleven

The Harrow captain's letter to Sussex Cricket Club, claiming JW's services (1856)

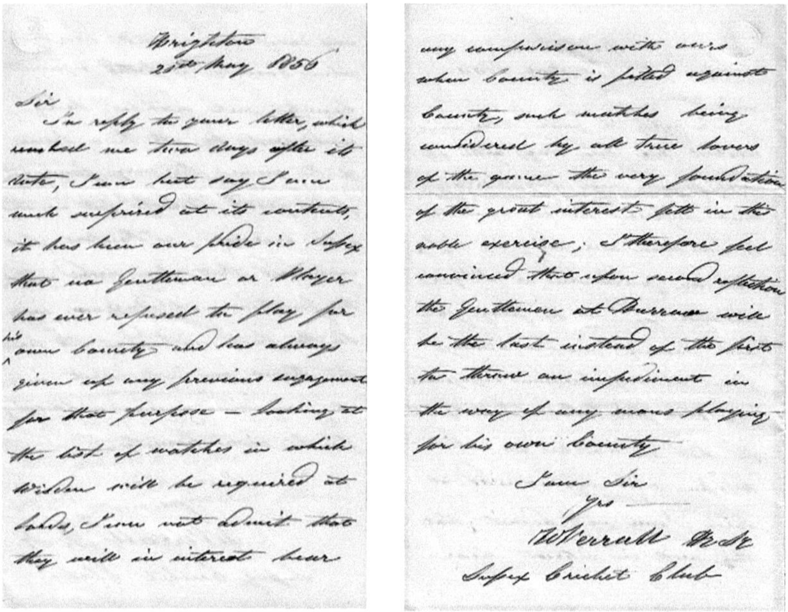

Brighton
25th May 1856
Sir,

In reply to your letter, which reached me two days after its date, I can but say that I am much surprised at its contents, it has been our pride in Sussex that no Gentleman or Player has ever refused to play for his own county and has always given up any previous engagement for that purpose. Looking at the list of matches in which Wisden will be required at Lords, I can not admit that they will in interest bear any comparison with ours when County is pitted against County, such matches considered by all true lovers of the game the very foundation of the great interest felt in these noble exercises. I therefore feel convinced that upon second reflection the Gentlemen at Harrow will be the last instead of the first to throw an impediment in the way of any mans playing for his own County.

I am Sir yrs
W Verrall, Hon Sec
Sussex Cricket Club

William Verrall's dismissive reply to the Harrow captain re JW's services (1856)

On the last day of July 1856 a curious pair of fixtures took place. At Luton, UEE took on Twenty-two of Luton (including James Lillywhite), while in Leamington, on the Parr & Wisden ground, eleven Players took on Fifteen Gentlemen of England, in a match staged for the benefit of George Parr and John Wisden. This clash of fixtures left the professionals with divided resources. Whilst Caffyn, Grundy, Dean and John Lillywhite played at Luton, Parr and Wisden, naturally, played at Leamington.

At Leamington the Wisden and Willsher bowling combination had reduced the Gentlemen to 29-8 when Edgar Willsher was taken ill and had to leave the field. At this point the not out batsmen, Hankey and Peel, took advantage of his absence and their scores of 35 and 46 respectively became the core of a total of 167, which later gave them an 11 runs first innings lead. After being set 135 to win the Players were bowled out for 91. The run chase was not helped by Parr being unfit to bat and the not yet fully recovered Willsher coming in as last man. As the match was staged for their benefit Parr could count the takings as he nursed his injury and JW was left to consider what he had missed at Luton where Caffyn (104) and John Lillywhite (51) had been the top scorers in an innings of 358, UEE winning by an innings and 82 runs.

The high total at Luton was another illustration of the developing trend of higher scores; the local side had scored 169 and 107. At the start of the following week Kent came to Hove to play Sussex on the Brunswick Ground. Kent scored 115 (JW 6/64) and 206 (JW 2/38) but lost by an innings after Sussex had scored 337 against an attack lacking the still ill Willsher. JW scored 89 and John Lillywhite 138 in a match defining partnership. At stumps on the first evening the pair were 12* and 17* respectively. When the partnership was resumed on the next day it filled all of the morning session until 2.15pm when John Lillywhite was caught at the wicket from the last ball before lunch. The pair had added 184. *Bell's Life* said that their batting was 'the very essence of cricket'. Through its officers the Sussex club arranged a collection for their benefit. In this match, for the first time in a quarter of a century, Tom Box was not selected to keep wicket for Sussex. This would have been a significant moment for JW given Box's role in his cricket education going back to his boyhood.

The higher totals were due, at least in part, to the improvements in the standard of pitches, itself due to increasing skills in groundsmanship and the availability of improved equipment. Two of the grounds most frequently showing this trend were the Oval and the Brunswick Ground at Hove. The trend was to accelerate in the coming years until it created a crisis point which triggered a whole series of changes with significant implications for JW, contributing to his decision to end his playing career.

Although the annual UEE programme of matches against local teams was getting under way there were still some county matches to be played. After the Kent match at Hove JW travelled to Manchester to play in a North v South fixture on the Broughton Ground. Sadly the weather got much the better of the game. JW took 1/28 in North's innings and was next-man-in when the match was abandoned. JW now had a free day, 10th August to hurry back south to Canterbury to join a combined Kent & Sussex team to play England. He took five wickets then two wickets in the England innings and having scored 16 in his first innings was at the wicket with 6* when the combined side won by six wickets. England had been 'MCC administered' and as was their practice at the time no records of bowling were preserved.[56] JW's final county match for the season was MCC's visit to the Royal Brunswick Ground. JW scored 13 (run out) and 2 in the two Sussex innings and took 4/61 in MCC's first innings. Once again the wet summer got the better of the cricket and rain caused the match to be abandoned as a draw with MCC at 92-4 (JW 2/41) chasing 143 to win.

Between the matches against England and MCC JW was part of the UEE side to play Reigate Priory starting on 14th August. Reigate Priory were possibly one of the strongest clubs that UEE played. William Caffyn was a long-standing member and for this match they had recruited the 49 year-old Alfred Mynn. JW had an indifferent match redeemed only by 8/32 in the host's second innings. Reigate won by 43 runs. A week later JW joined the UEE at Hailsham, East Sussex to play against twenty-two Gentlemen of Sussex. The match was staged as a benefit for George Picknell who farmed locally and had been a founding member of UEE. JW took nine wickets in the first innings, eleven in the second and scored 35 in UEE's second innings helping to set up a win by 67 runs.

At this time another significant change was taking place again with direct implications for JW. In the middle of June William Clarke played for the All England Eleven against Whitehaven. In the first innings Clarke bowled just a few overs at the end taking two late wickets. In

[56] See *Scores & Biographies V*, p. 246

the local side's second innings Willsher and Jackson bowled unchanged. This was to be Clarke's last match, so he had taken a wicket with the last ball that he ever bowled. In *Scores & Biographies*, Haygarth noted that Clarke 'is very weak'. In fact the old stalwart's decline had been noted and reported upon for some time; the *Nottingham Review* observing the previous summer that he was bowling too much. On 10th-12th July 1856 Clarke umpired in the All England v Melton Mowbray match and it transpired that this was to be his final appearance on a cricket field. After the match he returned to his base in London for treatment for his paraplegia. While AEE were playing a match in Loughborough news reached them that their leader was fading fast. Alfred Clarke left the match and rushed to be at his father's bedside but arrived too late. William Clarke's funeral took place five days later but the All England Eleven, his great project, remained in Hull to fulfil their fixture. At first sight this appears unfeeling but perhaps the enmity within the group went way beyond Clarke's antagonism towards JW. Clarke's demise was to adjust what might be called the 'balance of animosity' within the groups of professional players.

After a fortnight playing in a series of matches in the south-east corner of England the message was now 'Go west young man'. UEE were now to visit Wales meaning that they had now played in all of the four nations of the United Kingdom. The fixture was with Twenty-two of Llanelly[57] in Carmarthenshire. Tradition would warn that it was a wet summer to be venturing into west Wales and sure enough all of the first day was lost to rain. When play began on the second day JW won the toss and asked the local team to bat first. This no doubt gave UEE the opportunity to see how the wicket would play before they had to bat on it. JW worked hard bowling 37 overs for 5/23 in the first innings and 6/22 from 42 in the second innings. UEE won by four wickets.

Continuing the westward journey JW took his team across the sea to Ireland. They had made this journey each year since their first full season (1853) but this year they played a second fixture, making the travelling more worthwhile. Firstly they took on a side assembled by Earl Fitzwilliam on his Coollatin Estate before travelling to Dublin for the now annual fixture in Phoenix Park against Ireland. United thought that there would be 16 players on the Irish side but on the day 18 appeared. In

[57] This is the town renowned for its rugby football. There remain variations in the spelling of the name but the Ordnance Survey currently uses 'Llanelli' for this town and 'Lanelly' for the one in Monmouthshire.

a typical reaction JW agreed to let all 18 play but the concession proved critical as the hosts won by just six runs. JW had a good match personally scoring 29 and 18 and taking seven wickets in each innings.

On their return to England UEE embarked on a sequence of standard fixtures visiting Bradford, Hereford and Cornwall before arriving at Chichester in the final days of September 1856. Thinking that they were playing a team of 18, UEE assumed the innings complete when their opponent's 17th wicket fell. However, as they were walking off towards the pavilion a nineteenth batsman walked out to meet them. Again, UEE decided not to object but No 19 scored 5* and United lost by 3 runs. As the leader of the UEE team JW would have been mindful of the driving purpose of matches such as this – one of taking good cricket away from the major centres and to the wider population. Winning was not the dominant objective and a squabble would have spoilt the occasion. Fred Lillywhite was recorded as umpire in this match, so who was looking after the shop back in London?

During this summer Lillywhite & Wisden maintained a weekly block advertisement in the classified columns of *Bell's Life*. On 18th May they had added a second advertisement announcing that they had added pictures of R Hankey Esq and John Lillywhite to the portraits already available for sale. The advertisements appeared in a column with others for Frederick Lillywhite's scoring publications and the 9th edition of *Lillywhite's Guide*. Just below these was John Lillywhite's general advertisement. While the principals were away playing cricket the advertisements continued to appear weekly, unaltered, until 19th October. At this point L&W's advertisement switched to focus on cigars and winter sports.

The next retail initiative to be announced through the columns of *Bell's Life* proclaimed 'CHRISTMAS – Three Guinea Smoking Present'. This was a collection of smoking supplies and equipment assembled in a compact box for £3-3-0. The partners were prepared to send them carriage free, per rail, for up to 100 miles. Clearly Christmas shopping did not dominate the final months of the year to the extent that it does in the 21st century because the advertisement first appeared on 21st December and was repeated on 28th.

In fact Christmas presents were still being offered in the New Year but from 4th January 1857 Lillywhite and Wisden began to address a new client market. At this time Great Britain was maintaining an extensive empire and gentlemen soldiers were ever being posted abroad to effect that maintenance, often at short notice, to locations where cricket could be played and prosper. In part this explains today's spread of cricket playing countries. As cricketing outfitters L&W were offering officers and gentlemen to 'procure a complete outfit in a few hours' notice'. Much cricket had been played by troops on their way to the Crimea campaign.[58] Later both L&W and John Lillywhite were offering to kit-out whole regiments at short notice.

By March 1857, with the new season just a few weeks away, L&W offered another new service. The advertisement was headed 'CRICKET – bowlers and clubs – Professional'. The pair opened a register of cricket clubs and professional bowlers, seeking to match them up. In 21st century terms they were to become players' agents, the first of a number of services they offered, either jointly or severally, over the coming years that would assist or enable professionals to build a career playing cricket. With the ever-present eye on guaranteed quality, they stated 'bowlers must be of merit and good character'.

In 1851 there had been staged The Great Exhibition. Lillywhite Brothers ('now dissolved') had exhibited at the event, showing their 'triple whalebone and cane handle bats'. Breaking bat handles was a frequent problem at this time and these bats were designed to reduce the problem. By 1857 the L&W partnership had 'manufactured several hundred dozens … at their country manufactory' and were offering these bats to players going overseas where the repair of broken handled bats was not easily achieved.

As the season approached Page, Thoms, Payne and Mrs Dark were joining the ever-growing list of those advertising cricketing goods and services in *Bell's Life's* weekly columns.

In an intriguing reversal of the Army-Cricket relationship, amongst the set of the usual cricket advertisements was one for 'Crimean Tents'. They were said to be circular, 48 feet in diameter and in excellent condition. The idea was that they could be used as portable or demountable dressing rooms and pavilions. Supposedly good value at 30s to 50s the advertisement ran from 31st March to 24th May – had they all been sold by then?

During 1856, JW's elder brother William (jnr) opened a sports good shop in Brighton. It was situated just across the road from Middle Street School. In the role of sports outfitter William's company, Wisden Sports, was to outlast JW's.

---

[58] See *Cricket and Cannons* by David Shimwell, part of the ACS *Cricket Witness* series. One of the leading officers on this expedition was Lord Guernsey, JW's patron at Leamington.

12

THE CRICKETERS' FUND
FRIENDLY SOCIETY

No sooner had JW joined the ranks of professional cricketers in 1844 than he was being asked to 'put his hand in his pocket' to support a fellow professional in distressed circumstances. When the case first appeared in the national press it was headlined 'The Widow Dorrinton', and a young JW showed typical generosity in contributing 10/-, equal to a week's wages for, say, a farm labourer. William Dorrinton had caught an infection whilst playing cricket causing damage to his throat and leading ultimately to his death. Mrs Dorrinton was left without financial support for herself and her small children.

At this time cricketers who fell on hard times were reliant on benefit collections and appeals. They had to hope that the gentry whose entertainment and enjoyment they had enhanced would be suitably generous when the time of need came. It left the professional players in a subservient and at times demeaning position. Other appeals would be raised in the following years, even the multi-talented Felix (Nicholas Wanostrocht) ended up in the need of kindness from the cricket fraternity. Very often JW's London base in New Coventry Street was used as a collection point for donations to these appeals and it was very much in his nature to be of service in this way.

The instances of need had, perversely, increased with the success of the professional cricketers in expanding and controlling their own sport. In 1841 James Dean, who would be the beneficiary of the second ever AEE v UEE match, perhaps played as few as 20 days cricket away from his home. By 1856 that had increased to most of six months. He was not alone in this, many of the emerging corps of professional players were spending more and more days away from the craft, skills and professions which might support them in their declining years.

In the early years of JW's time as a professional player there had been attempts to create a benevolent fund to which professional cricketers would pay a subscription and from which they could draw benefits in times of need. In 1846 William Denison, the journalist, had tried to launch such a fund and had even collected donations from the gentry and gentlemen players. However, he was unable to get the players to agree to the necessary set of rules and the money was eventually returned and the project abandoned.

The MCC, a major employer of professional cricketers, also saw the need to provide some form of benevolence and also established a fund in the early 1850s. However, the players seemed to find the regulations irksome and the fund made limited progress.

William Clarke had done much to encourage and enable talented cricketers to give more of their time and energies to becoming professional players and ironically it was his death in 1856 which provided the opportunity to establish an acceptable benevolent fund. There had long been a public clamour for the two itinerant elevens, AEE and UEE, to play each other on an annual basis. As the professionals increased their skills the annual Gentlemen v Players fixtures, once a highlight of the season, were becoming increasingly uncompetitive. All England v United England was seen as a potential suitable replacement in the calendar. In his lifetime Clarke had resolutely refused to contemplate such a match, still holding the UEE players in contempt for 'deserting' his team. At the same time UEE had a policy of not playing in any match arranged by Clarke. In 1857 the leaders of the two elevens, JW and George Parr, were still business partners (through the lease of the ground at Leamington) and were able to agree conditions for both the launch of a fund and also the series of annual matches between the two elevens that could generate an income for the fund. It was at George Parr's insistence that the first match should be for the benefit of what was to become The Cricketers' Fund Friendly Society. So on Whit Monday 1857 the CFFS was successfully launched on a career that was to last for over 100 years. It was duly registered in accordance with the relevant Act of Parliament.

A possible explanation for the success of the CFFS as opposed to the other funds was the fact that its management was in the hands of the leading professional players. The first committee comprised Tom Box (Sussex) as chairman, George Parr (Notts.), Julius Caesar (Surrey), John Lillywhite (Sussex), George Anderson (Yorkshire), Edgar Willsher (Kent) and Alfred Diver (Cambs.). A selection of the great and the good acted as president, trustees and auditors so providing the governance. The treasurer was Mr JH Dark, operating from his base at Lord's. This combination of the players managing the fund but with the gentry providing an advise and support role had JW's imprint on it. There was not room for another Sussex man on the committee but with Fred Lillywhite acting as hon secretary and operating from the New Coventry Street shop, JW was well placed to monitor performance and progress.

There had long been a public clamour for the two Elevens to play each other on an annual basis. It would become the premier fixture of the season as the Gentlemen v Players matches were becoming increasingly uncompetitive.

JW could have a positive input to this project. He was a polite and courteous sportsman who had won the respect of those in privileged positions who controlled the sport at a national level. His days at Harrow School had generated many friends who warmed to his personality and respected his ability as both a coach and a player. At the same time he remained a professional cricketer and a leader of one of the larger groups of them. John Wisden in his shop in central London provided a neutral meeting ground for all those involved or interested in the game of cricket. Several of the men with whom JW first came into contact during his Harrow days would become major supporters of CFFS.

Across the kingdom, and indeed across Europe, these were politically turbulent times with workers organising themselves to have a greater say in the formulation of their terms and conditions of employment and remuneration. The first stirrings of a movement that would lead to the formation of trade unions were just beginning to appear on the scene. A trade union for cricketers would have done little to improve relationships with those who still controlled the game. MCC had shown a defensive wariness on each previous occasion when groups of professionals had sought to exert influence. However, the CFFS gave all professionals a common association, irrespective of their allegiance to a county club, a touring eleven or any other group. Whilst not a trade union it did have the potential to become an association of professionals.

Within three years of the foundation of CFFS its secretary Fred Lillywhite was in business on his own and starting to become increasingly irascible. The management of the fund was beginning to lose its way. Eventually the society agreed that JW would take over as secretary but Fred was not going to give up without a struggle and was obdurate in handing over the books. Eventually JW had to instigate legal proceedings against his former business partner. In October 1863 a formal hearing was only avoided when Fred Lillywhite arrived at the court building shortly before the case was to be heard and handed over the books.

JW then set about tightening the administration of the fund. Accounts were now regularly published so all could see both the money coming in, the investments being made and the payments going out. MCC still had their fund which was tightly controlled by the officers and committee but it was beginning to fail. Comment in the national press indicated a perceived lack of transparency and a belief that this was discouraging donations.

CFFS had two classes of membership. Those who earned a livelihood from cricket (players) paid an annual subscription and were ordinary members. Additionally there were honorary members, gentlemen, gentry and nobility, who made donations to the fund. The accounts through the 1860s showed that after the changes to the administration of the fund instigated by JW donations had doubled.

JW was still secretary and honorary treasurer of The Cricketers' Fund Friendly Society on the day that he died.

13

THE ESTABLISHED CRICKETER
AND LEADER

In a sense William Clarke quietly faded out of the All England Eleven. He played his last match in July 1856 and then some weeks later made his last appearance on the cricket field umpiring an AEE match. He then returned to London and passed away at the end of August. In his absence the Eleven carried on completing the match programme. In *Scores & Biographies*, as a footnote to the scorecard for the team's final match of the season, versus Twenty-two of Leeds (25th & 26th September 1856), it was reported:

> The England Eleven had a meeting on the evening of the 26th, when it was decided that the Eleven should be carried on as formerly when they were 'piloted' by the late William Clarke. A Committee of Management was formed, consisting of Julius Caesar, Edgar Willsher, George Anderson, Alfred Clarke and Heathfield Harman Stephenson; George Parr was elected to the office of Secretary.

So now the two strongest teams in the land, the two touring elevens, were being led by the partners in the Leamington ground venture. This gave the opportunity for a new beginning in the relationship between the two groups. For months, indeed years, there had been pleadings, usually expressed in the press, for the two elevens to settle their differences and play against each other. It was recognised, even if somewhat reluctantly in some quarters, that the professional players were now dominant in the best cricket. They formed the core of those teams playing in an expanding inter-county fixture list and had come to dominate the annual Gentlemen versus Players fixtures. There was the hope that annual United England XI v All England XI fixtures could join North v South as providing a platform for the display of the very best cricket.

The cricketing public did not have long to wait for a response to their pleadings. On 1st March 1857 *Bell's Life* announced that:

'The two celebrated Elevens of England will at length appear on the same field in friendly contest'. The date of Monday 1st June on the MCC fixture list for Lord's had been pencilled-in for a North v South match. Now it was to be replaced with All England v United. In 1857 this was Whit Monday. The match was to be played for the benefit of the newly formed, and also long overdue, Cricketers' Fund. There was also to be a second AEE v UEE match at the end of July, which would be for the benefit of James Dean, JW's long standing friend, assistant and team-mate. *Bell's Life* expressed the hope that people would 'rally round and support Dean – a faithful and public servant for 23 years'.

In the meantime JW began his 1857 season with a one-off engagement. On 28th & 29th April he, along with William Caffyn and John Lillywhite, turned out for Betchworth against Surrey Club. His contribution was modest, sharing the wickets with Caffyn and scoring 18* in the second innings as his team were well beaten. His next reported match was a wash-out when the UEE v Household Brigade fixture only reached the end of UEE's first innings before the rain brought it to a halt. Top scorer in that innings was Arthur Haygarth making a very unusual appearance for UEE. Ever eager to point out his own contributions his footnote to the match's scorecard in *Scores & Biographies* noted that he ran 152 runs while scoring 71. JW scored 51* mostly against the bowling of Bickley and Willsher, a formidable duo. In this match Haygarth was one of three gentlemen who played for UEE; F Burbidge and FP Miller being the others.

In the week before the AEE v UEE match at Lord's JW renewed his association with the University of Cambridge. He and John Lillywhite were included in a team titled Old Cambridge Men which included RA Fitzgerald, later to become secretary of MCC. Their opponents were Undergraduates of Cambridge. The Old Men took first innings and 74* from JW was the core of a total of 175. But despite taking seven wickets across the Undergraduates' two innings JW still ended on the losing side. Later in the week he visited Oxford University as a member of the UEE team to play Twenty of Christ Church. He made only a limited contribution to his side's comfortable win by six wickets; this may have been due to injury.

CRICKETTING OUTFITTERS.—Messrs F. LILLYWHITE and WISDEN have always on hand an immense STOCK of CRICKETING GOODS, comprising every article used in the game, and can procure a complete outfit in a few hours' notice. They beg to introduce to officers and private gentlemen going abroad the REGISTERED TREBLE WHALEBONE and CANE HANDLE BATS, which will be warranted not to break, and therefore particularly adapted for use where re-handling cannot be accomplished. Racket bats, foot balls, boxing gloves, dumb bells, &c, &c. Regiments, clubs, colleges, and schools supplied on the most advantageous terms. Address, Lillywhite and Wisden, 2, New Coventry-street, Leicester-square, London, importers of the finest foreign cigars only.

CHRISTMAS.—Three Guinea Smoking Present.— F. LILLYWHITE and WISDEN, of 2, New Coventry-street, Leicester-square, London, offer the following first rate ARTICLES, in a compact box, for £3 3s :—1lb foreign cigars, a valuable cigar case, Indiarubber pouch, 1lb very best tobacco, cricketing pipe and case, tobacco stopper and picker, leather bottle fuzee case, and a handsome carved meerschaum cigar tube. Sent, per rail, carriage free, under 100 miles. Every article connected with cricket and other games may be had at their establishment.—N.B. Cricketing outfitters.

JOHN LILLYWHITE'S CRICKETING and CIGAR DEPOT, Caledonian-road, Islington, London.—J. L. begs to inform his cricketing friends that he will forward a BOX of fine CIGARS and a POUND of VIRGINIA SHAG TOBACCO on receipt of a P.O.O. for £1 6s, payable to John Lillywhite, Battle Bridge, London.

Christmas Advertisement, 1857

At the time most of the sports outfitters placed advertisements of this style in Bell's Life. At peak times (pre-season) the cricket advertisements would stretch down a whole column. These advertisements were first placed on 21st December and repeated on 28th and 4th January.

The hope that all would be peace and harmony amongst the two itinerant elevens when they met at Lord's was dashed before the game had even started. JW was always seeking to maintain good relationships with the gentlemen cricketers, often acting as a link between the professionals and amateurs. Ever since the formation of UEE JW had sought to include amateur (gentlemen) players in the team; in fact FP Miller occasionally captained the side. Both Miller and Burbidge were in the selected UEE side but George Parr objected to their inclusion because they were amateurs and so two professionals had to be substituted for them. Parr spun the coin (apparently a two-shilling piece) and JW correctly called heads and elected to bat. As James Dean and Tom Hunt went out to open the innings there were, reportedly, 10,000 people on the ground. The match report in *Bell's Life* began with a long list of the nobility and gentry in attendance – it was that sort of event.

On a personal playing level the match was not a great success for JW. He came into the match carrying an injury, his second of the season, and broke down after having bowled only nine overs at the start of the AEE innings. In the UEE innings, batting at five, he scored only seven out of an acceptable team total of 143. However, without his bowling AEE were able to get a first innings lead of 63. UEE's second innings totalled only

140, leaving their opponents only 78 to win, which they reached for the loss of five wickets.

The *raison d'etre* for the match was well illustrated in the *Bell's Life* report of the match. Against the name of each member of the attending gentry was marked their individual contribution to the newly established Cricketers' Fund Friendly Society and after the bowling figures, at the foot of the scorecard, came details of both the daily takings at the gate and the final balance. After the 10,000 attending on the first day there were 7,000 on the second day but fewer on the final day as the match was close to conclusion. With total gate receipts of £291-3-0 and expenses of £130-14-0 the Cricketers' Fund was launched with a balance of £160-9-0. The match was a disappointment for JW as a player but as a leader amongst the professional players he would have been pleased with the public response to the fund-raising match and the funds accrued. This was a project close to his heart whose progress he would have closely monitored through the work of colleagues.

The second All England v United England fixture was scheduled for 27th July at Lord's. Between the first and second matches was the core of the county cricket programme.[59] UEE played just two matches between the two elevens' fixtures. On successive weeks at Lord's they played matches against firstly Cambridge University and then Oxford University, in each case the students' team being of 16 players. The University Match, Oxford v Cambridge, was played between these fixtures, Oxford winning by a comfortable margin. JW had a moderate match against Cambridge, 23 runs and nine wickets, but was more successful in the Oxford match where he had figures of 5/27 and 8/20. One of JW's attributes as a bowler was his consistent accuracy in both line and length. The fact that he bowled a wide in the match was so rare that it was deemed noteworthy in *Scores & Biographies'* report of the game, which also observed that JW had begun with 14 successive (4-ball) maiden overs. The accuracy of his bowling would become increasingly important as the pace of his bowling began to slacken.

The two matches against the University teams were part of the MCC's Monday programme; in both matches United included three leading amateur players. As well as the semi-regular FP Miller, they included A Haygarth and W Nicholson. By instinct JW sought to work within the established arrangements and playing the amateurs in the Monday matches was part of that.

[59] See Appendix C

155

UEE also avoided arranging fixtures that clashed with well-established fixtures such as the county matches. Clearly George Parr had fewer inhibitions about these clashes, and AEE played matches against Liverpool and Manchester Broughton while MCC played Sussex and Oxford University and Surrey played Cambridgeshire. Later AEE had matches at Sleaford and Uppingham while Sussex, Surrey, Kent and MCC played long-standing fixtures. In all fairness it must be observed that the traditional inter-county programme was very southern orientated, so AEE playing matches in the north created only minimal conflict in the demand for the services of the professionals. Apart from Lord's most of the county matches were played south of the Thames. Sadly this was a manifestation of cricket's North-South divide which was to create so much rancour during the 1860s and left JW having to work hard to keep the corps of professional players together.

At the beginning of July JW started playing in a sequence of first-class matches. About this time his match figures suggest that he might be beginning to find many of the UEE matches a bit of a necessary chore, but was able to motivate himself for the more demanding matches. In the first Gentlemen v Players match at the Oval he took eight wickets in the match and, batting at No 8, scored 46. However, in the second match between the teams at Lord's he was out-bowled by the emerging force of Edgar Willsher and took just a single wicket. His two innings yielded 16 and 5 runs; in the second case he was run out – yet again. Playing for a combined Sussex & Kent side versus England JW took nine wickets in the match and for Sussex against Kent scored 34 and 27. Set against this success was no wickets and just seven runs in an awful Sussex display against Surrey which saw them lose by an innings and 100 runs in a single day. Then he took just one wicket and scored only 11 runs for South in their match against North.

On Monday 27th July amid great excitement most of the leading professionals assembled once again at Lord's for the second All England v United England fixture. However, there was again a spat even before the match started when UEE objected to the composition of the AEE team. George Anderson had been due to play for AEE but had been ill for all of the previous week. AEE seem not to have made any arrangements to have cover for him and when he was declared to be unavailable at the last moment they attempted to include Ned Stephenson who was not one of their regular players. UEE objected to this change and the match began with the teams still not settled. Eventually James Dean was called away from collecting (his) gate money and joined the UEE team, releasing Tom Adams, who regularly played for either eleven, to switch to AEE.

Possibly motivated by the tension JW pulled out all of the stops and took 8/49 as he and William Caffyn bowled out AEE for just 99. Only George Parr (48) made any impression. UEE batted steadily, with JW contributing a useful 13 and gained a 27 runs first innings lead. At the end of the first innings the bookmakers were offering 4-5 on UEE winning. Thereafter, UEE's fortunes went downhill. AEE totalled 214 in their second innings and then on the third morning swept away UEE for 54 in a single session.

As with the first match large crowds gathered and one positive effect of this was a significant improvement in the catering arrangements which had been lacking at Whitsuntide. This was another step along the route towards a truly national, professional programme of matches.

Although he had a lean match in playing terms James Dean left Lord's that Wednesday afternoon with a smile on his face. The total of subscriptions and gate receipts earned him over £350, the equivalent of about seven years' wages from his original occupation as a farm worker. For someone who had given good service to the game it was a just and pleasing reward, a good advertisement for these matches and the work of the CFFS.

In earlier years the beginning of August would signal the end of almost all of the established, first-class programme and the field was left open for local matches and the fixtures of the travelling elevens. This was the space that William Clarke had identified, exploited and filled. However, the inter-county programme was expanding in two ways. Firstly most of the long established teams were playing nearly all others, home and away, but also new opponents and fixtures were being created. As well as Kent, MCC and Sussex, Surrey played Cambridgeshire and Oxfordshire, and Berkshire v Buckinghamshire and Herefordshire v Shropshire had been added to the season's list of fixtures.

Alongside this some powerful country estate teams had been assembled. One of these was the Earl of Stamford's XI, playing matches at his Enville Hall home in Staffordshire, and it was to this ground that the UEE travelled after Dean's match at Lord's. As well as including such gifted gentlemen as W Nicholson and A Payne the Earl also employed the professionals Edgar Willsher, Cris Tinley and John Bickley. Given the ability of many of Stamford's players it is surprising that the match was made 22 v 11. In that context it was understandable that UEE were beaten by an innings and 44 runs. As the main match had finished in two days a one-day match was arranged for Saturday. JW's innings of 59 would have given him some useful time at the wicket.

After the stay at Enville Hall many of the players returned to London for the Surrey & Sussex v England fixture. JW now found himself on a winning side as the combined counties won by an impressive 110 runs. The England XI were much weakened by the Earl of Stamford's belated decision not to release his employed bowlers, Bickley, Cris Tinley and Willsher. Because of the extension of the first-class programme the conflicting demands on the professional players were to become even greater.

Having taken 11 wickets when Sussex & Surrey again beat England, this time at Hove, JW travelled to Tunbridge Wells. The usual sequence of North v South matches had been disrupted by the use of the Whitsuntide date at Lord's for the UEE v AEE match. After the MCC-arranged match at Lord's in July, two individually promoted fixtures were arranged to be played at firstly Tunbridge Wells and then later at Nottingham. In Kent in mid-August the North had a convincing victory although it was a good match for JW on a personal level, taking 7/15 in the first innings and the only two North wickets to fall in the second innings as the North ran out easy winners. During the week JW had taken 20 wickets while conceding just 99 runs.

After playing for a well beaten Kent & Sussex team against England at Canterbury JW joined the UEE team for their match at Reigate. As a measure of the progress being made generally by the town teams Reigate were restricted to 16 players – although one of them was William Caffyn, a long-time member of the club. JW took seven wickets in each innings as UEE won easily. But this was just an interruption in the sequence of first-class matches and JW returned to Kent this time to Gravesend, with the visiting Sussex side. Kent batted first and scored 227 (JW 5/75) to which Sussex could only reply with 84. Forced to follow-on they managed a better 275 in the second innings before Kent won the match with 135-5. *Scores & Biographies* noted that 721 runs were scored in the match and gave it as another example of the shifting balance between bat and ball, in part a consequence of better pitches.

In the last days of the month there were signs of greater co-operation between JW's UEE and George Parr's AEE team. For 27th to 29th August UEE had a fixture with Liverpool while AEE were to play Priory Park in Chichester. James Dean wished to play at Chichester, just down the road from his Duncton home. To allow him to play at Chichester he exchanged places with Alfred Clarke who turned out in Liverpool for UEE. A rumbling noise could be heard from a grave in London!

Following a trip to Cardiff, then moving back to Lancashire where he and John Lillywhite were given men as Manchester took on Surrey (JW 12/70), JW crossed to Nottingham for the third North v South match of the summer. It was to be a painful one for JW in more senses than one.

In his book *A Cricketer's Yarns* Richard Daft recorded that in 1849 JW became engaged to be married to Ann Parr, younger sister of George. Nothing more is heard of Ann or the engagement until September 1857. On 5th September Ann Parr died apparently in the long established family home, The Manor House, Radcliffe-on-Trent. On her death certificate the cause is given as 'phthisis', and her occupation as 'Daughter of Samuel Parr, Farmer'. In the 1851 census Ann's occupation was given as 'dressmaker', so there is an implication that she had suffered a prolonged and debilitating illness while continuing to live in her original home.

On 7th September the players assembled at the Trent Bridge Ground for the match. George Parr had withdrawn from the North side, 'owing to a death in the family', reported *Scores & Biographies* but JW was in the South team and opened the bowling when the North batted first. Martingell and Caffyn took the wickets as North were bowled out for 50. South began their reply and towards the end of the first day's play JW was batting with Mr Miller when he attempted to drive a full length delivery from the fearsome John Jackson, missed and was struck painfully on the foot. The batting pair survived to the end of the day but on the second morning JW was unfit to bat and had to retire hurt taking no further part in the match. *Bell's Life* reported that on the third day JW took a catch to dismiss F Bell but *Scores & Biographies* recorded that it was in fact taken by WP Lockhart, substituting for JW.

Another catch by a substitute occurred in South's second innings when Caffyn's dismissal was listed as 'ct Daft, Esq., for Jackson, b Bell'. This was the first appearance in a first-class match of Richard Daft, son of Nottingham and resident of Radcliffe. Richard Daft was to become a dominant force in the game for the next 40 years, even in the era of WG

Grace. John Jackson was later to claim that 'taking nine of the South's wickets and forcing Johnny Wisden to retire hurt was as good as taking all ten'. In fact he took only eight of the wickets.

The third day of the match was also the day of Ann's funeral. Sadly all this coming and going of playing personnel makes it difficult to answer two questions. What was the state of JW's relationship with Ann and did he attend the funeral? The fact that he played in the match, while George Parr did not, suggests that the relationship had weakened, possibly as a result of Ann's protracted illness. His reputation elsewhere would suggest that JW would have done the decent thing and slipped away from the match to attend the funeral. Sadly, the only records of his movements at Nottingham are through the reports of the cricket match and he was no longer actively involved in that. JW remained a bachelor for the rest of his life.

As a result of his injury JW had to pull out of the Sussex v MCC match, Sussex winning without him. His next match was for UEE versus Twenty-two of Birmingham, the local side including Edgar Willsher, Cris Tinley and Charles Brown. Willsher not only took nine wickets in the match but was also the top scorer with an innings of 37. More significantly this match was the last time that Frederick Miller turned out for UEE. As well as acting as president of UEE Miller had also captained the side on occasions and his presence in the mainly professional team was an essential part of JW's efforts to build and maintain links with cricket's amateur establishment.

The 1857 season ended with a seven-day visit by UEE to Scotland with a stop-off in Lincolnshire (match drawn). The team won one and lost one of the matches and JW and Caffyn did an awful lot of bowling. On the final day of September they were free to head south, back to their homes and the opportunity to put their feet up.

It would seem that the business of the New Coventry Street shop had been left to carry-on on its own a little while the principals were away at the cricket matches. Fred Lillywhite kept a UEE scorebook and provided scorecards and a results service at other major matches, so he had been away from the shop as much as JW. He also stood as umpire in some UEE matches. Up until mid-July JW spent only a little time playing cricket away from London. This seems to be reflected in the advertising done by the partnership. From mid-March onwards the general advertising of cricket equipment and in some cases services went into full swing, with the major suppliers having weekly and occasionally several varying entries in the classified columns. The Lillywhite & Wisden partnership was now offering scorebooks and also printed sheets to facilitate the submission of match reports to *Bell's Life*. Both were to designs created by Fred Lillywhite; his training as a printer and his enthusiasm for cricket being of assistance to *Bell's Life* and of financial gain to the partnership.

In its issue of 14th June *Bell's Life* had made 'An Appeal to Cricketers, etc.' relating to 'Lillywhite's Collection of Scores from 1746, in preparation'. Club secretaries and other gentlemen were asked to submit old scorebooks and other information about the game to those compiling the collection. Back copies of *Bell's Life* and the Marylebone Club books had already been searched. The purpose of the project was to publish a complete history of the noble game. The output of the project would come to be known as *Scores & Biographies* and the work continues today. Any material was to be submitted to Frederick Lillywhite at Lillywhite and Wisden's shop at 2 New Coventry Street. Thus was beginning the move to fully record the game, both present and past, in which the names of Lillywhite and Wisden would be prominent.

Back in the spring the weekly advertisements for JW's business started to peter out at the end of May and ceased altogether in July as the demands of the matches increased. With the players' arrival back home in October a new winter advertisement appeared leading with cigars and tobacco followed by football and rackets equipment plus cricket kit for those going abroad. But after three weeks all disappeared.

After a long winter break advertising began again in 1858 with two classified advertisements in *Bell's Life* on 28th February. The first invited professionals seeking an appointment to send for and then complete and return a registration form. It also asked that existing clients completed a form and return it to Lillywhite & Wisden so that dates of birth could be confirmed to ensure that the ages given in the register were correct. The partners also offered a catalogue showing 'Twenty pages of cricketers' wants'. The next appearance of the advertisement was on 4th April when L&W added a reminder that club orders would be fulfilled at wholesale prices.

It would appear that the partners were confident that their client base knew who they were, where they were situated and what they had to offer as it was not until 8th May that the next advertisement appeared. On this occasion their patent catapulta was added. The machine was promoted as the ideal provider of batting practice for a gentleman. The image created is a Jeeves and Wooster one of the butler/valet feeding the machine with balls and the machine then providing the gentleman with batting practice. This then became the standard advertisement for the season and appeared weekly until 19th September, the last one for the year.

At this time the advertisements suggest that the shop and its associated activities were continuing in a steady state. The impression is that the shop was well known and had an established client base, to whom their services were well known. During the summer months the partners were away from the shop at cricket matches. On some of the days when JW was playing in county cricket Fred may well have been free to work at the shop. He certainly believed that he made greater input to the running of the partnership, later describing himself as having been the manager of the business. Census records suggest that the partners employed assistants living on the premises who kept the shop running on the days when both of the partners were away. The many days between UEE fixtures and the concentration of first-class matches close to London made it easier for JW, and at times Fred, to return to the shop to check that all was well.

JW's 1858 cricket season had a distinctly academic start. During May he made a series of daily visits to Harrow as he had done in May 1857. These were aimed at identifying and bringing together the players who would make up the school eleven for the summer. He then played in two matches against Oxford University. In the first of these he was a member of an England team. During his innings JW was caught off a no-ball. However, not hearing the call he set off for the pavilion. The students then ran him out. Some measure of revenge was gained when he took 5/26 in the students' first innings and England went on to win. At the end of this match he followed the students from Lord's to Oxford where he was part of the UEE team to beat Christ Church College by an innings and 35 runs; JW scored 35 to go with his seven wickets.

In 1858 Whit Monday was 7th June and as part of an emerging pattern UEE came to Lord's to play AEE for the benefit of CFFS, at the same time satisfying the demand for more matches featuring the best players to be staged at Lord's. JW had an indifferent match, just 20 runs and three wickets but would have been happy with his team's four wickets win. The big wicket taker for UEE was William Caffyn who had changed from being a specialist batsman into a very effective all-rounder. JW had helped Caffyn get started as a professional cricketer with a recommendation that he be employed at the Auberies. Caffyn had not so long ago transferred from being a member of AEE to playing for UEE.

At this time there was increasing evidence that the passing of the years and the cumulative effect of too many long spells of bowling were beginning to catch up with JW. Batting required less physical effort than fast bowling and he seemed now to be more successful at batting.

The CFFS match at Lord's was the first in the sequence of representative matches in which JW was to play that summer. Next was the first of the Gentlemen v Players matches, starting on 1st July. He opened the first innings for the Players and scored 42. He bowled little, although he managed to dismiss Haygarth while bowling lobs – his new low-energy style. The Players were set 170 to win but when John Lillywhite walked out to join JW they had been reduced to 54 for 6. At this point the Brighton pair got their heads down and lifted the score to 149/7 before JW was dismissed for 46. Julius Caesar now came to the wicket and the Players went on to win without further loss. Three wickets was a narrower margin than had been usual in recent matches between these two teams.

The desire to create more matches involving the most able cricketers saw some creative groupings and combinations introduced. When Kent travelled to Lord's to play England on 5th July Caffyn (Surrey), John Jackson and George Parr (both Nottinghamshire) were included in the visiting team. JW was included in the England team but contributed little as they eased to a 10 wickets win in one day. That gave him spare days at the shop to check that all was going well.

12th July saw the next in the sequence of matches staged at Lord's involving the stronger teams. This was South v North which the North went on to win by four wickets. JW had a quiet match scoring just 12 runs and taking only three wickets; he did though dismiss George Parr in each innings. A notable feature of the match was that it was Richard Daft's first match at Lord's. Daft would go on not only to have a long and successful playing career but he would also make a valuable contribution to CFFS, being chairman during many of the years that JW was secretary-treasurer. *Scores & Biographies* described Richard Daft as 'urbane and gentlemanly' which made him a good associate for JW.

A week later the Players overwhelmed the Gentlemen in the annual Lord's fixture. Having obtained a first innings lead of 63 the Players scored a massive 299 [60] in their second innings. JW scored 21* in his first innings and then opened the second with Alfred Diver. The pair put on 129 before Diver was out. JW was eventually dismissed for 58 with the score at 142 having had to run all of those runs. He was not needed to bowl as John Jackson and Cris Tinley, with a little help from HH Stephenson and Caffyn, dismissed the Gentlemen for totals of 52 and 77.

The last representative match for JW that season was as part of an England team to play Surrey at the Oval. A measure of Surrey's supremacy at this time is the margin by which they were able to beat a strong England team – an innings and 28 runs. A footnote in the *Scores & Biographies* record for this match[61] indicates that Fred Lillywhite scored the match as well as Surrey's scorer. The two books disagreed but Fred Lillywhite's book was taken as the better record.

After the Surrey match came JW's last major match at Lord's for the season, the second AEE v UEE match beginning on Monday 26th July. JW needed to return to bowling in his stronger round-arm style in this match. Coming on as third change he bowled 32 overs to take 2/39 as AEE scored a formidable 254. UEE were then bowled out for 87 and 70. AEE thus avenged their earlier defeat with an overwhelming win by an innings and 97 runs. The match was for George Parr's benefit which was increased by £1 by a donation from the French Ambassador, the Duke of Malakoff.

The UEE innings had been opened by Robert Carpenter who JW had recruited to the team earlier in the season. It proved to be an astute choice as Carpenter did much to keep UEE running in the mid-1860s in the years following JW's retirement from playing.

JW's matches for Sussex were spread across the season. After the first of the AEE v UEE matches at Lord's at the beginning of June, JW made the short trip to Hove to be part of a combined Kent & Sussex team which lost to Surrey by 24 runs. At the last moment Willsher was unable to play and was replaced by the young Sussex bowler Harry Stubberfield who took ten wickets in the match; JW took five of the others. Both bowlers were part of the Sussex team that returned to

[60] Probably equal to more than 600 in 21st century terms.
[61] *Scores & Biographies VI*, p. 101

London after the weekend to beat MCC by 48 runs. JW took 8/47 in the first innings and Stubberfield 7/50 in the second. A potential replacement for JW as a leading wicket-taker in future Sussex teams had been identified.

Early in July a return Surrey v Kent & Sussex match was staged at the Oval. On this occasion the combined counties provided a better challenge. However, the rain intervened and brought the match to a premature end when it was nicely balanced. JW and Stubberfield did the bulk of the bowling in Surrey's only innings and shared seven of the wickets between them. Stubberfield's wickets included bowling a well-set William Caffyn with a full toss.

When Kent came to Hove at the beginning of August JW had a much better match than in some of his earlier encounters, opening the bowling with Stubberfield as his new partner and taking 4/48 and 5/40 as well as scoring a second innings 30. However, it was not enough to save Sussex from a 32 runs defeat.

In mid-August Parr, Jackson and Caffyn were once again included in a Kent team for a match with England. JW was in the England team but he bowled little, took no wickets and scored just 12 and 13 in his two innings. In the end greater efforts from JW were not needed as England eased to a five wickets win. *Scores & Biographies* noted that the five gentlemen playing in the match contributed just eleven runs between them from their ten innings. Elsewhere the thought was expressed that Kent were trying to live on past glories when they tried alone to match sides such as England. The thought was they would be well advised to combine with another county in the way that they did with Sussex for matches against the powerful Surrey.

At the beginning of September JW played in a match which *Bell's Life* listed as 'The County of Sussex v Manchester (with Caffyn)'. The match had been arranged between JW and the Western Club, based at Eccles. It was afforded first-class status but the involvement of Sussex CCC seems vague. After Sussex had totalled 230 (JW 25) the hosts were dismissed for 47. The only player to reach double figures was WMN Kington whom *Bell's Life* noted was 'one of Wisden's pupils at Harrow'. Caffyn was taken ill with influenza and did not play on the second and third days leaving Manchester to bat with only ten players in each innings. Following-on from their first innings they totalled 142 to lose by an innings and 41 runs.

To complete their programme of county matches Sussex travelled to Tunbridge Wells for the return fixture with Kent. In a sense JW saved some of his best cricket for the last match. Batting at No 5 he scored 39* in a Sussex first innings total of 112. He then took 5/15 as Kent were shot out for 36. Batting again Sussex totalled 179 of which JW contributed 32 (run out). To complete the match JW took 5/36 to dismiss Kent for 63 to secure a 192 runs win for Sussex.

Aside from the matches at Oxford and Lord's the first of the UEE matches for 1858 was at Irnham Park in Lincolnshire starting on 21st June. UEE won by 177 runs with JW taking 15 wickets in the match bowling lobs. From this time on he mixed lobs with his standard right arm fast round-arm bowling. However what remained constant was his accuracy and the low number of runs conceded per over. The Irnham match was followed by one at Peckham Rye in which JW scored runs and took wickets in the first innings before the match petered out as a draw.

A month passed before UEE played their next match against a team of twenty-two, this time a trip to Spalding in the final days of July. In a very low scoring match JW took 12 first innings wickets and scored 14 first innings runs as UEE eased to a five wickets win. The loss of the third day to rain meant that the UEE fixture with Twenty-two of Bath (including James Lillywhite and James Dean) ended in a draw as did the fixture with Twenty-two Gentlemen of Sussex. JW made only modest contributions in each of these matches.

JW had an additional personal interest in UEE's match on 23rd August when they played a team called 'John Walker's Sixteen of Southgate', six of whom were from the Walker family. The ground was a private one but excellently prepared and maintained and attracted in excess of 10,000 people on the first two days. JW had a modest return, six wickets and nine runs, from a match dominated by VE Walker who had the top two individual scores and five wickets as Southgate won by 59 runs. JW had an on-going relationship with the Walker family having coached several of the boys during his time at Harrow School. Earlier in the season he had turned out to umpire the match Southgate v Rugby School on their ground and in later years VE was to become a trustee of CFFS.

From Southgate UEE moved on to Croydon where they played a side of 18. JW's 7/39 and 10/28 helped create a win by 43 runs. Over the weekend the group travelled to Nottingham to play Mr AW McDougall's Twenty-two on the Trent Bridge ground. Once more JW achieved little with the bat but his 10/44 in the first innings helped towards a four wickets win. Six men were dismissed 'run out' in the match but for once JW was not one of them.

The UEE season ended for JW with three gentle, classic UEE up-country matches. Twenty-two of Lowestoft, etc. were overwhelmed and beaten by an innings and 118 runs. JW took 8/13 as they were shot out for 28 in their first innings. A week later UEE travelled via Rochdale to Penzance where they beat Cornwall by an innings and 33 runs. On their way back they stopped off at Plymouth to play Twenty-two of South Devon and East Cornwall, UEE winning by 111 runs. JW did not bowl in the hosts' first innings but took 13/42 in the second.

As the core of the UEE squad headed north to Glasgow to meet Twenty-two of Scotland, JW made his way to the Hampshire-Sussex border. This match is titled in *Scores & Biographies* as 'On Westbourne Common, near Stanstead Park[62] (E Wilder, Esq) in Sussex' – the match being Priory Park Club with Stubberfield, Gilbert and Hodson versus Westbourne, with Dean, Adams and Wisden. The key element in this is the part in brackets – Edmond Wilder was a great supporter of cricket and cricketers, particularly the professionals, and President of CFFS. Dean and JW took all of their opponents' wickets between them and JW scored 23* to close out a seven wickets win in a low-scoring match.

Back in London advertisements for F Lillywhite & Wisden stopped in the middle of September, 1858. This may have been because of the increasing tension developing between the partners which came to the surface when the *London Gazette* of January 18th 1859 carried the notice:

> Notice is hereby given, that the Partnership lately subsisting between us the undersigned, Frederick Lillywhite and John Wisden, carrying-on business at No. 2 New Coventry-street, Leicester-square, in the county of Middlesex, as Manufacturers of Cricketing Goods and dealers in Cigars has been dissolved by mutual consent as and from the first day of January, 1859; and that the business will in future be carried out by the said John Wisden alone. – Dated this 13th. Day of January, 1859
>
> Frederick Lillywhite.
> John Wisden.

[62] This was in fact Stansted Park – a *Scores & Biographies* spelling error.

There is little explicit evidence relating to the break-up of the partnership. There are, though, some facts that give a clue. Throughout his lifetime there is a marked lack of negative comment about JW but one came from Fred Lillywhite when he said words to the effect 'Most of us have had to work for our businesses but Wisden had his given to him'. The source for Fred's gripe reached back many years.

JW's grandfather Simon died in 1842. At the time of his death the portfolio of buildings that he held was being poorly managed; in some cases rents had not been paid for months stretching into years. It took JW's father, William, many months to put matters in order. During this time one of the executors and some of the legatees died. This had led to a dispute over the phrase 'all my children' in the will. Particular concern centred around those potential beneficiaries who had died between the writing of the will and Simon's death. The case of Wisden v Wisden rumbled on through the courts for year after year until in March 1857 the High Court in Chancery directed the sale of the property portfolio (less those elements where family members retained a right of abode) and effectively liquidated the estate. On Thursday 23rd April 1857 the properties were sold by auction. The opinion of the local press was that they had fetched good prices.

Funds could now be dispersed to Simon's children and then, in the case of John's deceased father William, onto his grandchildren. JW inherited a useful sum of money. What is known of the partners' characteristics and attributes would suggest that there were differing views as to how some of this money might be best deployed. These differences would push the pair towards a parting of the ways and the new funds would make this possible. JW was able to buy Fred Lillywhite out of their partnership. Fred then used the money that he received to set himself up in a separate business in Kennington near to the Oval cricket ground.

Thus John Wisden & Co. was founded in January 1859 and it continues today. It has done many things for many sports in many places. Today it is a specialist imprint of the publishing conglomerate Bloomsbury. Fred Lillywhite's company was comparatively short-lived and was subsumed into what is now Lillywhites, with its prestigious London store in Haymarket close to Piccadilly.

It seems that it took some time for the new arrangements to settle into place. *Bell's Life* on 2nd February had two directly adjacent advertisements for Fred Lillywhite, one giving 2 New Coventry Street as his address with

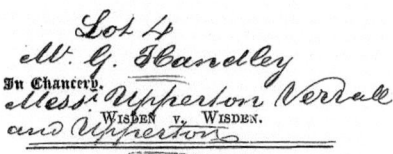

Lot 4
Mr. G. Handley

In Chancery.
Messrs Upperton Verrall
and Upperton
WISDEN v. WISDEN.

BRIGHTON.

Particulars and Conditions of Sale

OF

FREEHOLD
DWELLING-HOUSES

AND

SHOPS,

SITUATE IN

North Street, Upper Russell Street, & Grenville Place,

BRIGHTON,

To be Sold by Auction,

BY

Mr. CHRISTOPHER WREN,

AT HIS

ESTATE SALE ROOMS,

2, DUKE STREET, BRIGHTON,

On THURSDAY, the 23rd Day of APRIL, 1857,

AT THREE O'CLOCK IN THE AFTERNOON.

MEAD and DAUBENY,

2, *King's Bench Walk, Temple, London,*

Agents for JOHN DUNFORD,

71, *Ship Street, Brighton,*

Plaintiff's Solicitor.

C. STOCKS, Law Printer and Stationer, 6, Inner Temple Lane.

Sale of the Estate of Simon Wisden

Although Simon Wisden had died in 1842, his estate was still not settled by the start of 1857 when The High Court, in Chancery ordered the liquidation of the assets, particularly the properties.

To the left is the front cover of the published details of the sale of the properties. Below it is part of the accompanying map. Much of the area is now taken up by the Churchill Square development.

After the sale, The *Brighton Gazette* reported the prices achieved as:

Lot 1: 80 North Street – £1080
Lot 2: 81 & 82 North Street – £ 1210
Lot 3: 83 North Street – £610
Lot 4: 23 Upper Russell Street – £315
Lot 5: 24 Upper Russell Street – £285
Lot 6: No 1 in the Farm Yard – £140
Lot 7: No 2 in the Farm Yard – £150
Lot 8: No 47 Grenville Place – £300
Lot 9: No 48 Grenville Place – £290
Lot 10: No 49 Grenville Place – £680
Lot 11: No 19 Upper Russell Street – £365
Lot 12: No 20 Upper Russell Street – £200

The total realised by the sale was £5625 which was £1000 more than had been anticipated.

William Holdsworth of 2 Gloucester Place was the principal purchaser. Holdsworth was listed in the 1851 census as a 58-year-old proprietor of houses.

Under the terms of Simon Wisden's will Nos 81, 82 & 83 North Street (lots 2 & 3) were bequeathed to JW's father William. Under the terms of William Wisden's will the proceeds would go on to be shared between JW and his seven surviving siblings.

the other giving 15 Kennington Oval. By April locations had been sorted out and at that time JW placed his first advertisement of the season, discreetly adding 'late F Lillywhite and Wisden' after the name of his company. Fred was, at times aggressively, to assert his separation from Wisden for some years to come.

JW now placed a weekly advertisement, without change, until the end of June; it no longer mentioned tobacco. For the first week in July reference to the catapulta was added and that continued until mid-September when all advertising by John Wisden & Co. stopped for the year. In many ways this was consistent with a business ticking over while the owner was often away attending to other matters.

Before he became involved in the 1859 first-class cricket season JW played in two benefit matches. In mid-May he took a UEE team to play a team of 16 drawn from the Broughton Club, Manchester. The match was staged to raise funds for the widow of the long serving professional Thomas Hunt. Hunt was a well-regarded and ubiquitous professional based in the north playing for a wide range of clubs and teams. He had been the north's champion single-wicket player whose challenge JW had declined back at the beginning of the decade. Hunt had played for both AEE and UEE and had been involved in this tranche of cricket since its inception. He died in 1858 as the result of an accident near to Rochdale railway station shortly after he had finished playing in a landmark match when Twenty-two of Rochdale (including Hunt) played a combined AEE & UEE side (perhaps a sign of improving relationships between the two elevens). Thomas Hunt was just 39 years old when he was killed leaving behind a wife and a young family. This initiative to stage a benefit match was very much in the spirit of CFFS.[63]

There was a good turn-out of professionals from across the country – from North Yorkshire's Roger Iddison to Kent's Edgar Willsher.

Coming back to London UEE went to the Oval to play a team from The United Master Butchers' Club to raise funds for the latter's charitable institution. UEE lost the Manchester match but won the match at the Oval. JW's performances in both matches were undistinguished but good work was done for the beneficiaries.

Later in the 1859 season JW played in two more matches outside the usual list. A team called Middlesex played two matches against Kent. At

---

[63] CFFS was very much in its fledgling state at this time. No evidence has been found of the fund making a payment to Mrs Hunt.

this time there was no Middlesex CCC, and an *ad hoc* team was pulled together. It comprised five members of the Walker family augmented by JW and John Lillywhite on the basis that they currently lived in the county and the Sussex player George Wells because he had been born in Whitechapel. The first match was staged on the Walkers' Ground at Southgate and the second at Canterbury. Middlesex won the first by 78 runs and the second by an innings. In the first match JW contributed innings of 42 and 9 and took seven wickets. At Canterbury he got a duck and did not bowl but did show that he could still hold his catches.

The regular county matches began at the end of May and Sussex came to Lord's to play MCC. JW's 8/24 in the hosts' first innings was one of his best bowling performances of the year and he was undefeated on 8 as he marshalled the Sussex tail to gain a one wicket win. A fortnight later he was at Hove to be part of a combined Sussex & Kent team which lost to the increasingly powerful Surrey. In a season when his improving batting would offset declining bowling performances his scores of 25 and 13 were useful contributions.

Between these two matches was the Whit Monday at Lord's fixture between AEE and UEE. JW had a dual interest in this match, looking for both a win and a good gate – he achieved both. Although he did not bowl in a low-scoring match on a heavy ground his first innings of 26 was the top score in the match. UEE went on to win by 37 runs and CFFS netted £100.

A fortnight later JW was back at Lord's to be part of an England team that beat Cambridge University by a single wicket. JW's contribution might most kindly be described at supportive. No doubt as he stood at short slip waiting for the next catch to come his way he was able to dispense helpful tactical advice.

There then began a run of three matches over ten days which would go a long way towards meeting the popular demand for more matches involving the best players available. They would also display some of the emerging trends within the first-class game. Starting on Monday 27th June the South played the North at Lord's with the teams made up of 18 professionals and just four amateurs. However, it was the amateurs whose performances dominated the match. South batted first and totalled 215 with the critical innings coming from Arthur Haygarth (45) and Frederick Miller (43). When the North replied Carpenter, Hayward and Parr were dismissed for a collective dozen runs and they were indebted to A B Rowley (38*) for a major part of their paltry 107. North were required to follow-on and the fourth amateur, VE Walker, took 4/59 to go with his 3/30 in the first innings. South were left to score 8 for a ten wickets win, sending in Nos 10 and 11 to complete that task. JW had opened the batting in the first innings scoring 13 but did not bowl in the match. Skilful amateur players supplementing a strong professional core was a model for first-class teams that UEE had sought to develop and which was to survive for another hundred years.

These performances by the amateurs made the result of the Gentlemen v Players match at the Oval in the second half of the week all the more surprising. The Players batted first and scored 278 with JW batting at No 9 contributing 24. The four amateurs from the North v South match were in the Gentlemen's side but the team were shot out for 162 and 91 to lose by an innings and 25 runs in two days. Perhaps the stronger teams were created when the amateurs joined in with the professionals.

At the start of the following week, 4th July 1859, many of the same professional players re-assembled at Lord's albeit in a slightly different configuration. This was the second AEE v UEE match. The AEE team included six players who had played for the North and two for the South in the previous week. The UEE included five from the South and three from the North. Amateurs were excluded from these fixtures. In time this separation was to become more marked and create difficulties. An opening stand of 149 by Bob Carpenter (97) and Tom Hearne (62) was the basis of UEE's first innings total of 262 and set up a convincing win by nine wickets which helped assuage JW's disappointment in getting just two wickets in the match and scoring 0.

Earlier in the season, neatly slotted into appropriate gaps in the county programme, UEE played a series of their standard matches. They beat Peckham by an innings and 19 runs and then took a weak team to the Fairfield Ground, Croydon. JW took 12/63 in the first innings and having batted at No 6 in UEE's first innings held himself back in the second. When he walked out as No 11 UEE still needed 13 runs to win. JW scored 3* as he supported John Lillywhite in reaching the target in an exciting finish.

The first week of July saw a bizarre piece of fixture scheduling. The week began with the AEE v UEE match at Lord's which continued until Wednesday. Fortunately AEE's final wicket added only seven runs on the final morning and it took UEE just 20 overs to complete a nine wickets win. This allowed them to make an early start on a long journey to Scotland. By

Thursday morning UEE needed to be in Edinburgh to play Twenty-two of the Grange Club. After matching the Scots across the first three innings UEE were bowled out for just 37 in the final innings to slump to an 80 runs defeat. Both JW and Grundy were recorded as absent ill in the second innings. Perhaps an unusual form of travel sickness – or simply fatigue?

By Monday morning, 11th July, JW was back in London at Lord's as part of the England team that beat Oxford University by an innings. Then on the following Monday he was part of the Players team that crushed the Gentlemen by 169 runs. His contributions in these matches were minimal; no longer did he bowl unchanged through both innings.

After the Gentlemen v Players match many of the cricketers gathered up their kit from the Lord's dressing rooms and crossed the Thames to the Oval where an England team crushed the currently dominant county, Surrey. VE Walker had been a protégé of JW at Harrow and in this match the 22 year-old announced himself as a cricketer of quite exceptional ability. When England batted first he came in at No 9 and ran out of partners to finish on 20*, England totalling 172. He then opened the bowling in the Surrey innings with Nottinghamshire's fearsome bowler John Jackson. He bowled throughout the innings to take all ten wickets for 74 runs to shoot Surrey out for 131. At this time the Oval was emerging as a good ground for batsmen and the England team made the most of it and ran up the vast total of 390. In this innings VE was given the opportunity to show his skill as a batsman and contributed 108. He had clearly demoralised the Surrey team and faced with a target of over 400, they collapsed to 39 all out – Walker 4/17. JW scored 32 in the run feast. He did not bowl in the match but took a further three catches.

JW's last two matches of the year for Sussex were both against Kent, both won by Sussex by convincing margins. The first match starting on 28th July was at Tunbridge Wells and was a very low-scoring affair with neither side totalling 200 across their two innings. JW had one of his better bowling performances for the season at this level, taking 4/37 and 5/34. He was again at the wicket (5*) with John Lillywhite when Sussex won by six wickets. The following Monday the teams re-assembled on the more batsmen-friendly ground at Hove. After Kent had achieved an 8 runs lead on first innings Sussex set them 193 to win; JW scored 8 and 26 in the two Sussex innings. JW bowled just two overs in Kent's first innings but now he and young Harry Stubberfield needed just 16 overs each as they dismissed Kent for 23; JW took 3/13 while Stubberfield took 7/10. Master and apprentice?

As an indication of the sound basis from which UEE now operated while JW, James Dean and John Lillywhite were all playing for Sussex, the Eleven travelled to Yorkshire to play Twenty-two of Hull. The scores were very low (25 and 101 v 83 and 43) but the match was exciting as it ended in a tie.

Much of the remainder of JW's season was given over to UEE matches but there were still two more first-class matches to go. At this time it often took two counties to compete against the might of Surrey, so Kent combined forces with Sussex for a trip to the Oval for a match beginning on 8th August. Surrey batted first and JW (2/76) and Stubberfield (7/85) put in long stints but Surrey's lower order plundered a tiring attack, missing the support of Kent's Edgar Willsher to total 234. In reply the combined counties could manage only 88 and 143 to lose by an innings. The other match was a South v North encounter at Canterbury. JW made only a very moderate contribution with bat and ball but he did take three more catches. South very much missed the unavailable VE Walker and lost by 90 runs.

The first of the August tranche of UEE matches was against John Walker's team at Southgate on his own ground. The match was made at 11 v 16 but with the hosts built around VE Walker and his brothers they could have comfortably played at 11 v 11. Successive innings totals of 236, 320, 139 and 56/3 suggest a private ground in excellent condition. Southgate beat a very strong UEE side by 12 wickets.

After the game at Southgate UEE had four matches of a more usual style. They beat Loughborough by 62 runs, lost to Gentlemen of East Sussex by 20 runs and beat Walsall by 50 runs. They completed this part of the season with another trip to the west country where they drew with a combined Devon & Cornwall side at Plymouth. JW's 38* in this last match was his only significant contribution in this phase.

Unusually JW's English season of 1859 finished early at the end of August with the successful visit to Plymouth. There must have been excitement and apprehension in equal measure as he returned to London from the west country because he was about to undertake the biggest adventure of his life – a cricket tour to North America. Firstly he had a few days to check on the shop, tidy his affairs and bid farewell to friends and staff before making his way to Liverpool.

In a welcome sign of the easing of tensions between the two major touring elevens those players not going to America pooled their resources to put out teams to complete both groups' remaining fixtures.

14

NORTH AMERICA

Setting out on a tour of North America at the end of a cricket season was always going to invite meteorological challenges. And so it turned out. On the evening of 6th September 1859 JW joined five colleagues from the UEE team and six players from the AEE team at the *George Hotel*, Liverpool. He was the leader of the UEE group and his long-standing partner in the Leamington enterprise, George Parr, was the leader of the AEE group and captain of the touring team as a whole. Also with them was Fred Lillywhite, complete with his printing tent, who would record the expedition. This was the first ever overseas cricket tour and would have a pioneering element to it.

The party comprised: George Parr (capt.) Julius Caesar, William Caffyn, Robert Carpenter, Alfred Diver, James Grundy, Tom Hayward, John Jackson, John Lillywhite, Tom Lockyer, Heathfield H Stephenson, John Wisden and Fred Lillywhite.

The following morning the party went aboard their ship the *Nova Scotian* and before the ship sailed in mid-afternoon the party, dressed in their playing kit, had a team photograph taken. This is one of the few photographs ever taken of JW. It was taken by Thomas Hennah of Brighton and subsequently published by WH Mason. Fred Lillywhite was not included in the photograph.

The idea of an English team visiting Canada and the United States had been discussed for several years. Canada v United States is the world's oldest international cricket competition, pre-dating England v Australia by more than 20 years, and after the 1856 match the two sides had discussed the possibility of a joint invitation to tour to a group of English players. They opened correspondence with the Fred Lillywhite – John Wisden partnership in London. Although the English players were receptive to the idea arrangements could not be made. In the summer of 1856 William Clarke was still alive and the leading professionals in England were still divided into two distinct camps, making the formation of a single representative team difficult. The idea was raised again in 1858, by which time Clarke had died and the creation of and support

George Parr's side to North America, on board ship at Liverpool
Back row (left to right): R Carpenter, W Caffyn, T Lockyer,
H Stephenson (crouching), G Parr, J Grundy, J Caesar, T Hayward;
seated: J Wisden, J Jackson; in front: A Diver, J Lillywhite

for the Cricketers' Fund Friendly Society had brought the AEE and UEE closer together.

Although the team were to play matches in both Canada and USA the arrangements for the tour were made with Montreal Cricket Club of Lower Canada. Leading the negotiations from Canada was William Pickering, an Englishman living in and playing cricket for Canada. Pickering had been at school at Eton, playing in the 1834, '35, '37 and '38 matches against Harrow. He was captain in his final year before going on to Cambridge University where he played in the annual match against Oxford University. Throughout the 1840s he played gentleman's cricket at the highest level for MCC, Gentlemen (v Players), Gentlemen of Surrey and I Zingari, amongst others. In 1848 he met JW at the I Zingari v Auberies match. Pickering emigrated to Canada and spent the 1850s based in Montreal and playing cricket for both club and country. After he returned to England some years later he became a trustee of the Cricketers' Fund Friendly Society.

The Englishmen had a difficult journey across the Atlantic Ocean encountering rough seas, icebergs and at one stage getting lost, all leading to a much delayed arrival at Quebec. Fred Lillywhite wrote up an account of the tour in what was to become the first ever tour book.[64] The early pages are full of tales of the rough crossing and the steadily diminishing group of players who regularly sat down for meals. During this time JW proved to be a good sailor.

At 1.00am on Thursday 22nd September the players were woken by the noise of their ship docking. They then disembarked at 5.30am and were warmly welcomed by the Canadian authorities who eased their passage through customs. Waiting for them on the quayside were William Pickering and Mr Godfrey Baker (Ottawa CC), ready to escort them on the next stage of their journey – being taken by train the 179 miles to Montreal.

The players' base in Montreal was to be the *St Lawrence Hotel*, the largest and most prestigious in Canada. They found the hotel full of potential spectators who had been waiting since the previous weekend for the Englishmen to arrive and for the first match to begin. The following day was wet so it was still not possible to start the match. This was welcomed by the tourists as it gave them an additional day to shake off the fortnight at sea. Instead of playing cricket they spent the day in an activity in which cricket tourists would engage for the next 100 years and more – sightseeing. They were taken to see the newly completed Victoria Bridge which was a significant piece of civil engineering of an innovative design. As it spanned the St Lawrence River at a critical point it was to have great commercial benefit for the developing country.

On Saturday morning the players made their way down to the Montreal ground to be welcomed by a crowd in excess of 3,000 spectators who were intrigued to watch the players' match preparation routines. Elaborate arrangements had been made for the spectators with particular spaces for carriages and a separate stand for the ladies. The players also had their own accommodation.

George Parr won the toss and asked Twenty-two of Lower Canada to bat first, a decision which would give the tourists some more time to shake off the effects of the long journey. All the players had considerable experience arriving at venues after difficult overnight travel in England. From these experiences they had come to the conclusion that it was

[64] *The English Cricketers' Trip to Canada and The United States*

better to shake off the effects of travel while fielding than while batting. The match got off to a sluggish start not helped by the deadening of the pitch by the previous day's rain. The only significant stand of the innings was between Pickering and Daley, the former displaying the skills that he had developed in England and the latter a skilful young player whose score of 19 was more than double anything achieved by a teammate. The surprise of the innings from amongst the Englishmen was the successful bowling of George Parr whose slow bowling was very suited to the ground conditions. His bowling figures were 11-5-8-6 and JW's were 10-6-7-0. The bowling was described as 'sluggish' – the English players still needing some acclimatisation time.

The Canadian innings of 85 finished at 4.30pm so there was time for the English Eleven to start their innings with James Grundy and JW sent out as openers. Grundy was soon out, bowled, but JW and Tom Hayward safely saw out the rest of the day, bad light causing an early finish. The light had become unplayable when 'the sun went round behind the mountain' – not something that often happened in England.

There was, of course, no play on the following day, Sunday, and the tourists had another day of sightseeing, this time going around the mountain. The trip also gave them sight of the spectacular 'fall' of north-eastern America made by the trees and this being Canada the maple trees were very much in evidence. Another non-playing day gave the players yet more time to shake the voyage out of their legs.

When the match resumed on Monday JW (7) was soon dismissed but then Hayward (17), William Caffyn (18) and George Parr (24) set about building a useful first innings lead which was enhanced by a late flurry from Tom Lockyer (19*) and John Jackson (10). The innings closed at 117 giving the English Eleven a first innings lead of 32. When they went back out onto the field the tourists showed the benefit of the additional rest day and were much sharper in their bowling and fielding. George Parr's bowling was again most effective (20.1-9-19-10) as the hosts were dismissed for 63. JW bowled just six overs for six runs and no wickets. The tourists lost Hayward and Lockyer before William Caffyn and Alfred Diver knocked off the required runs.

Another advantage of the rest day on Sunday was the time it gave for all the players to recover from the night before. On Saturday evening over 100 people sat down to dinner. The lavish fare can be judged from the menu. As well as the sumptuous food there was much drinking and toasting. In his book Fred Lillywhite recorded that 'Mr George Parr rose and replied briefly'. JW proposed toasts to both William Pickering and to young Daley.

After the end of the scheduled match a second was started. The six UEE players were joined by five Canadians to play the six AEE players and five further Canadians, the match being a fund raiser for the tour party. On a fine Tuesday morning JW won the toss on behalf of UEE and elected to bat. The core of the innings came from JW (43) and John Lillywhite (53) leading to a total of 188. AEE were then bowled out for 90 (JW 2/29) and 44 (JW 5/18). Robert Carpenter was 'Man of the Match' scoring 32 runs, taking 3 wickets and holding seven catches.

Having arrived safely, experienced the warmest of welcomes and shaken off their sea-legs, the tourists settled into a sequence of weekly visits to major cities. Each of the visits seems to have followed a fairly similar pattern, so it would be best to look at just one in a little detail.

At 6.00am on Saturday 1st October the party left Montreal and set out for New York taking with them Messrs Pickering and Baker who were acting as tour couriers seeking to ensure that arrangements went as smoothly as possible. The journey might be described as multi-conveyance; various parts being undertaken by (stage) coach, railway train and river steamer. This all entailed many changes with the frequent off-loading and re-loading of passengers and luggage. By all accounts the luggage was roughly handled and led Fred Lillywhite to complain about the treatment of his equipment.

All the players were long standing members of one or other of the elevens that toured England and so were used to the challenges of travelling between match venues with both their personal baggage and their playing equipment. They would also be used to Fred Lillywhite and his printing tent tagging along with them. The additional difficulties of travelling in North America exacerbated the issues relating to Fred and his equipment; they certainly got under George Parr's skin. However, William Caffyn simply described the equipment as a nuisance.[65] There is evidence of steadily rising tension between Parr and Fred Lillywhite which was to continue after the party were back in England and spilled over into ensuing seasons.

An overnight passage on the steamer *New World* took the party from Albany to New York arriving at 7.00am on Sunday morning and reaching their hotel, the *Astor House* by 10.00am. The hotel was packed with

[65] William Caffyn's autobiography *71 Not Out*

thousands of guests, many of whom were in town to see the match. In the afternoon, with fine weather and amid great excitement the players took the ferry across to Hoboken to look at the ground on which the match was to be played. When they reached the ground they were greeted by 2,000 people anxious to catch a glimpse of the famous cricketers and excited about the forthcoming match.

At around 10.00am on Monday morning the scene at the front of the *Astor House* was one that we of the 21st century would more readily associate with boy band pop idols. It was at this moment JW and his colleagues were told that all was ready for them to make their appearance on the steps of the hotel and there was an immense stir amongst the citizens who had gathered to see the players. Their appearance raised a great cheer and then the players made their way down to their waiting transport, a four-in-hand. Both horses and carriage had been decorated in the flags and colours of both the USA and England and they made their way down to the ferry to take them across to Hoboken where they were enthusiastically greeted by another large crowd. Estimates of the size of the crowd vary but it may well have been 10,000 strong.

The St George's Cricket Club had made great efforts in staging the match. In his account Fred Lillywhite commented: 'The preparations for the convenience of the public were on the grandest scale imaginable and evidently had involved an immense outlay'. Fred went on to comment that the ground was newly laid and not up to the normal English standard. What Fred did not mention is that the American side included his brother Harry, who was the professional at St George's Club.

George Parr won the toss and asked the Americans to bat first. Almost as soon as the innings started England dismissed the president of the host club, Robert Waller, run out for 0. They used just two bowlers of distinctly differing styles: George Parr with his slow breaking lobs and John Jackson the hostile round-arm quick bowler. In just 57 overs they dismissed the Americans for 38, the highest individual score being 6. Parr took 9/26, Jackson 10/10, there being two run outs. Before the end of the first day's play the English Eleven's opening pair of Hayward (33) and Carpenter (26) established a first innings lead. The tourists' innings got off to an unfortunate start when Crossley, the Americans' best bowler, was precipitously taken-off after being no-balled. The umpire was John Lillywhite who was unfit to play because of a hand injury that he had received in Montreal. JW made only 3 before succumbing to his propensity for being run out although the American press described him as being 'unlucky'. Batting on into the second day England totalled 156, the openers being the top scorers with skipper George Parr contributing just seven runs, three of which coming from one of his famous mighty hits to leg – this one clearing both the playing area and the spectators. When the Americans batted again England used a different pair to bowl throughout the innings. JW took 4/24 from 34 overs and William Caffyn took 16/24 from his 34 overs.[66] The Americans were bowled out for 54 thus losing by an innings and 64 runs.

In recent seasons in England there had been much criticism about the short hours of play during matches involving the touring elevens; the core of the complaints being that two days of play were being spun out to last three days for commercial reasons. In this match the first day did not start until just before noon and finished at 5.00pm. Although the weather was good for all three days of the match the light closed in early at that time of the year. The second day did start at 1.00pm but the third not until just after 2.00pm. Even though Wednesday simply involved mopping-up the last few American wickets it attracted the largest crowd of the three days.

On the following day a new match was started. Once again the twelve English professionals were divided into two groups of six – in this instance the two wicket-keepers, Lockyer and Stephenson, making the selection. Other divisions were North v South and All England v United England. Then each group was topped up with five players selected from the host's squad. These eleven-a-side matches produced a different style of match and also gave the local spectators a chance to see the best English batsmen taking on the best of the English bowlers. All the bowling was done by the Englishmen, the role of the hosts being largely reduced to fielding. Having the English batsmen facing the English bowlers created an unfortunate consequence, although it was a positive outcome in many ways for JW. The pitches on which these matches were played were not up to the standard usually found in England and the wicket at Hoboken had been newly laid. John Jackson was a handful on any wicket and in this match he and George Parr were on opposite sides and he struck his captain a painful blow on the elbow. As William Caffyn recorded: 'He,

---

[66] There are multiple sources for scoresheets from matches on this tour, including *Bell's Life, Scores & Biographies* and Fred Lillywhite's tour book *The English Cricketers' Trip to Canada and the United States*. All sources provide different data so for this account the figures are always taken from Lillywhite's book.

however, continued his innings, but after a while his elbow swelled to an enormous size. I dressed it for him and continued to do so for many days; but he was unable to again take part in a match, which was a great source of disappointment to every one'.[67] At this point JW had to increase his leadership role within the party and took over the captaincy of the side.

JW played in Lockyer's XI in the second New York match and seems to have played a much greater part. He opened the batting (12) before taking 3/47 in Stephenson's XI's first innings and then 8/45 in the second. This match finished at mid-afternoon on the Saturday, which gave the tourists time to return to their hotel for a meal before catching the evening train to their next venue. This was a well-rehearsed routine for English players.

Fred Lillywhite's presence meant that the tour was fully, indeed copiously, reported and it also meant that the first ever English cricket tour generated the first ever tour book. In a temptation, to which international cricketers are still falling 160 years later, Lillywhite used his book to settle some scores and get some grievances off his chest. JW and Parr did not get a kindly write-up in the book. There are social responsibilities imposed upon the captain of a touring cricket team, especially abroad, and George Parr found these demanding. Fred was ever ready to point out his shortcomings and reluctant to acknowledge the handicap caused by the serious injury to his elbow.

Carpenter, Grundy, Caesar, Wisden, Parr, Stephenson, Diver, Lockyer, Caffyn, Hayward

[67] William Caffyn's autobiography *71 Not Out*

Lillywhite also harboured a lingering resentment at the break-up of his business partnership with JW that continued until his death in 1866. The pages at the back of Lillywhite's tour book contain a vast selection of advertisements for cricket outfitters. All the major suppliers and outfitters seem to be there except for John Wisden & Co.

Although William Pickering had had to leave the party and return to Montreal the tourists were accompanied on their journey to Philadelphia by Messrs Godfrey Baker and William Ellis who were keen to ensure that the tour continued to progress as smoothly as possible. The tourists were also accompanied by some of the American players from the New York match who were to be part of the opposing Twenty-two of the United States in the next match.

The train journey to Philadelphia was one of 90 miles which took three hours and the party arrived at the *Girard House Hotel* at midnight. Wherever they went the players were enthusiastically received and their hosts took every trouble to make them comfortable.

At this point the good weather, which had so far followed the English party, faltered and when they arrived at the Carmac Woods ground for the match The English Eleven v Twenty-two of the USA, they found that heavy overnight rain had rendered the ground unfit. Despite his injured arm George Parr was there to lead the England team. When play eventually got underway at 3.30pm the hosts batted first and by stumps at 5.30pm England had reduced the US team to 41-9. The following day, Tuesday 11th October was the occasion of an election in the city so no cricket was scheduled. When play began again on Wednesday Parr was absent; his injury was causing increasing concern and he was advised to stay in bed. At each of the tour matches one of the English party was scheduled to stand down from playing and act as umpire. For this match it was Julius Caesar's turn but on the Wednesday morning he was back on the field acting as substitute fielder for Parr. Mr Ellis took over as umpire.

When the US innings got under way again JW was captain of the England XI as he was to be for the rest of the tour. The change of captain also brought about changes in the deployment of players. Up until now, except in the UEE v AEE match, JW had tended to bat at the top of the order but now, as captain, he went in at No 9. There were changes to the bowling as well. In the first US innings Wisden bowled just eight overs (out of 134) and James Grundy none at all. In the second US innings JW bowled unchanged from one end and Grundy 23 overs from the other. Part of this may have been the necessity to replace Parr's slow under-arm lobs which had caused the American players so many difficulties. JW was to bowl in his slow lobs style for the whole of the tour.

The US innings was fairly quickly and easily brought to conclusion for 94 runs. Then Hayward and Carpenter got the English reply off to a good start and the 10 men of England mustered 126 in reply. When the US batted again only one player reached double figures and they were dismissed for 60. JW's figures were 39.1-20-39-8 and England went on to win by seven wickets.

At the conclusion of this match a North v South match was arranged. Caesar stood down so that the England squad could be divided five and five with each side having six US players added. Grundy (seven wickets) bowled out the South for 59 and then Jackson (60) and Carpenter (34) dominated the batting as the North moved to 120-5. But by mid-afternoon the deteriorating weather killed off any lingering interest and the match was abandoned. This gave the players time to return to the *Girard House Hotel* and get ready for another lavish celebratory dinner. The Philadelphians seemed delighted with the week's cricket and the English players (and scorer) were most appreciative of the fulsome hospitality that they had received. Although nobody seems to have recorded it, it would seem expected that JW was more comfortable than Parr in making the after-dinner speech to thank the hosts.

The following day JW and his colleagues boarded a train for Buffalo, the first stage of the journey to Hamilton where the next match was to be played. By all accounts it was a tedious journey with a complete lack of food and drink so the breakfast taken at Buffalo at 8.30am on Sunday morning was most welcome. With no play scheduled a trip to the impressive Niagara Falls was arranged but the cricketers missed the train so the journey had to be made by stage coach; the 22 miles took five hours. However, on arrival they found the best-appointed hotel so far and William Pickering waiting for them. On the Monday morning the party returned to Canada to be greeted by another great throng of people and deteriorating weather; by Thursday it was so cold that the customary benefit match, to follow the main match, was abandoned. The main match against Upper Canada followed the usual pattern. The hosts batted first and scored 66 (JW 2/19) and 53 (JW 14/24), with England replying with 79 and 41-0.

The match against Upper Canada was the final one of the original schedule but while the English party were in America arrangements were made for a fifth match against a combined Canada & USA team. Ever since they had arrived in North America the England party had been under pressure to add fixtures to the programme and JW and George Parr negotiated with more than one group. The conversations would have been interesting – George Parr was very aware of his value as a player and a personality and JW was very commercially astute. Eventually they reached an agreement with the club at Rochester (USA). At least that town was on a route back to their ship home.

So on the Thursday evening (20th October) the players again boarded a train for another overnight journey, this one of 210 miles, arriving the following morning in Rochester. As in their days back home with the touring elevens they were expected to begin playing on the day of their arrival. The weather was getting worse and was not really fit for cricket; at one stage the fielders were wearing greatcoats. It was also raining so play did not start until 3.00pm but there was enough time for the hosts to be bowled out for 39 and for England to reach 35-2. There was then a two-day interval as snow prevented play on the Saturday. To fill in the time the players engaged in a game of baseball; Caffyn performing with distinction and the local press noted Lockyer being as effective as a catcher as he had demonstrated as a wicket-keeper during the tour. The cricket match was completed at the start of the following week. England scored 171 and bowled out their opponents for 62. JW and John Jackson bowled unchanged throughout both innings. JW took 16/17 and 13/43.[68] During one over in the second innings he took a wicket with every ball. As he had taken wickets with the last two deliveries in his previous over that amounted to six-in-six or a double hat-trick. Statistically this was a formidable achievement but it many ways it was a miserable match. There was time for one more game of baseball before the Englishmen started the journey home.

On the afternoon of Tuesday 25th October the party boarded the train for the first part of the journey back to Montreal which took them to Rome (Canada) where they were to find the hotel full. After a few hours sleeping on the lounge chairs and floor and with a hearty breakfast they set off for Kingston via Cape St Vincent. Here changing trains involved

[68] *The English Cricketers' Trip* records JW as bowling slowly so they were probably lobs.

carting (literally) their luggage overland to the next train. As a significant part of this luggage belonged to Fred Lillywhite he was, reluctantly, delegated to be part of the squad that supervised the carting. The train took them to Montreal where they had a one day stay in a familiar hotel before moving on to Quebec where they boarded ship for England.

They sailed home in the *North Briton* a sister ship to the *Nova Scotian* which had brought them out. The first part of the journey through what is now the St Lawrence Seaway provided the welcome relief of a settled base, regular meals and time to relax. However, the peace and quiet was to be short-lived. Soon after the ship moved into the open waters of the North Atlantic they encountered storms. These were worse than the ones that they had experienced on the outward journey. While uncomfortable for the passengers these were to have tragic consequences for one of the crew. A storm broke a mast and while the storm-lashed crew were attempting to repair it an anchor shifted and smashed the legs of 63-year-old John Evans. Despite the best attention from the on-board doctor Evans died as the ship was reaching British waters.

Led by the ever-restless Fred Lillywhite the players organised a charity concert and benevolent collection to support the injured sailor, with the cash raised going to his widow to support his family. This ready support for colleagues and contacts facing difficult times was an attitude that had led these players to setting up the Cricketers' Fund Friendly Society and which JW would harness in the years to come. As the annual cricket programme expanded players would increasingly lose contact with their professions/trades which meant that sudden, career terminating injury had ever more dramatic consequences.

On reaching dry and stable land many of the cricketers expressed the view 'Never again!'. However, some of them seem to have quickly forgotten the discomforts and within two years they were away on an overseas trip again, this time to Australia. Caffyn reported that he earned £90 from the North America tour. He was to make two further tours, both of them to Australia, where he then remained for a while as a coach. JW declined an invitation to tour Australia in 1861-62.

Although they had been well rewarded in financial terms and received lavish hospitality the 12 English cricketers and Fred Lillywhite had certainly suffered significant discomfort. The weather had been bitter for the last two matches and both sea crossings were difficult. What did the tour achieve? Cricket was not to become a national game in either

Canada or the USA. This is despite mass emigration from the British Isles. Hobsbawm[69] records that between 1851 and 1880 3.5 million people emigrated to USA, 0.5 million to Canada and 1 million to Australia. It was the latter who were to challenge England's cricketing supremacy.

In the longer term the greatest impact of the tour seems to have been felt in England. Subsequent events would suggest that relations between the AEE and UEE had not been improved by the tour; there had been no lasting unity in adversity. In December an elaborate celebratory dinner to honour the seven tourists from Surrey and Sussex (JW was invited but unable to attend through illness) was staged at the *King's Arms* in Godalming. The dinner was chaired by Henry Marshall, the president of Surrey County Cricket Club. These were predominantly UEE men so they were separated from the mainly AEE players from northern counties. The next decade of cricket was to be littered with squabbles and feuds. JW was to spend much of his time trying to keep the peace and maintain a semblance of unity within the ranks of the expanding band of professional cricketers.

The tour was the final cricket act of the 1850s. The decade had begun with the burgeoning of the touring elevens and had seen a great expansion of cricket across the country, much of it inspired by these elevens. The cricket season had become more structured and had developed into three phases:

> **April:** The focus of attention was on schools, colleges/ universities and some military establishments. Many professionals spent the month coaching at these establishments, especially the educational ones.
>
> **May – July:** The central part of the season which began with the MCC annual meeting. Most of the matches at Lord's were played during this period as well as many of the inter-county matches. The touring elevens made fixtures to generally fit into the gaps in the rest of the programme.
>
> **August – September:** Much 'up-country' cricket. Some inter-county matches and some MCC 'away' matches. The travelling elevens played almost continuously (except Sundays, of course) through these months whenever their players were not needed for, essentially, first-class matches.

A pattern of fixtures had evolved and the conflicts in the demands on the best professionals were held in check although by no means eliminated.

[69] Eric Hobsbawm *The Age of Capital: 1848-75*

Some of the professionals had clearly developed a taste for overseas touring. HH Stephenson led a team to Australia in 1861-62 and then George Parr took a team there in 1863-64. A consequence of these tours was that many leading professionals were not back in England for the early part of the following season with the effect, amongst others, that the established touring elevens were not able to operate in normal mode. This created a gap in the market which new enterprises were eager to fill.

Several new travelling elevens were created during the 1860s, many with either 'North' or 'South' as part of their title. In one way it made sense to restrict the geographical range over which any eleven toured. However, much of it went deeper than that. The developing feud between Nottingham(shire), led by the 'queer tempered' George Parr and Surrey CCC rumbled on. An element of the differences may have been cultural and had a resonance with the parting that created UEE as an alternative to AEE. This was the time when Elizabeth Gaskell became a significant female social novelist. One of her best-known novels is *North and South* which relates the struggles of people coming from a southern environment acclimatising to work in the north. Northern cricketers may have been happy to accept William Clarke in 'mill-owner-mode' and tolerated his autocratic demeanour as long as he paid sufficient wages. JW and his colleagues from southern counties had come from an environment where the boss/owner/master, perhaps the farmer, laboured in the fields alongside his workers creating more empathy with and understanding of those he employed. From a family owning and running a business that worked in small groups JW knew that there was a better way to manage men than Clarke's autocratic approach which Parr was to replicate in many ways.

Undoubtedly the tour to North America proved to be a watershed in the development of cricket, particularly at a professional level. It crystalized several of the trends and attitudes that had been developing over recent years. The first half of the 1860s was a period of turmoil for cricket during which JW sought to play his part in managing the impact of events. By the end of the decade first-class cricket looked very different with county teams, numerically dominated by professional players, making up a significant part of the annual programme. Later in the decade a Champion County would be nominated annually by various publications.

15

RACQUETS AND SHOTGUNS

JW did not play cricket during the 1860 season. The reason given in the national press was an injury to his right wrist. Newspaper descriptions of the injury varied but in modern terminology it might be described as significant soft tissue damage to his wrist which had occurred as a result of a bad fall during a rackets match. (Given the impact on his cricket, it is assumed that it was his right wrist that was injured). When in mid-season it was becoming noticeable that Sussex were badly missing JW's bowling the *Brighton Gazette*[70] expressed the hope that he might be able to play again shortly. Sadly that did not happen.

If you were going to sit-out a cricket season 1860 was a good one to choose. The scorecards and match reports during the year were littered with accounts of sodden pitches, matches were left unfinished because of the weather and whole days and more lost to rain.

It is difficult to determine exactly when and where JW took up the sport of rackets. At this time it was one of several racquet[71] and ball games being played on courts both indoors and out. There had been a real tennis court near his home in Brighton and a racket court at the Brighton cricket ground. When he came to Leamington the social base for Lord Guernsey, his patron, and his friends was the Leamington Tennis Court Club (a real tennis venue). However, there is no evidence to suggest that JW played at either of these places.

In the 1850s Harrow School was a major centre for the game of rackets with several courts available to the boys. In an article on 8th May 1853 *Bell's Life* reported on the outcome of a rackets tournament at the school. Of those who reached the final stages of the competition Lord Garlies, Digby, Hon R Stewart and Crawley played cricket for the school in the prestigious match at Lord's that summer. Clutterbuck and Lord Royston played in following years. One of the Walker brothers (no initials given) was listed in the rackets results; all the brothers went on to play cricket for the school.

---

[70] *Brighton Gazette*, Thursday 28th June 1860

[71] The convention within the sport is that the word 'rackets' is used for the game and 'racquet' for the hand-held implement.

It is clear from all the reports and comments about matches in the national press that JW was greatly involved with the boys in the development of their cricket and he was always a welcome guest and/ or companion in the higher social circles. It seems entirely reasonable, even probable, that his relationship with the school's cricketers provided his introduction to the game. While playing cricket JW had gained a reputation as an athletic and agile sportsman. His close catching skills were testimony to his good hand and eye co-ordination and these skills were useful when playing rackets.

Rackets and similar games such as fives seem to have been sports which attracted cricketers. In the 1850s Lord's had courts for both real tennis and rackets. Elsewhere, William Clarke had lost an eye as the result of an accident while playing fives on the court at the back of his *Bell Inn* in central Nottingham. Further evidence of able cricketers being involved in the game can be seen in this piece from *Bell's Life* on 18th April 1858:

Rackets

LORD'S CLOSE COURT.[72] – During the week we have witnessed many interesting matches in this court. The players, although amateurs at this game, evidently showed that they have paid much attention to "points" which the renowned Frank Erwood has taught most of them. The matches were played by Wisden, Lillywhite, Royston, V.E. and A.H. Walker, all well-known cricket players, who were sometimes assisted by Erwood. Several matches, we understand, will take place this week, one, Wisden v F. and J. Lillywhite, the former having been backed for a stake against the two.

Given the date (1858) it is to be assumed that it was not James but John Lillywhite who partnered brother Fred. As well as all the listed players being cricketers, with the exception of Fred Lillywhite, they all had a well-established connection with Harrow School. No results of these matches are known but if JW managed to beat the two Lillywhite brothers it probably did little to bolster his faltering relationship with his then business partner Fred. After the Rackets Court at the Oval was revived in 1862 Fred Lillywhite took on its management.

[72] This court was on a site that later became The Tavern and its associated stand and is now occupied by the Mound Stand.

Rackets is a game similar to modern day squash and experienced a popularity boom in the mid-19th century. However, at this time it was largely restricted to Great Britain, Canada and the United States. In his writings on the 1859 cricket tour of North America Fred Lillywhite recorded the following about the players' time in New York:

> During our sojourn we were invited to the Racket Court, on Thirteenth Street, and saw several good games played, and it is quite likely that, ere long, our champion player will be showing his prowess in that establishment.

Given the anonymity of the 'champion' and Fred's slightly sniping tone in this note we may assume that the champion player was JW.

Racquets was a game often played in prison yards, especially those holding debtors, for whom it was a useful way of passing the time while family and friends cleared the debts. Later the walls of the yard would be replaced by purpose-built courts.

One of the Lillywhite & Wisden partnership's first offerings apart from cricket was for rackets equipment. In *Bell's Life* on 19th October 1856 their advertisement led with 'RACKET BATS and BALLS (of the first make only and selected by George Erwood)'. This was the same emphasis on quality that had been attached to the selling of Gilbert's footballs.

George Erwood was the brother of Frank and his place as a national champion was later taken by Henry John ('Harry') Gray, who then went on to become world champion. Harry Gray was also an able cricketer. He was one of five brothers, all able sportsmen, one of whom played first-class cricket for Middlesex. Harry Gray made and sold rackets and cricket equipment while playing in Cambridge and went on to found the company that, after more than 170 years of operation, bears his name today. Sets of brothers have served the company well and today Jason, Neil, Nick, Paul and Richard Gray lead a company that is probably best described as a sports' goods conglomerate. A brochure produced in 2015 to celebrate 160 years proudly notes:

> A notable acquisition was John Wisden, including its famous Cricketers Almanac which was under Grays' ownership from 1970-1999.

This period of ownership included the centenary of JW's death in 1984. Bill Gray, then the head of the company, joined with David Frith of *Wisden Cricket Monthly* to erect a fine, black marble cover stone and headstone to top JW's then unmarked grave. Grays' generosity in funding this work has shown its value as 35 years later the headstone stands proudly black and shining against the background of sepia-like buff, grey and brown of the surrounding graveyard and monuments in Brompton Cemetery.

Today one of Grays' most visible products is the Gilbert branded footballs used for international rugby union matches, the successors to the balls that JW was keen to promote in his earliest trading days. When JW first started selling Gilbert balls they were being made in Rugby where John Lillywhite was the school's cricket professional/coach. When retailers began to add illustrations to their weekly advertisements in newspapers such as *Bell's Life* and *Sporting Gazette* John Lillywhite chose a football bearing a marked resemblance to that held by William Webb Ellis on his statue outside Rugby School. In the 1850s there was an expanding network of professional sportsmen and sports good retailers, who a decade later provided crucial assistance to the game of football following the founding of the Football Association in October 1863.

JW's excellent hand-eye co-ordination gave him success in another sporting pastime. During close seasons he often travelled to Duncton to take part in shooting competitions. These were either singles events or pairs with James Dean who was a good shot and may have been the one to introduce JW to the sport. Many of the competitions took place in this part of West Sussex.

James Dean was JW's team mate, colleague and best friend from the time they first played cricket together in the 1840s. James Dean was very much a countryman but was a successful coach at Westminster College where this photograph was taken in 1862.

It seems that JW took a fancy to the countryman's life. In August 1877 an article in *Baily's Monthly Magazine* provided extracts from a book *The Biography of a Huntsman* explaining that the author had 'served at Petworth'. A quoted extract from the book said:

> I have seen Wisden, old Jemmy Dean, and George Wells the cricketers and also Challen and Sopp, all taking a breather after the hounds.

In fact James Challen and Edmund Sopp were also Sussex county cricketers.[73] Dean (Duncton), Wells (Wisborough Green), Challen

---

[73] Sopp and Challen are surnames with an abundant local presence. Cricket evidence would suggest that Edmund and James are the correct members of the families.

(Kirdford) and Sopp (Petworth) all lived locally and had strong connections with the local farming community and industry. Petworth House was a strong and active cricketing centre having played a key role in the development of the game in the first half of the century with the park staging inter-county matches.

The expansion of the network of railways was a feature of the middle years of the 19th century. It served JW well. The London to Brighton Railway was completed in September 1841 at the same time that the railway station at Brighton was opened. This railway gave JW easy access to London and beyond when he started to play cricket away from his home area.

By the late 1850s the operating company had become the London, Brighton & South Coast Railway. In 1859 the company completed the extension of a branch line from Horsham to Pulborough and then along the Rother Valley firstly to Petworth and later on to Midhurst. From Midhurst the London and South West Railway took the route through to Petersfield where it met a London to Portsmouth route. As the new track passed along the Rother Valley it kept to the south of the river which meant that the station for Petworth was sited well to the south of the town and was effectively as close to Duncton as it was to Petworth. Duncton was now well connected with a trip from Leicester Square to the *Cricketers' Inn* involving a straight forward train journey with a very manageable walk at each end.

In its entry for Petworth *Bradshaw's Descriptive Railway Hand-book* for 1863 lists two hotels: *The Swan* and *Half Moon*. *The Swan* was the original name of *The Cricketers* but the *Swan* mentioned by Bradshaw was the hotel in the centre of Petworth. So when JW changed the name of his inn he not only created a connection with his sport but he also removed a possible confusion.

It would look as though JW had become part of the local community in Duncton beyond merely being the owner of the inn at Duncton. In 1861 he went with James Dean to Broadwater supporting the Petworth cricket team in their match against Worthing. He was staying at *The Cricketers* on the night twenty years later that James Dean died at the inn.

16

WINDING DOWN

1860 began with an attempt to draw a line under the debate about the arrangements for the North America Tour. On New Year's Day *Bell's Life* had published a letter from Rob Waller of New York concerning the arrangements for the tour. A week later a response from George Parr and John Wisden was published clearly stating that the arrangements for the tour had been made solely with Montreal CC. The given address was 2 New Coventry Street and other evidence suggests that JW wrote it with Parr's support. *Bell's Life* added a line underneath terminating the publication of comment.

At the 1860 annual meeting of MCC at the beginning of May the honorary secretary reported on a letter received from St George's Cricket Club, New York. It stated that the cricketers of USA had learned much from the Parr & Wisden tour and had improved their skills. A visit by HRH the Prince of Wales had also done much to create a favourable atmosphere and they now hoped to arrange another tour by twelve gentlemen cricketers. The suggestion was that a nine week (including travel time) tour should begin in mid-August, so there would be no playing cricket on snow covered grounds or wearing great coats on the field. The footnote that a similar letter had been sent to the other great club in England, Surrey CCC, may not have been well received.

The North America tour and the events that followed it served to highlight JW's role in this pioneering event. George Parr had begun the tour as the leader 'on the field', although JW had to assume that responsibility after Parr's injury. During the second half of the tour and on the party's return home JW's skills as administrator-organiser became increasingly visible. His skill in dealing with these matters enhanced his position as leader of the cohort of professional cricketers in England. In the following years, as his cricketing skills began to decline his leadership skills would come increasingly to prominence.

The balance between JW's playing time and his organiser's role was inadvertently adjusted by his rackets injury. Being unable to play for a whole season he had plenty of time for his organisational duties.

In June there was one further event associated with the tour – a sort of reunion match. Those who had toured North America played a team that in school terms would be described as 'the next eleven'. The match was played on Manchester's Old Trafford Ground and was plagued by the wet weather that dominated much of the season. With JW not available through injury there were no selection problems – the other eleven all played. The ground was wet and dead and the 101-7 that the Next Eleven scored in their winning innings was the highest total of the match. The winning factor was Cris Tinley whose slow lobs proved ideal for the conditions. Given the number of overs of slow lobs George Parr had bowled in North America it was strange that he did not bowl in this match.

Although not playing himself during 1860 JW still had responsibilities relating to UEE. He clearly travelled with the team and on occasions was recorded as one of the umpires for a match (sadly the names of umpires were not routinely recorded at this time). A match for which he did stand as umpire was the defeat by MCC at Lord's of a Sussex side clearly struggling in his absence. Sussex lost by an innings and 15 runs and they only totalled 112 across their two innings.

When JW umpired the UEE v Mr John Walker's Sixteen of Southgate his fellow umpire was James Dean who was now standing as umpire in a great number of matches. Another of JW's friends and colleagues from the Sussex team was John Lillywhite who was at this time mixing playing with umpiring; he played in the Southgate match. The match held an additional interest for JW as seven of the Southgate team were Walker brothers, many of whom were coached by him during his days at Harrow. JW maintained his contact with these people who were to prove supportive of his various efforts in later years – VE Walker being involved in the Cricketers' Fund Friendly Society.

In November 1860 the UEE held a meeting in London to give thought to the 1861 season. They agreed that if JW was fit he should be the sole secretary (and thus captain and leader) for the coming season and that the existing committee should continue in office. John Lillywhite, whose career both playing and commercial had so closely matched that of JW, was to continue as treasurer.

With reduced playing commitments JW was able to devote more time to his business. It is unclear exactly who was left to look after the shop while JW was away for two or three consecutive days at a cricket match. However, as 2 New Coventry Street was a home as well as a place of business there is some information available. The 1861 census, taken on the night of 7th/8th April, lists those living at 2 New Coventry Street as (the final column being place of birth):

John Wisden	34	Head	Cricketer	Sussex, Brighton
Eliza Wisden	25	Sister	Housekeeper	Sussex, Brighton
Joseph Williams	18	Bachelor	Porter	Middlesex, London
Jessie Wisden	19	Cousin		Bath

There is no indication as to the length of Jessie's stay at New Coventry Street or what her role may have been. Over the years several of the Wisden girls lived at one or other of JW's shops. Their presence there is indicative of the self-supporting ethos of the Wisden family. Jessie's father, Joseph, had been bailed out of bankruptcy by his father, Simon.

The picture of the shop on the front of the 1862 catalogue for John Wisden & Co (*see page 133*) suggests fairly small premises which would have created competing demands for the storage of stock and for living accommodation. When JW was issued with a general game certificate (gun licence) around this time the given address was 9 Sydney Alley, which was a street that ran parallel to and behind New Coventry Street. During the 1860s he was also charged poor and sewer rates for 7 Sydney Alley, so perhaps the '9' is a writing error. The trade directories of the time suggest that several of those businesses operating out of premises fronting onto New Coventry Street also held supplementary accommodation in one of the Sydney Alley properties. John Wisden & Co may also have had day-workers living in their own homes.

At this time the columns of classified advertisements in *Bell's Life* suggest a company in sound health. The last advertisement in 1859 had appeared just after JW set sail for North America and then no more appeared until 11th March 1860. This was the quiet period for the business, still dominated by equipment for cricket, although it did add 'also, rackets, foot balls, dumb bells, boxing gloves, quoits, foils. Bowls, lawn billiards, skittles, marquees, tents, nets and all articles for British sports'. There was no longer any mention of tobacco. When the weekly appearances of the advertisements began again for the 1861 season the wording was very little changed during the following weeks.

However, in early June details of a new stock item were added to the advertisements as 'Mr John Wisden, 2, New Coventry Street', is announced as the 'agent for WH Mason, Repository of Arts, Brighton'. Specifically being offered were copies of the photograph of the North

America tour party that had been taken on-board ship just before sailing. Copies were offered for one guinea or two guineas framed and glazed. Two guineas was a week's salary for such as, say, a skilled engineer, so sales were restricted to the more affluent members of society.

During the summer months of 1860 a column within the classified advertisements of *Bell's Life* was filled with a plethora of advertisements offering cricket equipment and services by a long list of suppliers. As autumn passed to winter the number of advertisements dwindled until only JW's and John Lillywhite's businesses were making regular appearances. In the case of both of these retailers the continuation of the advertisements reflected the broadening of the range of goods that they offered. For instance, JW was offering racquets and racket balls, while John Lillywhite promoted football and boxing. This was the early stage of a trend that was to continue and develop for several years.

When UEE began their 1861 match programme on 30th May JW was fit to play and opened the bowling at the start of the match against Sixteen Undergraduates of Oxford. This was JW's first match since North America and the match report said 'Wisden appeared himself again' which was, no doubt, good news to the cricket-following public, especially those who followed Sussex. However, his figures of 15-?-22-1, as the students piled up a massive first innings score of 314, suggest that after a season's lay-off he may have been easing himself in gently. UEE were then bowled out for 122 and 153. JW scored 21 in the second innings joining Grundy (72*) in a late partnership in an unsuccessful attempt to stave off defeat. The next day, Sunday, was used to travel to London where on the Monday morning UEE were to play their annual fixture versus AEE at Lord's for the benefit of the Cricketers' Fund Friendly Society. JW did not need to bowl in the first innings as William Buttress and William Caffyn shot out AEE for just 74. In their reply UEE managed only 61 with none of the batsmen getting into double figures. In the second innings more normal scores were achieved. JW came on as first change but again did not make the impact that he had done in previous years, with figures of 7-?-18-0 as AEE totalled 152. UEE rallied second time around but fell six short of their 166 runs target. JW was cheered by the £137-9-0 surplus from the match which CFFS immediately used to purchase £150 worth of new three per cent stock.

Clearly eager to make up for lost time, the following day JW played for the Household Brigade in a match at Eton College. He took eight wickets and held a couple of catches.

The following Monday, 10th June, JW was back at Lord's to be part of the Sussex side to play MCC. Although Sussex lost by 85 runs JW had a better match, batting at No 5 and scoring 19 in the second innings as well as taking six wickets in the match. For the second half of the week UEE had a fixture at Sleaford in which JW did not play. Then on the Sunday the UEE players spent the day making their way across the country to Cheltenham to play Twenty-two from the College. Although travel was easier these days it was still a sizeable undertaking for a Sunday.

College Playground

Cheltenham College cricketers had for a number of years been coached by James Lillywhite, JW's boyhood friend. Whether fond memories influenced the terms & conditions for the match it is not possible to tell but the terms offered by UEE turned out to be far too generous. The College won the match by an innings and 86 runs. As would be expected of a team led for so long by JW, UEE were courteous guests and well received and accommodated wherever they went. The final sentence of *Bell's Life's* match report recorded:

> On Monday night a large number of old collegians, together with the President, entertained the United Eleven in a very hospitable manner, for which they return their most grateful thanks.

James Lillywhite, who claimed eight wickets in the match, would also have been thankful. He had been at the College since March 1856 and had made a success of both his ground and supervisory duties and his coaching. He was now keen to expand his activities but the college authorities were apprehensive about the implications of opening the college gates to the general public and any disruptive behaviour that might result. UEE had been an astute choice of visiting team for the first match to which the public could gain admission. They were polite and courteous opponents and the public had watched their efforts in a civil and orderly manner. The experiment was a success and the College authorities were sufficiently reassured and continue to stage cricket of the highest order on their grounds to this day with the general public continuing to enjoy the Cheltenham festival.

This series of matches well illustrated JW's new playing performance level. At first-class level he was no longer the formidable strike force he once had been and in UEE matches he was no longer able to sweep away local teams in the way that he once did. He was, though, still able to make a useful contribution. As his contribution to the North America tour showed so well he remained a true leader both on and off the field. He had an inclusive approach to the management of his players. Off the field he offered true leadership through his administration of the team and its affairs and was ever agreeable to their hosts and opponents.

A week after the Cheltenham match JW was back at Hove to be part of the Sussex side to play Kent. The match was to show that JW's decline in form was having a significant impact on the Sussex side that had for so long relied upon him. His modest scores of 18 and 6 and his bowling figures of 10-?-13-2 and 26-?-21-2 showed that while he remained steady and economical he was no longer the strike bowler of the 1850s. His fielding, however, appeared to be as sharp as ever as he still usually held at least one or two catches per innings.

JW was not selected for either of the 1861 Gentlemen v Players matches played at the beginning of July. A few years earlier he was an automatic selection for all matches of this status and his exclusion is another marker of his declining effectiveness. The two matches were played in the same week. On Monday and Tuesday 1st & 2nd July the sides met at Lord's where the Players won by an innings and 60 runs. After a rest day on Wednesday the teams crossed the Thames and played a second match at the Oval. The result was almost identical, the margin of victory being just eight runs more. In the match at the Oval the professionals batted first and scored a massive 358 (equivalent to at least 700 in 21st century values), and so despite respectable totals of 154 and 136 the amateurs were well beaten. This was the second high-scoring match within a couple of weeks at the Oval. When Surrey played Cambridgeshire, relative newcomers to the county cricket circuit, they were beaten by two wickets despite scoring 228 and 259.[74] Cambridgeshire had been 10 for 2 in their first innings before Carpenter and Hayward, each scoring a century, put on an unprecedented 212 for the third wicket. Scorecards and match reports were beginning to attract comment about the ever-increasing size of totals and the lack of balance between bat and ball. This was all to come to a head in the coming year or two. As more bowler than batsman this shift in the balance between bat and ball would have had JW considering his future as a player.

In the early years of the 1860s there was a change in the structure and style of teams playing cricket at a first-class level. There were fewer matches involving teams based at country houses or estates or promoted by members of the gentry and more teams either representing or bearing the title of counties. Many of the sides were Gentlemen of ...... shire either playing against the Gentlemen of a neighbouring county or, in many cases, the Players of their own home county. From here it would be a simple step to bring together a side wholly representative of the county. Also, by this time Nottinghamshire were playing the longer established counties such as Sussex and Kent more regularly. Cambridgeshire had joined the circuit and teams bearing the name 'Yorkshire' were becoming more representative of the whole county.

It was beginning to seem as though the trip to North America would be the pinnacle of the importance of the AEE/UEE duopoly. New All England Elevens were popping up at regular intervals. In part this was encouraged by the advent of further overseas tours. After each of the 1861/62 and 1863/64 tours to Australia the core of the established home professional touring elevens arrived back after the start of the English season. This created a vacuum which other professionals were only too ready to fill. However, there appeared to be little co-ordination between these competing ventures as one bizarre match was to show. Early in September 1861 there was a match between New All England Eleven (F Caesar's) and New All England Eleven (T Sherman's). The prize for the winners of the match was to be sole use of the title New All England Eleven. Caesar's team won by 10 wickets, so it was assumed that Sherman's Eleven became extinct at the end of the match. Caesar's Eleven did not play any matches during the following season.

---

[74] At this time run totals need to be multiplied by at least 2 to make them comparable to 21st century totals.

The situation surrounding the strongest sides in the land can best be described as fluid. There was need for a strong co-ordinating lead from the centre but MCC's influence amongst the professional players was weakening and there was a new assertiveness coming from south of the Thames. While Surrey CCC were increasingly setting a trend, their leaders were not only creating discord amongst their own people but now had a long running dispute with George Parr, many of his Nottingham-shire team mates and other professional cricketers with northern bases.

As the schedules and arrangements for first-class cricket changed it was becoming increasingly necessary for CFFS to provide a strong common focus for all professional cricketers. As JW was now CFFS's principal officer his input became increasingly important.

In a wet season Old Trafford was always going to be a risky venue. So it proved to be in 1861 when it was chosen to stage the second AEE v UEE match of the season. Only ten minutes play was possible on the first day, 11th July, and only 2¾ innings were completed. Coming on as first change in each of the AEE innings JW had figures of 43-25-33-2 and 26-9-37-3 (only seven wickets fell in AEE's second innings). These were useful contributions. After this match most of the players travelled to Lord's for the North v South fixture but JW was not included as the pool of players was strengthened by the inclusion of a number of amateur players.

While the match went ahead at Lord's JW together with James Dean and Julius Caesar travelled to Hampshire to be part of a Westbourne team raised by Edmond Wilder to play Southampton. Wilder was a great patron of cricket and cricketers and gave great support to the professionals through his involvement with CFFS. JW took nine wickets in the match and the other two guest professionals took the rest of them as the match ended in a tie.

JW's next match was ten days later, 25th July, when he was a member of the Sussex team to travel to Tunbridge Wells to face Kent. His importance to Sussex was underlined by the fact that his much improved performance made Sussex much more competitive. Although he scored only 1 run across two innings his bowling figures were much more like old times: 39-20-40-4 and 29-9-40-5. Kent won the match but only by 34 runs.

In the first week of August JW was in the UEE side to play in their second match with AEE at the Oval. The match was for the benefit of Thomas Barker. JW made no contribution to UEE's first innings total of 171 and was not needed to bowl as AEE were dismissed for 106. In

UEE's second innings he scored just 14 out of a total of 260 but returned figures of 18-4-34-4 as AEE could make only 210 to lose by 115 runs.

In the 1840s when William Clarke created the first touring eleven the best cricket in the south of England tended to be county-based: Kent, Sussex, Surrey, etc. The early origins of, certainly, the Sussex and Kent teams had been in the country estates within essentially agrarian counties. However, in the north most of the best cricket came from teams with town or city origins. Nottingham played Leicester and Sheffield who also played Manchester. Clarke's AEE had tended to focus on teams and venues associated with towns more often in the north. When JW set up UEE it had been not so much in opposition to AEE but as an alternative. JW tended to allow odds that created participation rather than those that minimised the risk of defeat. UEE also played against a wider range of opponents, playing schools, colleges, universities, regiments, etc.

Both of the touring elevens had played their part in stimulating interest in cricket across the British Isles. UEE's fixtures for September 1862 included matches against teams titled Devon and Isle of Wight; the previous September they had played a side representing Hampshire as well as the Gentlemen of Hampshire. The Gentlemen teams provided opportunities for amateur players to play at a high level as the professionals came to increasingly dominate the full county sides. While the professionals hoped to attract paying spectators to county cricket and thus fund their fees, the amateurs wished simply to play for their own personal enjoyment. The wishes of the amateurs led to the creation of a series of nomadic clubs. I Zingari (The Gypsies) had been the first in 1845. JW had played in the first Lords & Commons team in 1850 and for Leamington in the early fixtures of Gentlemen of Worcestershire. UEE played Free Foresters in 1861. So, as well as a significant increase in the amount of truly representative inter-county cricket, there was a re-alignment of the layer of cricket immediately supporting it. All this would feed into the turbulent flux that was to dominate cricket in the middle years of the 1860s.

For the last two months of the 1861 season JW's cricket was almost all for UEE. There were two exceptions. On 19th August he was included in the Sussex team that entertained MCC at Hove and he had a good match, scoring 45 in the first innings and 66 in the second. He opened the bowling in each of the MCC innings returning figures of 45-8-103-7 and 4-1-8-1 in the second leading Sussex to a 197 runs win.

Scores & Biographies noted that 839 runs were scored in the match. In the following days the Gentlemen of Sussex v Cambridge Quidnuncs match on the same ground resulted in 867 runs scored in the match with all four innings totalling more than 200 runs.

In contrast to conditions at Hove, when JW went to Aston Park, near Birmingham for a North v South match *Scores & Biographies* described the new ground as 'terribly rough, quite unfit for cricket'. He achieved little with the bat but returned bowling figures of 15-?-11-1 and 22-?-37-5. He bowled throughout the North's second innings and led the South to a 43 runs win in a match that yielded fewer than 400 runs. The likes of Daft, Parr, Hayward and Carpenter were unable to achieve much in the poor conditions. JW's nagging accuracy exacerbated the difficult conditions for some of the best batsmen in the country. In its interim report on the first two innings of the match *Bell's Life* noted that the information had been submitted by electric telegraph.

After Barker's Benefit match UEE went to Southgate for a match with Walker's XVI, the hosts winning by fifteen wickets. JW achieved little but was pleased to see the lads from his Harrow days doing so well; six of the Walker brothers played. A week later, on 15th August, UEE travelled to Portsmouth to play Twenty-two of East Hants Club, who were boosted by the inclusion of James Lillywhite junior and Harry Stubberfield from Sussex. JW's main contribution to the match was first innings bowling of 38-?-83-4.

Having travelled to Lancashire on 26th August UEE began a fairly concentrated sequence of matches. The first was on the Western Ground at Eccles where the opponents were Sixteen Free Foresters, a fixture which indicated the social acceptability of JW and UEE. JW made useful contributions with 36 runs and seven wickets across the match but it was not enough to prevent a four wickets defeat. Immediately after this match JW led the UEE players to his own ground in Leamington to play Twenty-two of Leamington where his eleven wickets in the match helped to achieve an eight wickets win. Of the Leamington players only Page, the ground professional, remained of the players who appeared when the ground was being set up ten years earlier, so perhaps the ground and club was being successful in bringing forward a new generation of cricketers.

UEE used Sunday 1st September to travel north to play at Bradford. Their opponents were allowed twenty-two players which seems to have been excessively generous given the developing strength of these Yorkshire teams. And so it proved to be as UEE lost by an innings and six runs. JW's most significant contribution was 29 runs in UEE's second innings. James Dean stood as umpire in this match as he had done in the previous one.

After an interlude to allow the North v South match to be played at Aston Park, UEE completed their season with two matches in Hampshire. At Southampton they beat Twenty-two Gentlemen of Hampshire by 87 runs (JW 9 wickets) before travelling to Winchester where the match with Twenty-two of Hampshire ended in a draw. Once again Harry Stubberfield appeared in a Hampshire side. So on 14th September both JW and UEE ended their 1861 seasons.

The fact that JW could give more attention to the shop now that he had finished playing for the season was reflected in the classified advertisements in *Bell's Life*. During the cricket season the same advertisement had been repeated week by week as had those of many of the other advertisers. Now there was a change. In part this reflected the change in the sporting seasons but there was also a change in the wording suggesting that a review had taken place. Also, from 27th October John Wisden & Co were offering a 'Carte de Visite Photograph of the eleven of England cricketers that are on their way to Australia'. By 17th November a range of photographs were also being offered by John Lillywhite and M'Lean, Melhuish and Haes, who were based a short distance away from JW's premises at 26 Haymarket. By December, JW was the only one still placing a weekly advertisement.

JW maintained his advertisement in *Bell's* Life throughout the winter then, on 6th April, the impending start of the 1862 cricket season was heralded by a significant increase in the overall number of entries due to Fred Lillywhite, who had six separate entries. Within these advertisements Fred described himself as 'The best and cheapest house in London' and 'THE GREATEST CRICKETING OUTFITTER in the world'. Having a character capable of such self-aggrandisement meant that Fred was never going to be an easy partner for the self-effacing JW. Fred Lillywhite promised that the first volume of *Scores & Biographies* would be available in mid-May, then in June and finally on a more specific publication date of 10th July. Fred appears as something of a dreamer who struggled to fulfil his promises which would have put him at odds with the organised and commercially astute JW.

During 1862 JW was to play less cricket than he had since the mid-1840s (with the exception of 1860). For his first match he was part of a team raised by the Sussex CCC secretary Bridger Stent to play in a twelve a-side match against Sussex Colts. The colts' side include James Dean's nephew, James, and James Lillywhite jnr. By now Harry Stubberfield was no longer considered a colt and opened the bowling for the secretary's team with JW. Considering the reputation of the Brunswick Ground on which it was played the match was extremely low scoring: 59 and 54 played 20 and 67. JW took 3/12 in the Colts' first innings.

The Colts' match was one of only two that JW played for Sussex during 1862. In the MCC v Sussex match at Lord's in mid-June he picked up another injury, a sprained leg, and did not play again until September. The match at Lord's was another extremely low scoring one, in part due to the very heavy conditions. In MCC's first innings the youngsters Harry Stubberfield and James Lillywhite jnr (14-57 on his first-class debut) bowled out MCC for 46 in 50.3 overs. In reply Wootton and Grundy took 60.3 overs to dismiss Sussex for 64. In MCC's second innings it took the young Sussex pair 71.2 overs to dismiss them for 52. This set Sussex 35 runs for victory and they decided to send in the younger players to get the runs. When they had been reduced to 13-6 it was decided to change tack and captain John Hale, who had opened the first innings, and JW were sent out to win the match – which they did without further loss. As the leg sprain was sufficient to keep JW out of cricket for two and a half months, he presumably hobbled through the final innings.

JW played in just two other first-class matches during the season. Every time that JW went to Manchester for a match it seemed to rain, as in this case when he was in the South team to play the North. The second of the three scheduled days was completely lost to rain. When the South added a second innings of 137 to their first innings lead of 56 they set the North a daunting target in the conditions. Edgar Willsher and JW each bowled just 11 overs each as the North closed at 39-3.

JW's other first-class match was when he led UEE in their annual match with AEE at Lord's. UEE set AEE just 53 to win but reduced them to 14-6 before George Anderson with support from Alfred Clarke saw them to a four wickets win. The match raised a further £214 to be added to CFFS funds. But ominously, the planned matches to be played at the Oval and in Manchester did not take place. It was a sign of the increasingly difficult relationships between various groups of players.

Before he was injured JW played for UEE against Twenty-two of East Hampshire when UEE had the better of an unfinished match. He also played in the unfinished match with Twenty-two of Dudley. Setting their hosts 196 to win they were 35-16 at stumps. JW had bowling figures of 42-?-42-10 and 27-?-22-9. An interesting feature of this match is that in the first Dudley innings JW bowled more than half the overs.[75]

Although unable to play until his injury healed, JW still accompanied UEE to matches and stood as umpire. He travelled to Chichester for the match with Priory Park and then to Wolverhampton before another fixture with the Walkers at their Southgate ground.

In mid-August JW travelled with UEE to Plymouth and stood as umpire in the match versus Cornwall and Devonshire and then one against Hampshire. UEE won at Plymouth by six wickets but the match at Winchester was drawn with the local twenty-two making, 256 in their second innings. In reply UEE opened their second innings with a stand of 121, providing further evidence of the need to think about the balance between bat and ball.

By the first day of September JW was fit enough to play again. Between the two fixtures at Plymouth and Winchester UEE travelled to Birmingham to play Twenty-two of Aston Park. JW batted at eleven (17) and bowled only two overs, giving further evidence of his steady move to the back seat and perhaps nursing his only recently healed leg. After the Hampshire match in Winchester, UEE made the short journey north to play Twenty-two of Odiham. JW batted once, at number eleven, and bowled only 23.2 overs across three days. However, he did take four catches – so that aspect of his game was still sharp.

After the two matches in Hampshire, UEE travelled to Tiverton to take on Twenty-two of Devonshire. However, the composition of the local team showed up the weakness in the status of the emerging county teams. Very few of this twenty-two had played in the combined Cornwall and Devon team. Sides still had some way to go to be truly representative. JW took a slightly more active part in this match, scoring 18 (No10) in his only innings, his long-time colleague John Lillywhite batting at No 11. JW bowled 17 overs in each innings and took 3/26 and 8/14.

UEE's final match of the season was on the 15th-17th September at Newport on the Isle of Wight. Both JW and John Lillywhite had quiet matches as the visitors won by an innings. Wherever they went UEE were courteous visitors and most acceptable guests, and on the evening between the first two days' play they were treated to theatre and a fine dinner. Not surprisingly, they promised 'to be back'.

[75] The Laws at this time permitted a bowler to deliver consecutive overs from opposite ends.

17

A CHANGE OF DIRECTION

It was by all accounts a pleasant late summer's evening at Kennington Oval on 26th August 1862. The players were approaching the end of the second day of the Surrey v England fixture when umpire John Lillywhite called No Ball! against Kent's Edgar Willsher who was bowling for the England side. Lillywhite had earlier in the afternoon made known his misgivings about Willsher's action, judging that the bowler's arm was above his shoulder thus making the delivery illegal. He called No Ball! a further five times after which Willsher threw down the ball and stormed off the ground. He was followed by the rest of the professionals in the England side, bringing the day's play to an unscheduled end.

Sadly, for neither the first nor the last time, management failed to support their official. John Lillywhite refused to retreat from his position and Willsher refused to continue with him as umpire. The players won the argument and Lillywhite was replaced by George Street as umpire for the final day, despite there being a wide consensus that many players were currently contravening this law and that Willsher was a frequent offender.

Cricket is a game of balances: bat v ball, heat v moisture, runs v wickets or even runs v wickets v time, with the weather the occasional fourth factor ('dimension'?). Bat v ball translates into batsmen v bowlers which in 1862 then often translated into amateurs v professionals and further into Gentlemen v Players (both the teams and the classification). The Gentlemen were seen as the representatives of the establishment running the game and the Players the emerging force comprising the country's most skilled performers. The Players were looking to restructure the way in which the game was organised so as to create for themselves the opportunity to make a good living from their skills.

Maintaining the balances within the game was creating tensions which were moving inexorably towards breaking-point. John Lillywhite's actions were to tip some of them over the edge. Lillywhite had a reputation as an honest straightforward man which gave added weight to his actions. There were even suggestions that he had been put up to it by senior people who wished to see a change in the laws that took account of the new balance between bat and ball. As the changes that ensued had a significant impact on JW's life it is worth exploring them here.

Ironically, the primary reason for the need to change was brought on by an improvement – that in the preparation and condition of the grounds. Over the previous ten seasons there had been a steady improvement in the state of the grounds, in particular the parts of the playing surfaces used for pitches. This was none more so than at Lord's where the pitch had been notoriously uneven for many years. Much of the improvement had been created by the new machinery that was becoming available for the maintenance of the grounds. These improvements were adjusting the bat v ball balance in the favour of the batsmen and leading to the steady increase in the number of runs scored in any innings or match.

In the match in which Willsher was no-balled England's first innings totalled 503. In *Scores & Biographies*[76] Arthur Haygarth recorded that the innings took up 9 hours 55 minutes of a match scheduled for three six-hour days. Inevitably it ended in a draw. To appreciate the size of the score it would be fair to say that 1860 scores could be multiplied by two to equate to, say, 1980 scores. The balance between batsmen and bowlers was not only a feature of matches. At this time the gentlemen amateurs concentrated on their batting leaving most of the hard work of bowling to the professional players. Thus a shift in influence from ball to bat would see a shift in influence from players to gentlemen, giving advantage to those who had always controlled the game and taking it from those who were anxious to increase their influence on the game that provided their livelihoods.

Until Clarke launched his All England Eleven in 1846 the gentlemen ran the game, arranged the fixtures and involved the professional players at their absolute discretion. Since that date the professionals had realised and developed the influence that their expertise gave them; as already recorded, a group of twelve all-professional players had recently expanded the game by making the overseas tours to firstly North America and then to Australia. As the professionals developed their skills the annual Gentlemen v Players fixtures had ceased to be a meaningful contest and for some years *Bell's Life* had been publishing letters suggesting that the fixture should lose its pre-eminent place in the calendar – or even be abandoned altogether.

[76] *Scores & Biographies Vol. VII*, p. 406

Another consequence of the activities of Clarke's All England Eleven and then the Wisden-Dean managed United All England Eleven, was the expansion of inter-county cricket. An *illustration* of this development is in the table below showing which counties were having their fixtures listed in the Cricketers' Register feature in *Bell's Life*, along with the major touring elevens.

1852	1863	1864
11th July	*5th July*	*18th July*
MCC	MCC	MCC
I Zingari	Surrey	Surrey
All England Eleven	Sussex	Middlesex
Surrey	Kent	Kent
Sussex	Devon	Sussex
	All England Eleven	Lancashire
	United England Eleven	Nottinghamshire
		Hampshire
		Warwickshire
		Devon
		Shropshire
		South Wales
		Carmarthenshire
		All England Eleven
		United England Eleven
		New All England Eleven

Whilst this listing is a useful illustration it is far from the complete picture. Herefordshire happen not to be listed, but were in the process of developing a county team. The Warwickshire listing is not for a fully representative county side (not established until 1882) but represents the fixtures for the all amateur Warwickshire Gentlemen.

Many of Clarke's fixtures had been against what might be described as shire towns – the matches in Yorkshire and Lancashire being an exception. In order to boost their strength many of the town clubs had drawn in talented players from the surrounding area. The seed having been thus sown meetings began to be called to discuss the more permanent arrangement of a county cricket club. This development was augmented by existing clubs/teams such as Nottinghamshire and Cambridgeshire tightening their organisation and arranging more regular fixture lists. This *ad hoc* extension of the programme led to an inevitable over-crowding of the national programme with conflicting demands on players, especially the more able professionals. An incident illustrating the tensions occurred when the gentlemen running the Surrey County Cricket Club summoned three professionals to leave a northern tour by AEE and return to London to play for their county.[77] The professionals calculated, correctly, that the fees and expenses paid by Surrey would not even cover their travel and subsistence costs let alone compensate them for the loss of their AEE match fees. They declined to return and play, much to the annoyance of their county club. The professionals were much in demand and aware of how to exploit the influence, indeed power, that it gave them. A complicating factor was that George Parr was not only the master of AEE but also held sway over Nottinghamshire CCC. Frequently described as queer tempered, Parr was also running a personal vendetta against Surrey CCC and using every avenue available to him to conduct it. His view was that Burrup's efforts to tighten the financial regime at the Oval and make Surrey CCC financially viable had moved from sustainability to wealth creation. This raised the question as to who should be accruing the wealth – the traditional clubs or the new professionals. This was a motivating factor in a long-running feud between George Parr and his northern colleagues against Burrup and the Surrey CCC committee.

At this time there was also a rapid expansion of the gentlemen's amateur, usually nomadic, clubs. I Zingari had been the first in 1845, followed by Lords and Commons in 1850 (JW had been a last minute replacement in their first match). Now as the professionals, with their superior skills, came to increasingly dominate representative teams, the amateur gentlemen organised teams and matches to suit their preferences. In the 20 years since the founding of IZ, wandering clubs such as Quidnuncs (1851), Harlequins (1852), Free Foresters (1856) and Band of Brothers (1858) had been founded.[78]

The 1863 cricket season continued the extensive debate on the subject of what to do about illegal bowling. In the run up to the AEE v UEE fixture at Lord's the players were warned that Law X would be rigorously enforced; there was speculation as to whether Edgar Willsher would again be no-balled. However, the outcome of the pressure to amend the bowling law (Law X) was as inevitable as it had been in 1827 when the battle was fought to raise the limit of the height of delivery from below the elbow to below the shoulder. Ironically, John Lillywhite's father, William, had been at the forefront of that battle. In June 1864 Law X was amended to allow the over-arm bowling style that is still in use today.

[77] July, 1855

[78] Fully recorded in *Gentlemen, Gypsies and Jesters* by Anthony Gibson and Stephen Chalke.

*By the 1860s the Oval was well established as London's second major cricket venue.
It had an excellent batting surface which led to increasingly large scores. It was the scene of
the developing Law X crisis which became a factor in JW's decision to retire from playing.
The painting is by Felix.*

It is difficult to determine at what point JW decided that 1863 was to be his last playing season. It may well have been in his thoughts from early spring; a sequence of events suggests that he may have been taking stock of his position as he played in early season matches and that his attention and energies were beginning to drift away towards other activities. During May he played in four matches for UEE. In these matches he only once batted higher than No 9 and his highest score was 15. He picked up a few wickets here and there but seldom bowled in both of the opponents' innings in any match. During this sequence of matches, for the first time ever, he was not included in the UEE for the match against AEE at Lord's

After this match a meeting of the professionals was held in the pavilion. It was to consider the current state of CFFS. In the chair was Tom Box who had recently taken up residence in London and the vice chairman was JW. JH Dark who was the founding treasurer also attended the meeting. *Sporting Life* reported[79] 'somehow or other (like other things at Lord's), it has been neglected no one taking charge of the books'. Dark

[79] *Sporting Life,* 30th May 1863

212

is further reported as saying 'There is now (August 6, 1862) £1,300 stock and dividend from 1860 to be accounted for by me'. Dark then proposed, seconded by George Parr, that John Wisden be appointed honorary secretary. This was passed unanimously. All the books were to be called in and delivered to JW who was to have them audited. He was then to give a full statement to the CFFS committee at Lord's on the Tuesday of the North v South fixture. HH Stephenson (Surrey) and Robert Carpenter (Cambridgeshire) were added to the committee.

On the day after JW turned out for UEE for one of the more demanding matches, that against twenty students from Christ Church College, Oxford. JW did not bowl in the students' first innings 160 before UEE were bowled out for just 83. Then in the students' second innings JW and George Atkinson bowled unchanged, JW returning figures of 30-?-37-8.

JW's cricket in June got off to a slightly bizarre start. On Monday 1st he played for UEE in a fairly standard match at Ealing. After this match he immediately travelled overnight to Manchester to play for All England Eleven against Broughton on the Old Trafford ground. On the assumption that the Adelphi declared opposition to William Clarke's matches was transferred to all AEE activities, this must be seen as unusual. Several newspapers reported the match and JW's presence and achievements but none offered any explanation for JW's first appearance for AEE in 12 years. His journey may have had a wider purpose. At the recent meeting at Lord's he was charged with sorting out CFFS affairs and getting it back on track. He was now lead administrator for the society and would meet regularly over the summer months with the professionals who were part of UEE. By playing in this match he had the opportunity to consult with the AEE group. On the final day of the match JW played a significant part in saving AEE from defeat. In their second innings Edward Grace opened the batting and carried his bat for 97*. JW (12, run out) was the only batsman to stay long enough to build a good partnership with Grace which was to leave Broughton with too many runs to get in too little time to win the match where much time had been lost to rain.

On the following Monday morning JW was back in London to be part of the Sussex team to play MCC. It had rained in London as it had in Manchester to produce a 'dead' Lord's pitch and a generally miserable match. Spirits would not have been lifted by Sussex's two innings totals of 36 and 56 as they lost by an innings and 52 runs. To play in this match

JW had left UEE to travel to Seaforth (just north of Liverpool) to play Northern Club.

No cricket was scheduled for Wednesday with Sussex due at the Oval on Thursday to play Surrey. It seems that JW spent part of it writing a difficult letter to Bridger Stent the Sussex CCC secretary to resign from playing for the county team. Stent accepted it in respect of the Surrey match to start later in the week but not thereafter. JW was back in county team when they played Kent towards the end of June.

Sporting Life urged JW to explain himself, but no such statement seems to be forthcoming. Was it that JW was beginning to become disillusioned with playing following two matches played in poor, wet conditions and a limp batting display at Lord's by Sussex? These events may well have helped develop the thinking that led to his retirement at the end of the season. Was it that JW's resignation letter might be described as a 'notice of retirement'? Could it be that in rejecting the resignation Stent had persuaded JW to postpone his retirement to the end of the season while allowing him to sit out the Surrey fixture at the Oval.

The following week UEE were MCC's opponents. For once UEE's fixture planning had failed to avoid a clash as Surrey were playing Hampshire on the same day. This left UEE with a depleted team and allowing MCC to field 15 players was a questionable judgment. Jemmy Grundy and Fred Reynolds bowled unchanged for UEE and JW's only significant contribution was 26* in the first innings. He had reached the stage where he seemed to be contributing more with his batting than with his bowling.

Two mid-summer matches serve well to illustrate JW's declining status as a player. On Monday 13th July the return Sussex v Surrey match began on the Royal Brunswick Ground. The pitch was reported as being in splendid condition; the bowlers had remarked that it was too good. Surrey batted first and totalled 234 and JW had bowling figures of 6-2-15-0 – though he did have Caffyn dropped by an amateur fielding at mid-off. The Sussex reply totalled a massive 369. Of these John Lillywhite, who did not bowl in the match but opened the batting, contributed 91. The last wicket partnership of 63 illustrated the changing of the generations. While making his 43 ('a fine innings'), JW was accompanied by the young James Lillywhite (27*) – known as James junior. Surrey's second innings totalled 383, during which JW again bowled little and without success (18.2-3-45-0). By the time that Surrey's innings had been completed not enough time was left for the match to be finished and it petered out into a draw. It must have seemed strange for JW to bowl so little, especially as James Lillywhite jnr bowled 120.3 overs and Charles Ellis 108.1 overs; the latter had started the match as wicketkeeper and finished by taking 15 wickets.

The following Monday the South met the North at Lord's. In a fixture where he had often starred, JW was not initially selected. However, William Mortlock had not recovered from a leg injury picked up in the Gentlemen v Players fixture (JW not selected) and JW became a late replacement. He bowled just 11 out of 168.3 overs – although he did take a wicket – and batted at No 11 in both innings (6 and 0).

In 1863 allegiance to counties was a little more flexible than it was later to become. JW qualified by birth to play for Sussex but he now also qualified by residence for Middlesex. So on 27th July he once again appeared at Lord's but this time for Middlesex in their match with MCC. JW batted at No 4 and his first innings score of 26 was described as 'all good cricket'. He was not required to bowl in either innings as Middlesex slumped to a 165 runs defeat.

JW's final season as a player had three clear phases. During May and the first week of June he played in a series of standard UEE matches. From then until the end of July he played in first-class cricket which included the MCC v Middlesex match. From the beginning of August he returned to UEE fixtures with a break to turn out for Sussex.

In August the UEE matches began with what was now becoming almost an annual fixture at the Walkers' Southgate ground. The match was now part of what was being described as 'The Southgate fete'. This time the opponents were titled Southgate CC by some and John Walker's XVI by others. It included six of the Walker family and the highly successful amateur Frederick Miller, who had in the past captained UEE. UEE used eight bowlers to deliver the 170.3 overs of the hosts' innings but of these JW bowled just seven for a miserly five runs. In its match report the *Sporting Gazette* noted that JW 'was not quite up to old form'. Having allowed Southgate sixteen players UEE lost by an innings. JW had not been selected for the Sussex v Kent match that had taken place a few days earlier.

On Monday 10th August JW appeared for UEE at Otley. In the last two months of his career he seldom rose above No 9 for UEE, even though he had successfully batted higher in the order for Middlesex. JW's 16* in UEE's second innings was not enough to force Otley to bat again and they won by an innings. This match raises questions about the organisation of UEE's itinerary. Having been badly beaten at Southgate UEE spent the Sunday travelling to Yorkshire. With a weakened team they faced the standard complement of 22 local players and were again well beaten. The match had originally been scheduled for two days but was then extended to three despite the fact that UEE had a fixture in Southampton for the Thursday. The thought occurs that perhaps JW already had his mind on other matters and was not giving sufficient attention to the detail of UEE's match programme. The Southampton match was against Twenty-two Gentlemen of Hampshire who comfortably beat UEE by 17 wickets; JW did not bowl and scored just five runs in two innings. By the end of the month moves were being made to form a Hampshire County Cricket Club.

His last first-class match was for Sussex v MCC on 17th-18th August 1863 on the Royal Brunswick Ground at Hove. He scored 8 and took 2/35 in a match that barely got beyond halfway with the third day completely lost to rain. It was a rather damp end to an outstanding career at this level. There was no clear indication as to whether JW had decided to go ahead with retirement. If he had so decided he had not made the fact generally known.

Almost as if anticipating that a great career was coming to an end on 27th June *Sporting Gazette* printed a single tributary sentence: 'From his general demeanour we know of no professional who is more respected in the cricket world by those whose good opinions are worth having than John Wisden.'

After the MCC match JW continued his way along the south coast where UEE were to play Twenty-two of Hastings. Again, the loss of the third day meant that the match ended in a draw. JW bowled long enough to take four wickets to go with his seven runs and the usual catch.

Having spent two and a half weeks on the south coast JW next led a strong UEE squad to Yorkshire to play Bradford, whose playing strength was such that they were now restricted to sixteen players. Yet again the weather ruined the match with the whole of the first day being lost to rain. If JW had not already decided to retire at the end of the season, tramping up and down the country to play in uninspiring matches on damp grounds would have done little to encourage him to carry on. However he noticeably seemed able to raise his game for the more interesting, higher-skilled matches; witness the two late summer matches against MCC.

At the conclusion of the match at Bradford UEE immediately set off south as they were due at the Cattle Market Ground in Islington to start a new match on the following morning. As the journey was from one large conurbation to another it was likely that almost all of the journey was made by train, with the hope of catching up on some sleep. Although the railway network had expanded rapidly journeys between matches were often started and finished by stage-coach. Their opponents had been drawn from Middlesex clubs and included one Thomas Wood Box, son of JW's mentor Tom Box. JW got more involved in this match and had figures of 36-21-30-7 which led to the clubs' side having to follow-on. They were still 34 short of making UEE bat again at stumps on the final day. The third day of the match was JW's 37th birthday. Presumably he got some time at home.

On the morning of 7th September UEE made their way to play Godalming. The locals had a strong side which included EM Grace, Julius Caesar and HH Stephenson but were still allowed sixteen players. The competitiveness of the match seems to have stirred JW into some action. Having scored 8 batting at No 11 in the first innings, he promoted himself to open the second innings but his 9 runs were not enough to prevent UEE losing by 44 runs. They had not won a match since those early season fixtures.

To complete the season UEE went on a two-week tour of north England. They played against twenty-twos of Stockton and Middlesbrough (lost by an innings and 26 runs), Newcastle (draw), Prescot (draw) and Alnwick, Northumberland (lost by 10 runs). During these matches JW scored 30 runs in seven innings, held two catches and took one wicket.

JW's cricket career ended on the evening of 23rd September 1863 with the defeat at Alnwick.

There seems not to have been any great announcement about his retirement and there were certainly no valedictory assessment-tributes in the national sporting press. In fact some people appeared not to have known about it until he did not appear the following season. In its spring 1864 review of Sussex CCC's prospects the *Sporting Gazette* forecast that the friends John Lillywhite and John Wisden would give Sussex yeoman service in the coming season. Instead of turning out for Sussex JW put his time and energies into the CFFS and running UEE. He was frequently listed as an umpire for UEE matches, sometimes with his life-long friend James Dean at the other end.

This Illustrated Sporting News image shows JW during his final playing days. After he stopped playing he continued to act as secretary to the United England XI. He occasionally stood as umpire in their matches, often in partnership with his friend James Dean.

18

THE LAUNCH OF THE ALMANACK

For what was to become such a pivotal year, 1864 started quietly. In the 2nd January issue of *Bell's Life*, John Wisden & Co., 2 New Coventry-street, W. announced that *The Cricketers' Almanack* for 1864 was 'now in press'. It would cost 1s 1d post free. An advertisement in the *Sporting Gazette* on 16th January announced that *The Cricketer's Almanack* would be ready on 8th February. Already, just a fortnight into the book's existence, there was confusion about the possessive apostrophe – an issue that would take several seasons to resolve.

When the Almanack finally arrived in the bookshops and bookstalls in early February it was well received; being generally deemed to be worth its 1s. There was at this time a popular enthusiasm for such publications. Alongside the advertisement for JW's *Almanack* were ones for a Rowing Almanac, a Sportsman's Almanac, *Ruff's Guide to the Turf* and *Baily's Turf Guide*. AH Baily was also publishing *The Cricket Chronicle* (at a price of 2s 6d). It would prove to be short-lived.

There seemed to be little comment about the choice of information that went into the Almanack; certainly in no way comparable to the raised eyebrows of the 21st century. It could be that readers and commentators had a fuller understanding of the origins of the book; it is difficult to be certain. It is a feature of mid-Victorian sports journalism that there was often detailed recording of an event and sometimes endless comment and argument about its outcomes; witness the UEE breakaway. However, there was hardly ever any analysis of the causes of any action or event.

From the late 1840s up until 1863 Fred Lillywhite had dominated the cricket handbook market; *Lillywhite's Guide* as it was commonly known had a status similar to that of *Wisden* today. He had led the way in improvements and enhancements in the recording, reporting and performance analysis of cricket. However, as the 1860s progressed it was becoming increasingly obvious that Lillywhite was struggling both personally and professionally. Publication dates were being missed and then pushed back to the following week or month. There was also evidence that he had taken on too much work including involvement with the publication of *Scores & Biographies*. He had lost the support of the establishment (essentially MCC), particularly through a series of ill-chosen and acerbic comments about leading cricket personalities. He had also been eased out of his duties with the Cricketers' Fund Friendly Society, to be replaced by JW. This had hurt him and an application for a court order to hand over CFFS records was only forestalled when, in late October 1863, Fred arrived on the steps of the court house in the hour before the hearing to hand over the books etc. to JW. On top of or because of all this Fred's health was declining.

JW was aware of all these factors. He had known Fred Lillywhite since they were boys together in Brighton and then had been business partners in London. JW was astute both socially and commercially; he knew that Fred's personal decline would lead to the decline of the *Guide* and thus create an opening in the market for a new annual cricket handbook. It must be assumed that others had seen the same decline and opportunity as both AH Baily and John Lillywhite (in 1865) looked to fill the gap.

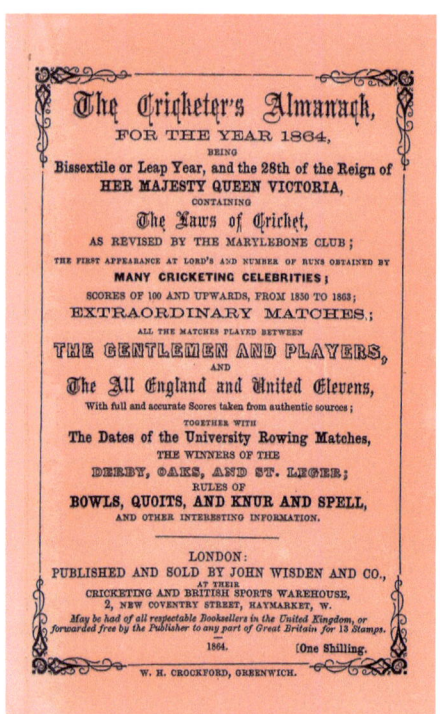

Cover of the very first Almanack, published in January, 1864

The first *Wisden's Cricketer's Almanack* was a marker or a place filler – essentially a statement of future intent. There is no indication as to when JW first started thinking about publishing a handbook; it may have only been mid-autumn 1863 after he had finished his final playing season. The handbook is a collation of readily available information and this would support the notion of hurried preparation. Most current commentators are of the opinion that although the *Almanack* is universally known by his surname, JW's long-term role was confined to that of publisher, promoter and book-seller. Rice and Renshaw[80] list WH Crockford and WH Knight as the editors. There is, however, evidence that JW may have had a fuller role in sourcing data for the first *Almanack*. Francis Elwes was a contact of JW's and a frequent visitor to his shop. He maintained a diary that showed listings of dates similar to the opening article in the 1864 *Wisden*, a calendar for 1864. The *Almanack* also used the calendar as a vehicle for listings of births and deaths of cricketers. In the days of the Lillywhite and Wisden partnership they had been appealing through such media as *Bell's Life* for information from gravestones to give dates of births and deaths of cricketers from bygone years. Elwes's diary also contains a table on university rowing matches which has content and layout almost identical to the listing that appears on page 108 of the *Almanack*. The data for the section headed The Two Elevens (pp 84-97) was easily found in the UEE scorebook(s), which were presumably in JW's possession.

The scorecards for Gentlemen v Players matches could have been obtained from a variety of sources, not least from the recently published first two volumes of *Scores & Biographies* (copyright permitting). The more recent scorecards could be sourced from the bound copies of past issues of *Bell's Life* which were stored and generally available at 2 New Coventry Street.[81] JW is often considered to have had a commercially sensitive eye on his society customer base. However, publishing the Gentlemen v Players results would serve to illustrate how his fellow professional cricketers were beginning to dominate the game, thus serving another of his client groups, those professional players.

At this time Victorian society had an enthusiastic interest in data listings. Match reports in *Bell's Life* frequently included lists of past

---

[80] Jonathan Rice and Andrew Renshaw in *The Wisden Collector's Guide*

[81] In its edition of 7th March 1858 *Bell's Life* had responded to a correspondent named Winton by stating 'Lillywhite and Wisden have back numbers of "Bell's Life" bound up, and no doubt you can refer; we cannot find the time'.

results in fixtures which had established a long running sequence: Eton v Harrow, Sussex v Kent, etc. The non-cricket lists in the *Almanack* were clearly 'fillers' but would have been of interest to what may be imagined as the target readership.

After several delays, *Lillywhite's Guide* for 1864 was eventually published in mid-May.

When the 1864 cricket season got underway there was much change within the cricket that involved the professional players. George Parr's team that had toured Australia during the English winter was still on its way back home. Three of the team were UEE players and the rest were from AEE. Whit Monday arrived early in 1864 – on 16th May but it was agreed that the annual AEE v UEE fixture at Lord's should go ahead as usual. Although JW had retired from playing he remained the secretary/manager of UEE and needed to put a side into the field. He had the easier task of the two managers, being able to field nine regulars. As was his instinct he used the two remaining places to blood two young colts. In his new role JW was free to mingle with those beyond the boundary including the sometime Lord Guernsey (now Earl of Aylesford), RA Fitzgerald, one of his boys at Harrow, and the Ponsonby brothers, always strong supporters of his work. For this match his efforts were well rewarded: the sun shone, the ground was much improved, UEE won a good match by two wickets and CFFS profited by £125.

Others had noted the absence of, in particular, AEE in the national fixture list and saw the gaps as an opportunity to develop their own touring elevens. Edgar Willsher, who had captained AEE at Lord's in the match against UEE was now to create The English Eleven, a team name that had previously been used during the tour of North America. His team was short-lived, as were many other 'new elevens'. The net effect was to hasten the decline of many of the Elevens through overkill. Over the previous twenty years AEE and UEE had had an enormous and beneficial impact in raising awareness, in raising standards and creating career opportunities for professional cricketers. One of the responses to the arrival of an Eleven in their town was for local people to try to raise ever stronger sides to compete in following years. This involved delving into ever increasing catchment areas and so, for instance, Hereford soon became Herefordshire. The fragmentation of the touring elevens' programmes created a space in which more inter-county matches could be played. Most counties selected increasing numbers of professionals until the ultimate model was established at the end of the century when the dominant Yorkshire side had Lord Hawke as its general, Hon FS Jackson as his adjutant, and a squad of a further nine, battle-hardened, professional troops comprising a highly successful team.

JW's task in maintaining the UEE v AEE Whitsun fixture at Lord's was not his only work for the team. He continued as its secretary and inevitably its leader, at least off the field. Sadly, recording the names of umpires at matches was not yet common practice, so there is an incomplete record, but it is clear that he often stood as umpire for their matches, sometimes with James Dean at the other end. He continued to be amongst cricketers and was aware of their views and their concerns about their world of employment. Employment in general in England and beyond was experiencing significant tensions and change. The UEE programme for 1864 that JW and Dean had arranged was much reduced from the previous year, just 11 matches compared to 20. After the match at Lord's and one at Christ Church College, Oxford there was a single match against C Absolon's team before they embarked on the traditional sequence of visits to towns. This year the range was from Hastings to Newcastle upon Tyne – but no late season trip to Scotland.

At the start of the decade there had been just two Elevens and a handful of county clubs with an established set of matches. By 1864, the significant increase in county sides and the late return of groups making winter tours of Australia[82] had helped to break up that dominance. Several attempts were made to set up new Elevens, generating a warning in the *Sporting Gazette*[83] that the supply of Elevens might soon exceed the demands of Twenty-twos. The changes in the pattern of fixtures led to some thought about the activities of the touring sides. Did all of the Elevens need to travel over all of the kingdom?

In the autumn of 1864 the players of UEE were clearly having second thoughts about the need to travel annually to Scotland. Their conclusion was 'No', and a significant block of them resigned their membership of UEE to form the United South of England Eleven. Those moving across included John Lillywhite who as well as being treasurer of UEE was a leader of the group both on and off the field. *Sporting Gazette* reported that moving across with Lillywhite were 'Thomas Hearne, William Mortlock,

[82] From mid-July onwards
[83] *Sporting Gazette*, 9th April 1864

Thomas Lockyer, Thomas Sewell jnr, George Griffith and H Jupp'.[84] JW decided to stick with UEE; by instinct he was attracted to the *status quo* and he was aware of his responsibilities towards all the expanding body of professional cricketers. CFFS was the one organisation that brought them together and he was providing an ever clearer lead within that society. In October[85] JW published the restructured rules of the Society. Although the announcement carried the names of Thos. Box (Chairman), James Dean and George Atkinson it was clear that this was an announcement by JW. JW and 2 New Coventry Street were now at the centre of the world of professional cricket

Up until the 1860s *Bell's Life* had been the house journal for cricket. But at the beginning of the next decade a new newspaper, *Sporting Gazette*, began publication and brought an alternative style to publication. *Bell's Life* had played a significant role in popularising and expanding the game through its inclusive approach to reporting matches at many levels. Much effort had been made to encourage and facilitate the reporting of club matches across the British Isles. The consequence was that *Bell* was frequently pressed for space and became cramped in its layout. The *Gazette* took a more selective view as to which matches it reported and so was able to generate a 'cleaner' page and devote more space to major matches. *Bell's Life* had traditionally been a Sunday paper but from the beginning the newcomer published on Saturdays and *Bell* was eventually forced to follow suit. Like many other sporting activities the world of sports publishing was changing.

An advertisement in *Sporting Gazette* of 16th April 1864 announced a further development in sports reporting. In future (some) sporting intelligence would be distributed by The Electric and International and Magnetic Telegraph Companies. The advertisement was signed by 'C. V. Boys, Manager, Intelligence Department, Central Telegraph Station, Telegraph-street, London'. It was another aspect of the reform of sports reporting.

Although he continued to attend UEE matches JW now had more time and energy to devote to his commercial activities. New initiatives show up in the enhanced range of advertisements placed by the company and the expanding range of newspapers in which they appeared.

John Wisden & Co first advertised in *Sporting Gazette* in the issue of 27th June 1863. The content was the same as the advertisement for that weekend in *Bell's Life* but the space given to it was greater and the printed

[84] *Sporting Gazette,* 26th November 1864
[85] *Bell's Life,* 15th October, 1864

impression clearer. The *Bell's Life* advertisements continued through the autumn and winter of 1863/64 but for 16th January JW moved his advertisement for the new *Wisden's Cricketer's Almanack* from *Bell's Life* to the *Sporting Gazette*. From 1st February the company also placed an advertisement in the monthly issues of *Every Boy's Magazine*.

In the 1860s, at least as far as London was concerned, the dominant companies in the sports goods market would appear to have been the cricketing outfitters, who had had a head start on those specialising in other sports. Equipment for many other sports had a status perhaps best described as 'also supplied' in their weekly advertisements in the newspapers' classified columns; JW and the Lillywhite family had long been principal players in this market. In October 1863 a meeting had been held to form The Football Association. A driving motive for establishing the Association had been the need to establish a common set of laws for the game. John Lillywhite gave a lead by publishing the new laws and the other suppliers anticipated the opening up of a new market as the game expanded. In January, 1864 'FOOT-BALLS' appeared as the header of a JW advertisement lifting it from 'foot-balls' down amongst the also supplied. By autumn 1864 other traditional cricket suppliers were advertising football equipment. A whole new range of possible sports goods was there for suppliers to develop.

Another business development was in the field of pictures. During the 1850s, apart from oil paintings, engravings of water colours had often given the best representations of the leading players. The work of John Corbet Anderson had been central in this field and the Lillywhite & Wisden partnership had published and sold many of them. A notable exception to this had been the photograph of the players about to set off for North America taken by Thomas Hennah aboard the *Nova Scotian* just before the players set sail. Now photographs were becoming more generally available and although they had their limitations groups of players sitting still for team photographs made ideal subjects. The company's 16th January 1864 advertisement in *Sporting Gazette* went on to offer:

> Photographs of the Twelve Cricketers now on their way to Australia, price 10s. 6d.[86] also Carte de Visites [sic] of the professional Players, price 1s.

[86] 10s 6d was the equal of a week's wages for a labouring worker.

The advertisement also mentioned that at 2 New Coventry Street 'models of the Patent Catapulta[87] can be seen and worked'. Given the restricted size of the premises this might have been an interesting experience.

There was no longer any mention of cigars.

A new feature of advertisements available in *Sporting Gazette* was the inclusion of images in addition to the plain type, so the column containing JW & Co.'s Cricketing Outfitters' advertisement was headed by a large image of John Lillywhite's Football (looking very much like a Gilbert's of Rugby make of football).

The first issue of *Wisden's Cricketer's Almanack* must have been a success as JW's advertisement on 12th November 1864 in both *Bell's Life* and *Sporting Gazette* said that the 1865 issue would be ready on 1st January – price held at 1s 1d. On 19th November, JW invited secretaries of cricket clubs to send him their addresses and the names of their clubs so that they could be included in the 1865 *Almanack*. On 26th November in the books section of the *Gazette*, John Lillywhite announced the publication of the new *Cricketers' Companion* due out in the early spring of 1865.

Being as good as his promise, JW placed advertisements in the 7th January, 1865 issues of both *Bell's Life* and *Sporting Gazette* to say that the 1865 edition of the *Cricketer's Almanack* was now ready. At this time only the last one-fifth of the company advertisement mentioned sports equipment. The advertisements were repeated at regular intervals in both papers throughout January and February and into March. For 11th February a line was added: 'A few copies of last year's almanack (the first number) on hand'. Thus the process of collecting *Wisdens* had been given a kick-start leading to a hobby involving costs that now can run into at least tens and possibly hundreds of thousands of pounds. It has also become a highly profitable business line.

JW & Co's *Bell's Life* advertisement of 11th March 1865 was boxed in by, above, a Fred Lillywhite advertisement saying that the 20th edition of his *Guide* would be published on 15th April, and below by John Lillywhite saying that his *Companion* ('the best work on cricket ever published') would be sent to subscribers on 27th March and available to the public on 8th April. *Baily's* failed to appear so the scene over the next couple of years for the publishing of cricket handbooks was taking shape. The *Guide* eventually appeared on 29th April and was available from

[87] The catapulta was an early bowling machine.

either Fred Lillywhite's new base at 41 Ship Street, Brighton or 201 The Borough, London where his partner Ward was based.

Up until the middle of March 1865 the focus of attention for the advertisements seems to have been on the annual cricket handbooks but on 18th March *Sporting Gazette* in an article about the coming season announced that those wishing to make fixtures with UEE should contact Mr John Wisden at 2 New Coventry Street. Clearly, many did apply and a programme of nine matches was played (compared to 11 in 1864).

JW had arranged a single match, versus Trinity College, Cambridge, before fielding a UEE team to play AEE in the annual Whit Monday fixture at Lord's on 5th June. Fine weather and a well prepared ground made for a good match. JW's disappointment as UEE lost by 66 runs was offset by the takings of £267-9-6 at the gate and £15-3-0 in donations; all funds for CFFS.

On 13th June the 1865 AGM of the CFFS was held at Lord's and the attendance list shows a good spread of members from across the three main professional groupings: AEE, UEE and USEE. Richard Daft was elected as chairman and JW as honorary treasurer, already being the salaried secretary. The committee also included George Parr and John Lillywhite so that all the groups were represented. Amidst all the churn and turmoil in professional cricket at this time CFFS, with JW at its centre, would be common ground for all professional players.

After the Lord's match UEE's next fixture was with Lansdown, Bath. JW and James Dean accompanied the team to Somerset and stood as umpires. This match gave a new meaning to the phrase The Three Graces (EM, H, WG) and in hindsight allowing the host's eighteen players was yet another example of JW/UEE generosity as they lost by an innings and 113 runs. EM scored 121 and the 16 year-old WG took 4/33 in UEE's first innings. With JW and Dean stepping back to take the supportive role of umpiring and the Grace brothers dominating the play this match in many ways signalled a changing of the generations.

There was then a single UEE match at Peterborough at the beginning of July before the high-summer series of fixtures started on 31st July at Aston, Birmingham. After Birmingham UEE travelled north to play at Buxton.

Now, unlike seasons past, matches were spaced out at least a week apart, so it is reasonable to suppose that the players no longer toured from match to match but travelled to each independ-ently. The season's programme was completed with matches at Clayton, Birkenshaw and

Leeds. JW was recorded as umpiring at Buxton and Clayton but given the lack of completeness in the records he may well have stood in other matches as well.

For JW 1865 had been a quiet season on the cricket field and so it is a little surprising that there is not more obvious sign of development of the business. In the *Sporting Gazette* of 14th October JW was still saying that the 1865 Almanack was 'now ready', with an advertisement that had remained unchanged since 7th January. By comparison John Lillywhite's advertisement was now dominated by the big illustration of a football. In a second advertisement Lillywhite acknowledged the change of season and thanked clients for their support through the cricket season just past. He believed that his first *Companion* had been a success and was starting work on the second. He promised that 'my *Companion* .... will contain nothing offensive'. This was, no doubt, a 'pop' at brother Fred who had recently needed to publish a letter defending controversial remarks in his *Guide*. *Wisden's Almanack* was taking a similar stance to John Lillywhite's and so a lack of comment was a feature of the handbooks for several years.

December brought the, no doubt anticipated, announcement that the *Almanack* for 1866 would be published on 1st January. The status of the publication appears to have risen in that it appeared in both the sports/ cricket sections of the newspapers and also in 'Literature' under books received. Although there were now three cricket year books for 1866 it seems that the Victorian public had an insatiable appetite for such publications. Immediately following JW's advertisement were ones for Almanacks from *Bow Bells*, *Johnson's*, *Gardener's*, *Moore's* and *Punch*.

The sports newspapers of the first weekend of 1866, 6th January, announced the publication of the third *Wisden's Almanack* – on time as ever. A pedantic change was that the cricketers possessive apostrophe was moved from the singular position to the plural one. In a section 'To The Reader' it was noted: 'J. W. and Co. have carefully avoided making any remarks upon play or players, as the purport of this little work is to record the scores of the matches published as a book of reference.' This clearly related to the acrimony created by some ill-chosen comments in Fred Lillywhite's *Guide* a few years earlier. The policy was later dropped. The book was well received in the newspaper reviews, the consensus of opinion being that it was informative and good value for money. With the *Almanack* JW was beginning to set the standards for such handbooks. John Lillywhite announced that his *Companion* would be published on 14th February, which was earlier than previously, and would be priced at 1 shilling, or 1s 1d, post free – another aspect in which JW had set the standard.

At this time there was no word from Fred Lillywhite about his *Guide*. However, there was a further indication that people wished to assume his role at the centre of cricket reporting. WH Knight was already into his third year as one of the joint editors of *Wisden's Almanack*. He announced:

> CRICKET REPORTING in 1866. – To Editors, or Managers of Daily, Weekly, Metropolitan, or Provincial Newspapers. – The yearly increase in popularity of cricket – "the national pastime" – among all classes, from the "marquis to mechanic," is one of those signs of the times that all prudent managers of newspapers take note of and encourage; for if they do not their journal will assuredly give way in popularity and circulation to those that do. I have had many years' experience in "taking cricket notes and having them printed," and am desirous of forming additional ENGAGEMENTS for the ensuing season. I will punctually supply editors with accurate and original reports, wherein nothing shall be extenuated nor aught set down in malice, and will furnish managers of provincial papers – per parcel or telegram – with notices – copious or condensed – of the great matches to be played at Lord's, the Oval, and Middlesex Grounds. My address is W. H. KNIGHT, 46, George-street, Hampstead-road, London, N.W.[88]

This seems a development of the service that Fred Lillywhite had been providing through the letter post for fifteen years or more. It could be termed a cricket reporting agency, even if The Cricket Reporting Agency was still some years away; it only came into being when WH Knight died. It was a development with an already established link (WH Knight) with JW and the *Almanack*. The Cricket Reporting Agency would be associated with the *Almanack* for very many years to come.

It would seem that by this time JW & Co. was feeling well established in the market. Instead of the weekly repeats of block advertisements in classified columns they began in January with a 16 lines advertisement, 14 of which dealt with the *Almanack*, one with fives and the address and sports goods occupy the other line. There were then memory-jogger repeats at roughly monthly intervals. By May advertisements had stopped altogether.

---

[88] *Bell's Life*, 6th January 1866

The wish of northern based cricketers to distance themselves from the south continued at this time and they were now supported by their own handbook. In the *Nottingham Guardian* of 23rd March, 1866 there was an editorial piece announcing the second issue of *The Cricketers' Handbook* this being for 1866. It compared itself with *Wisden's Almanack* and *Lillywhite's Guide* but stated that there was a focus on the north of England.

If JW's commercial activities appeared to be coasting, there was a step change in the activity of UEE. After two quiet seasons 1866 saw a significant expansion of the UEE fixture list to 22 matches, more than the previous two seasons combined. The programme began at Lord's on Monday 21st May. The continuing popularity of the AEE v UEE fixture was such that the first day attendance was reported as being the largest ever recorded for the fixture. UEE went on to win by 69 runs but no doubt JW was just as pleased with the £267-9-0 in gate money and £11-0-6 in donations going into the CFFS coffers. However, this was to be the last time that this fixture was played at Lord's. Although it continued for a further three seasons it was in future to be played away from London.

The following Monday UEE took on a new fixture, in the Channel Islands, having stopped off for a match in mid-Hampshire on the way from London. JW's presence was not recorded but James Dean took the opportunity for a once-in-a-while match, batting at No 11 and not bowling. It is recorded that the pair were together, umpiring, when UEE visited Midhurst early in July, close to Dean's home.

For the first time for several seasons the UEE fixture list did not include a match against a University-based side, a feature that had waned since its introduction in the mid-1850s. After the visit to the Channel Islands and apart from teams labelled Shropshire and South Leicestershire, all of their other opponents bore the names of towns. After the Midhurst match the group were back to playing two matches per week. Although there was no trip to Scotland the travelling was wide ranging taking in both north and south-west Wales and the Isle of Wight. The players were back to the 'treadmill' arrangements of fifteen years earlier.

The marked changes were probably due to alterations in the management of the Eleven. JW had recruited Robert Carpenter to UEE early in 1858. Carpenter was based in Cambridge and his first appearance at Lord's (always a milestone in the careers of cricketers at this time) was when he played for UEE in the 1858 Whit Monday match against

AEE. The original management of the team had centred around JW and James Dean, with support from John Lillywhite, who had become a UEE pet (to use a phrase beloved of the press). Lillywhite had now left to become treasurer and player for the new USEE. JW had retired completely and Dean spent more time umpiring than playing. Carpenter was a highly skilled top order batsman and fine fielder. He was also a skilled and energetic administrator. He was to fill JW's place as captain of the eleven and also to share with him the role of secretary. In the first ever *Lillywhite's Companion* (1865) Carpenter was listed as Secretary of UEE and JW as its Treasurer. But in the same edition JW was also listed as a professional player so the editor may not have entirely caught up with recent changes.

A good example of the need for, and value of, JW's work with the CFFS occurred in mid-summer. At the Surrey CCC annual dinner in May members had been told that the fund that had been set up to sustain Felix in his retirement had now been exhausted. It was suggested that thought be given to replenishing it. Then in its issue of 16th June 1866 *Bell's Life* reported that Felix was paralysed and in straitened circumstances. The editor suggested that a fund be established and offered to temporarily hold any early donations. The following week *Bell's Life* published a letter supportive of a fund and also suggesting that the professionals be encouraged to set aside their current squabbles and differences and stage a North v South match for the benefit of the fund. Given the work that Felix had done in the early days of AEE this would have been a fitting tribute. Sadly, it did not happen.

Law VIII of the CFFS rules excluded Felix from receiving benefit payments because he had not 'derived a living from cricket'; this multi-talented man had been able to fund his life in cricket from his other activities. His contribution to maintaining some sense of peace and good order in and around AEE had been immense. Now support for him was dependent on setting up *ad hoc* arrangements. It was not until December that these arrangements were sufficiently effective to make it possible to pass funds to Felix. However, in the end the support was effective and allowed him to live on until 1876 when he died aged 71 years.

In 1866 the *Almanack* was not the only book to bear JW's name. Darton & Hodge published the book *Cricket and How to Play It*. The authors were given as John Wisden and Captain Crawley. Crawley was a *nom de plume* of George Pardon, whose sons Charles and Sydney made significant contributions to the development of the *Almanack* in the latter part of the century. It was stated that all the technical input came from JW and that the 'literary part' came from Crawley. The book was part of a series of instructional handbooks on recreational topics being published at the time. No doubt having JW's name on the front cover was seen as a bonus for sales.

Fred Lillywhite had by now moved home to 41 Ship Street, Brighton. In August *Bell's Life* announced a Fred Lillywhite bankruptcy sale and newspapers also reported that a guard had been posted outside his Ship Street premises to make sure that there was no asset stripping before the sale. Then on 15th September 1866 *Bell's Life* announced the death of Fred Lillywhite and on 17th *The Racing Times* followed suit. Only a week later there was an advertisement in *Sporting Gazette* to say that James Lillywhite & Brett were setting up in The Borough, a short distance from Fred's former base at the Oval. An unseemly dash to set up in Fred's shoes had begun. During his life time Fred had been regularly berated and derided. Some of this he had brought on himself; the obituary in his local newspaper described him as 'his own worst enemy', but he deserved a better testimonial. His contribution to the improvement in the recording and reporting of cricket can be measured by the eagerness with which one-time competitors sought to get their hands on his surviving assets. This scramble would bring JW to court.

Since that evening in August 1862 when John Lillywhite had called those fateful No Balls the world of professional cricket had passed through a series of significant changes. Law X had been amended and bowlers were now able to raise their delivery hand above their shoulder, creating overarm bowling. This would contribute to re-adjusting the balance between bat and ball. The recording and reporting of cricket had passed from, essentially, Fred Lillywhite and *Bell's Life* to the cricket handbooks published by JW and John Lillywhite and the cricket reporting service of WH Knight. Publications increasingly included pictures as well as text. Reporting away from London was also on the increase. The dominant position of AEE and UEE was waning and a range of new teams – county, nomadic amateur and touring professional – were all seeking a place in the annual programme of fixtures. All was now ready for the development of professional and first-class cricket to move to the next stage – the creation of a county cricket competition.

19

THERE MAY BE TROUBLE AHEAD

A regular comment on JW's commercial skills amongst commentators and historians was that he knew who his clients were and where his market lay. So it was no surprise that in early 1867, when advertisements in the usual sports papers began to be less regular, there was still a weekly advertisement in the *Army & Navy Gazette*.

At this time the promotion of *Wisden's Cricketers' Almanack* for 1867 was moving away from classified advertisements to short editorial pieces appearing in newspapers across the whole country. Often just a single paragraph, they announced publication, briefly listed contents and gave the book their approval. While the cover price remained 1s, postage had risen to 2d. Copies of previous issues were still available, even for 1864, so perhaps the habit of collecting the whole set was taking time to get going.

As welcome as this support from newspaper editors was, February brought some less welcome news on another front. Sporting Gazette of 9th February, 1867 carried the following announcement:

> The match on Whit-Monday, June 10th, Middlesex v England, will be played this season for "The M.C.C. Professional Benefit Fund". The Earl of Sandwich, President of the M.C.C., has given notice that at the anniversary meeting[89] on May 1st, he will bring forward a resolution to the following effect:- "That taking into consideration the conduct of certain of the professional players last season, it is no longer desirable to extend the patronage of the M.C.C. to the Cricketers' Fund[90] exclusively, but that a fund be now formed, to be called 'The M.C.C. Professional Fund' which shall have for its object the support of those professional players only who have, during their cricket career, conducted themselves to the entire satisfaction of the Committee of the M.C.C." – By order of Committee.
>
> R.A. FITZGERALD, Hon. Sec. M.C.C.

[89] Effectively the Annual General Meeting
[90] The Cricketers' Fund Friendly Society

The message to the argumentative players seemed to be: conform or risk poverty in later life. At a time when working people across Europe were seeking to improve or enhance their employment rights and their working conditions, this would not have been well received by groups within the ranks of professional players.

This was unwelcome news for JW, not least because it was taking away the biggest money-spinner that he had in terms of building up CFFS funds. The Whit Monday match at Lord's had been at the very heart of the creation of CFFS but would never again be played on that ground. AEE v UEE fixtures would continue for a couple more years but never at this historic venue which had been part of its financial attraction.

Another unwelcome aspect of this announcement was that it signalled that the Gentlemen had run out of patience with the squabbling Players. From early on in his career as a cricketer JW had sought to create a personal network of good contacts amongst the gentry, going back to the day in 1850 when the Lords & Commons were one short on the morning of a match and he was the one called to fill in at short notice. His years at Harrow School had also been useful in developing his contacts.

Since the mid-1840s there had been various attempts to set up benevolent funds for cricketers. All had foundered with the exception of CFFS. A common factor within all of the unsuccessful attempts had been the resistance of the professional players to the extent of control to be exerted by gentlemen amateurs, whether the latter were cricketers or administrators. From its very beginning CFFS had been under the day-to-day management of the Players, but always within the oversight of the Gentlemen, whose presence gave assurance to donors that funds were being well managed and appropriately distributed. JW had positioned himself to be the link-man between the would-be donors and the potential needy. When the latter started to irritate the former his task was made that much more difficult.

The bad behaviour referred to by Fitzgerald was a product of a long running conflict between the cricket community in the north and their counterparts in the south. Although the dispute was largely developed and maintained by the professional players with bases in the north of England, administrators, particularly although not exclusively in the south, exacerbated the situation.

The schism (as it was frequently described) gained increased prominence following a meeting of Surrey CCC in January 1866. It was the subject of a lengthy report in the issue of *Bell's Life* of 13th January and then further correspondence in that newspaper on 10th and 17th of February. It was clear from this report that there were several aspects to this dispute.

The origins of the dispute between the north and the south and its attendant animosity probably went back to the early 1850s. It had almost become a vendetta, the origins and progress of which few could recall with any certainty. It began to seep into every aspect of the game; when some of the UEE players led the creation of the USEE, they were accused of 'taking the bread out of the mouths' of the northern professionals. Ten years previously Elizabeth Gaskell had written a well-received book titled *North and South*, a central theme of which was the geo-cultural differences between an industrialised north and an essentially rural south. This was now being played out on the cricket fields across England.

On Tuesday 8th April 1867 the management committee of CFFS held a meeting at *Gregory's Hotel*, Rupert Street, Haymarket, London. They resolved that this should be the venue for both future committee meetings and any general meetings of members. For JW this was conveniently close to his home and shop which served as a regular venue for casual meetings of cricketers. The day to day running of the society was now left more and more to JW and at this meeting he was further authorised to make prompt payments to meet immediate needs – thus avoiding long drawn out processes such as those that had so markedly slowed-up the collection of funds for Felix. Under the chairmanship of Richard Daft the committee comprised George Parr, HH Stephenson, George Anderson, John Lillywhite and Edgar Willsher, thus maintaining a balance between north and south and amongst the principal touring elevens. With this good spread of representation CFFS acquired the role of a forum for all professional cricketers, a role discharged in the 21st century by the Professional Cricketers' Association. JW now acted as both secretary and treasurer of CFFS. He reported that he held £3-12-8d in cash on behalf of the society and £2304-18-11d in new 3% annuities. With the maximum payment set at £2-0-0d per week, this would be enough to support 20 plus cricketers for a year.[91]

When the AEE v UEE matches were first played the custom was for the proceeds from the annual Whit Monday match at Lord's to go to CFFS and the matches later in the season to go to other beneficiaries. In the second match of 1857 the beneficiary had been James Dean. Although

---

[91] At this time £100 pa was the median wage in England.

UEE played AEE in each of the years 1867/68/69, CFFS had to share proceeds with other beneficiaries. Thus by the autumn of 1868 there was rising concern that for the past two years the fund had paid out more than it had taken in. Working with AC Murton, the CFFS's solicitor, JW arranged a meeting to attempt to address the issues. He prompted Edgar Willsher to write to George Parr to have a clear the air meeting. Parr passed this letter to Richard Daft, who replied to it but then failed to arrive at the meeting. Once they had gathered at *Gregory's Hotel* on 31st December 1868 and addressed some administrative issues the usual routine of blame and counter-blame began. A motion to dissolve the society was opposed by all the southern based committee men. As those from the north declined to vote the society survived. However, when it was proposed that a new series of North v South matches be initiated, each of the northern players present in turn declined to raise a side. JW was thus left to continue to manage and maintain the society relying on accruing interest and using his contacts to encourage donations from honorary members and subscriptions from the ordinary (playing) members to sustain the fund.

JW used his Harrow contacts to keep the honorary element of the fund working. When one of the trustees, Charles Hoare, died in the spring of 1869, JW recruited VE ('Teddy') Walker as a successor. Teddy Walker had been at Harrow during JW's days. JW had maintained his links with the Walker family, taking UEE to play on their Southgate ground and also umpiring other matches that they staged. A recently recruited trustee at this time was William Pickering who had worked with JW and Fred Lillywhite to set up the 1859 tour to North America and had played a significant part in ensuring the success of the venture.

The need for the fund was well illustrated by a report about John Jackson, the Nottinghamshire quick bowler, who had so terrified batsmen in the 1850s. He had ruptured a blood vessel in his leg playing for Nottinghamshire in 1866 and was now (1869) unemployed, homeless and virtually destitute surviving on the 5s 6d that JW sent to him weekly from the CFFS funds.

The efforts to restart high profile matches for the benefit of CFFS would be frustrated by the slow decline of UEE. After the 22 matches played in the bumper-revival season of 1866 the fixture list went into slow decline. Also the essence of United dissipated to the extent that when a fixture labelled AEE v UEE was played at Old Trafford, Manchester, *Bell's Life*

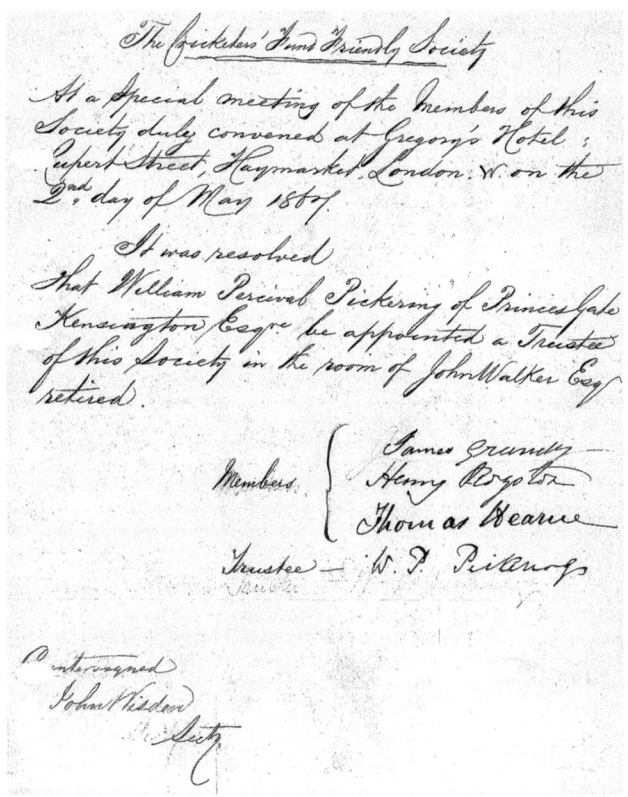

William Pickering was an Englishman working in Canada at the time of the 1859 tour. He did much to facilitate the arrangements. Back in England, JW recruited him, as a gentleman cricketer, to become a trustee of CFFS. Thomas Hearne, a player and a member, would take over as secretary/treasurer on JW's death.

was moved to comment that it was little more than the foremost talent of the north divided into two teams. This match was not played for the benefit of CFFS. Although for 1867 the UEE fixture list comprised 17 matches played at venues across the country, including the island of Guernsey, the following year saw only seven matches and in 1869 just the solitary AEE v UEE fixture. Despite being fully involved in the administration of the game there is no record of JW umpiring matches after 1866; however, this may be due to incomplete record keeping rather than lack of appearances.

Given the determination of George Parr and his followers to abrasively assert their northern identity the decline of UEE was an inevitable outcome. Professionals from the south would feel better placed in USEE. Therefore there was little point in having two teams operating in the north and as Parr was the leader of AEE it would be the survivor. JW's efforts to maintain a centre ground faded away. Strength on the field was also moving north. From 1869 the *Almanack* began nominating either Nottinghamshire, long the home of AEE, or Yorkshire as the unofficial champion county. In the case of the latter, the impact of both UEE and AEE in visiting Yorkshire clubs, and drawing the best players together to make fixtures competitive, had had a beneficial effect.

After UEE disbanded many of those players joined the United South of England Eleven. Here they are gathered at the Priory Park Ground in Chichester – not far from the home of James Lillywhite jnr, the future England captain.

Others were having to work hard to maintain the concept of the itinerant eleven. AEE and UEE had played a significant role in developing a country-wide set of county cricket clubs. The counties were dominating to the extent that publishing scorecards and match reports of county matches forced reports of matches played by the itinerants from the pages of the national sporting press.

There was a brief but sadly short-lived attempt to revive the annual fund raising fixture in July 1870. A team calling itself United North of England Eleven came down to Lord's to play USEE and were rewarded with a handsome win by an innings and 40 runs. However, any report on the cricket or the funds raised for CFFS seems to have escaped the sporting press, both nationally and regionally.

The *Almanack* now seemed to have found a settled place in the annual cricket calendar, being published in the first few days of January each year, with the only change being the increase in the charge for postage. However, JW's business seemed to be going through a difficult patch. Without warning or explanation the advertisements began to be headed 'Wisden & Maynard'. Winder[92] describes Frederick Maynard as a hay merchant. The partnership was short lived and was dissolved when Maynard was declared bankrupt. The advertisement also mentioned Sydney Alley (the road behind the shop on Wisden's side of New Coventry Street). There is other evidence that the operations within the fairly small shops facing New Coventry Street had spread backwards and moved into the properties immediately behind them. The space was needed to demonstrate a catapulta – assuming that they were not permitted to take it out to either street and fire it along the roadway. When JW was granted a shotgun licence it was to the Sydney Alley address. Evidence from censuses and local directories suggests that some of the New Coventry Street neighbours made similar moves to expand their premises.

Fred Lillywhite had been much derided in his life time, particularly by some of the professional players whom he sought to support. He was certainly an innovator but he was also unable to deliver on all his ideas and promises. He was a bankrupt when he died in 1866 and so his assets had to be disposed of in such a way as to discharge his debts, at least in part. In the 21st century some of his assets would be described as intellectual property. One of his innovations had been to design a scoring sheet that recorded all the data from a cricket match. A particular feature of this sheet was the detailed recording and analysis of the bowling in the match. Part of his case for recording this additional information had been that this level of detail was needed to create the data to properly assess professional bowlers prior to employment. The design had first been published and granted copyright in the early 1850s. At this time the Harrow School scorebook was simply a set of pages with parallel ruled lines – the sort of book a present day pupil might use for writing a history essay. Lillywhite's new design would be familiar to and useable by those who currently keep the score for club cricket matches. (Even the print-outs from new electronic

[92] In *The Little Wonder*, p. 52

JW had known Fred Lillywhite since the latter's birth, and their careers followed parallel paths. Fred's approaching death in his mid-thirties was a factor in JW's decision to launch the Almanack. Fred's legacy continues today in the design of match scorebooks used by many cricket clubs.

scoring software use a very similar format). At the same time Lillywhite had designed a sheet for submitting the outcome of a match to *Bell's Life* (and, presumably, other newspapers). During the years in which JW had been in partnership with Lillywhite, they and the editor of *Bell's Life* had been an effective trio in raising the profile of cricket through publishing fixtures and reports on matches played at various levels across the country.

Edward J Page was a cricket outfitter based in Kennington. He believed that he had paid those administering Fred's estate £20 for his stock of scoresheets and scorebooks and the copyright that Lillywhite had established over the design. He soon discovered that the purchase was a profitable one. The then partnership of Wisden & Maynard had made an unsuccessful bid for the stock and copyright and now during the 1867 season paid Page £30 for a partial stock of the sheets and books for resale to their own customers.

Following this JW moved to publish his own scoring sheets and books based on Fred Lillywhite's design. Page responded by suing for breach of copyright. The case proved to be a legally complex one in part because Fred had not been careful to observe all the legal details as ownership of the copyright was transferred from the original Caledonian Road operation to his own business and then updated as changes were made to the design. Also the design had to some extent drifted into common usage in the 15 years since it had first appeared.

The case came to court and was heard by Vice-Chancellor Sir R Malins at the Rolls Court on 8th March 1869 having been instigated nearly a year earlier. In defending the case Wisden & Maynard presented affidavits from James Dean, George Parr and William Pickering. *The Times* report of the case ran to only just short of 2,000 words and recorded his Honour's judgement with:

> Then came the important question of the copyright, and his Honour's opinion was that here there was neither sufficient novelty nor importance to make it a fit subject for copyright. It would be absurd to hold that there was a copyright in a particular mode of ruling a book, and yet this was little more, and there was some analogy to a solicitor's bill – a mere common arithmetical operation.

This seems to be a slightly bizarre judgment. A good knowledge of cricket was needed to create the design and make it possible for the match scorer(s) to easily record the match as it progressed. There was more to the design than the ruling of a few lines. Judging by the claims to copyright printed in the books used for 21st century cricket, it seems Malins' judgment has subsequently been reversed. The longevity of the essential elements of the design are testimony to the value of Fred Lillywhite's original work.

Having successfully defended the claim, JW left Page to meet the costs of the case. By the end of May John Wisden & Co was making the sale of 'Scoring books half the usual price' a central element of the usual advertisement in *Bells' Life*. They were also offering scoreboards, 'The New Telegraph, very portable, weight 25 lbs'.

Shortly after this case on 4th May the *London Gazette* announced the dissolution of the Wisden and Maynard partnership. This event was sufficiently newsworthy to be reported in such as the *Liverpool Mercury* and the *Nottingham Guardian*.

After the court case and the change in ownership the shop settled into a period of steady routine. It appeared that additional attention was being given to the weekly advertisements that were being placed in the sporting newspapers. Perhaps, now that he did not have such a high profile on the cricket field, JW needed to draw more attention to his business through paid for publicity. The advertisements for early January 1870 were of the usual format but then in mid-April, as the cricket season approached, more expansive announcements appeared. While *Bell's Life* advertisements were still set out in close-packed small black type of a single font size, those in *Sporting Life* were given more space and the variation in type face made them more attractive.

Other sports were now being given increased attention and so the advertisement for 7th October 1871 did not start with the owner's name but with 'FOOTBALL!! FOOTBALL!!' and listed a variety of kit and equipment available. It did, however, not forget to mention that the next *Almanack* would be ready on 1st January 1872 and that back issues were still available.

When the 1871 census was taken it recorded JW as staying as a guest in a house on the Isle of Wight. Those back in London, living in and attending to, the shop were listed as:

Charlotte E Gibson	38 years	Housekeeper
Joseph Williams	27 years	Porter

Joseph Williams was a long term employee of John Wisden & Co. He had been working at the shop at the time of the previous census (1861) and was still there 10 years later. But soon everybody would be on the move.

On 16th December 1871 the following announcement appeared in the 'Cricketing, &c.' section of *Bell's Life's* classified advertisements:

> JOHN WISDEN and Co. beg to inform their customers and the public that in consequence of the expiration of the lease of their present premises they are about REMOVING their old established cricketing business to 21 Cranborne-street, Leicester-square. During the necessary alterations the business address will be as usual, and due intimation will be given by advertisement as to the time of removal. – JOHN WISDEN and Co, 2 New Coventry-street, London.

Immediately underneath this came the announcement: 'In preparation, and will be ready on January 1, 1872, THE CRICKETER'S ALMANAC for next year (being the ninth year of publication)'.[93]

---

[93] The 'k' at the end of almanack seems to have become optional and the possessive apostrophe has slipped back to the position for the singular case. Cranbourne was soon to lose its 'e'.

20

CRANBOURN STREET

On 13th January 1872 John Wisden & Co placed an advertisement in both *Bell's Life* and *Sporting Gazette* to confirm that they were in the process of moving from New Coventry Street across the top of Leicester Square to 21 Cranbourn Street. They also reported that the 1872 *Wisden's Almanack* was ready, the price being held at '1s, post free 1s 1d'.[94]

John Wisden, the successful businessman, poses in the doorway of his new, larger, premises. It was also his home.

Available maps and drawings suggest that the new premises provided greater space than the old. When at New Coventry Street JW had paid rates on a property in Sydney Alley, suggesting that his own and some of his staff's accommodation were provided separately from the shop. Now he was being charged only for Cranbourn Street so it must be assumed that they were all living, literally, above the shop. In April, as the cricket season approached, JW's advertisement in *Bell's Life* was a 'special notice' reminding his customers that he had moved premises.

[94] The phrase is a hang-over from earlier days, even though Rowland Hill's scheme of pre-paid postage had been in operation for over 30 years.

From the earliest days of the Lillywhite and Wisden partnership there had been efforts made to encourage the fullest possible scoring and reporting of a match. Now JW was promoting his own scoring forms, of a now established design, both as single sheets and also multiple sheets bound into book form. The shop was still offering a new model of the telegraph (scoreboard).

The change of venue seems to have prompted a review of operations, possibly facilitated by additional storage and display space. There was a move away from the strong focus on cricket. In mid-September a revised advertisement in *Bell's Life* was headed 'BRITISH GAMES – JOHN WISDEN & Co.' and offered football jerseys at either 7s 6d and 8s 6d each or 75s and 80s per dozen. It also offered footballs, 'round and Rugby', with cases and insides sold separately if desired. In March 1872 the first FA Cup final was staged on Surrey CCC's Oval ground. Harrow School, through its alumni, made a significant input to the creation and early development of The Football Association. The first winners of the FA Cup were Wanderers, a side whose origins lay at the School. A member of that first winning side was CW Alcock, Harrow old boy and secretary to Surrey CCC. For many years Harrow School had had well organised team games and innovative internal competitions. JW's work in tightening and enhancing the structures for cricket and its coaching had contributed to this. Inevitably alumni drew upon their school experiences when creating new structures.

Although no cricket equipment is offered at this time there is a reminder at the bottom of the advertisement 'Cricketer's Almanac – ready 30th December and back numbers available'. One element that remained unchanged was the ethos of 'Best goods from best makers at most reasonable prices'.

At this time the majority of sports' goods retailers came from a cricket background. But this network of shops and other outlets did much to assist in the development of association football into a national game. In his biography of Charles Alcock[95] Keith Booth records a match being delayed because Wisden had failed to deliver the footballs. When Wanderers won the first FA Cup competition their jerseys were hooped in orange, black and violet, colours borrowed from the Butterflies Cricket Club.

The texts for advertisements were now changing more frequently and just five weeks later (19th October) a newly worded one was headed

---

[95] *The Father of Modern Sport*, p. 45

'FOOTBALL and CRICKET – JOHN WISDEN and Co'. Football takes up the bulk of the text with the small amount of cricket content being focused on the *Almanack*. The block of advertisements in *Bell's Life* was still headed 'Cricketing. &c.' but below JW's advertisement John Lillywhite's began with 'FOOTBALL!', twice and James Lillywhite, Frowd & Co's with 'FOOTBALLS!'. The range of games may have been changing but it was still the cricketers who were supplying the kit and helping to make the ever expanding number of matches possible.

Although the company maintained a strong advertising presence in London newspapers, serving the city where the shop was located, it also advertised across the British Isles, not only at the major cricket centres such as Nottingham (in the *Nottingham Journal*) and Huddersfield (*Huddersfield Daily Examiner*) but also down in the west country and even across the Irish Sea in Ballymena (*The Ballymena Observer*). For these readers price lists and a postal service were available.

An advertisement was placed in *Bell's Life* for 21st December 1872:

WISDEN'S CRICKETERS' ALMANAC (greatly enlarged) for 1873, will be ready early in January, and parties desirous of having early copies on sending their names and addresses, with the requisite amount in stamps, may rely upon being supplied the first day of publication. The book (of which this is the tenth edition) would have been ready for the 30th inst. but for the extraordinary number of figures and the anxiety of the publisher that it should be complete in every detail, and with reliable information to the latest date. The scores of all the important matches of 1872, including those played in America, and the proposed alteration in the qualification of cricketers will be found in this edition. Price 1s, post free 1s 2d. Also can be had copies of the preceding nine years; price 1s, post free 1s 1d each. – John Wisden and Co, 21, Cranbourn-street, London.[96]

The *Almanack* was, in the end, just a fortnight late. In the early years, possibly as a reaction to the erratic publication dates of the existing *Lillywhite's Guide*, the *Almanack* had made an effort to be reliably available in the first few days of January. It is interesting to note that the reason given for the delay was the need to be comprehensive and totally accurate despite the ever

[96] Switches between the spellings *Almanac* and *Almanack* appear to be arbitrary choices.

increasing amount of data that needed to be included. Amongst reviewers and commentators the accuracy and completeness of the *Almanack* was an attribute that set it apart from its competitors. In the coming years the *Almanack* would experience a number of publication delays.

After some fluctuations in the earliest editions the *Almanack* had settled down to a size of around 160 pages. Now the 'greatly enlarged' edition was to increase the size to beyond 200 pages. In part this was a sheer necessity created by efforts to report all important matches. County cricket was gaining momentum with more clubs playing more matches (all creating more employment for professional cricketers). As well as the increasing number of overseas tours cricket from places as far distant as North America and Australia was being reported and recorded. Presumably it was the increased size that led to the increased postal charge. A general consensus from the published reviews in newspapers etc. was that while the sport was well served by several annual handbooks, *Wisden's Almanack* was the best of the field, was creating the model and setting the standard against which others would be assessed. There was now also a *Scottish Cricketers' Annual and Guide* and a *Handbook of Cricket in Ireland*; imitation is said to be the sincerest form of flattery.

England at this time was a prospering country creating more wealth and more time for recreation. A series of Acts of Parliament restricted the length of the working day and created half-days and statutory holidays, all freeing up more time for leisure and sport. This in turn was creating an expanding market in sports goods which showed up in an increasing number of providers placing an increasing number of ever more elaborate advertisements in newspapers. Logos and illustrations were now becoming commonplace within the advertisements.

JW had always displayed an astute and carefully focused sense of business. He resisted following the trend of more outlandish advertisements, choosing instead to focus on slowly extending the range of goods included. An advertisement in 1874 had proclaimed 'CRICKET, FOOTBALL AND BASEBALL' offering to supply the emerging number of baseball clubs in the country. The initiative was short-lived. However, of longer duration was the company's commitment to Germain's Lawn Tennis, a newly established sport.[97]

[97] The first Lawn Tennis Club was established in the grounds of the Manor House Hotel, Leamington which was just a few minutes' walk from what had been the Parr & Wisden cricket ground. Dinners had been held in the hotel during cricket matches on the ground.

A reminder of the location and purpose of 21 Cranbourn Street before the expansion of the Leicester Square underground station subsumed the Wisden shop. It remains the only piece of 'corporate marketing' on the London Underground except for LU itself.

In the earliest of the New Coventry Street days JW was an enthusiastic supplier of rackets equipment. This was probably in part due to his own enthusiasm for the game. Now, tennis seemed to have replaced rackets amongst the company's offerings – commercial advantages overcoming any lingering attachment to his previous sport. A more constant feature, though, was the company's commitment to be 'outfitters to the Army and Navy'.

Early in November 1874 JW experienced another personal sadness when John Lillywhite died after a very short illness. The two Johns had been born in Brighton within a couple of months of each other and both enjoyed the days helping out at William Lillywhite's coaching sessions. They had played together for Brighton Schoolboys and their careers had run along parallel paths for many years. Later their similar sports good businesses had run in apparent harmonious co-existence. A divergence came when John Lillywhite left UEE to become one of the leaders of the United South of England Eleven. After John Lillywhite's death, elder brother and fellow Sussex county cricketer James came up from Cheltenham to support his sister-in-law and her children. In the report of the funeral JW was not included in the short list of mourners but it was in his nature to stand unobtrusively at the back of any graveside gathering and so avoid being noted in any report. Of those who had enjoyed the summer days of coaching on the Montpelier ground in Brighton only James and JW now remained. James was to die on 24th November 1882 at his home above his shop in Cheltenham.

Scores & Biographies, the great work of cricket reference, had begun life as an initiative by William Lillywhite which was then taken up by his son Fred who was involved in the publication of the first four volumes in the early 1860s. However, it was Arthur Haygarth who had continued collecting the data and compiling the texts and now (1876) MCC were getting ready to publish volumes V and VI. JW advertised himself as an agent for the new books whose publication was being stalled by the need to update biographical details; accuracy of current data was an attribute of both *Scores & Biographies* and *Wisden's Almanack*.[98]

Aged cricketers and their relatives were being asked to contact MCC with current information. In the days of the Lillywhite & Wisden partnership the cricketing public had been urged to search out and inspect gravestones to determine key dates.

In June 1877 John Wisden & Co embarked on a new venture – publishing a book of the complete scores of all of the Oxford v Cambridge university cricket matches. It was priced at 1s 6d with the usual additional 1d for postage.

As owner and publisher of the *Almanack* JW had one particularly sad duty to attend to; he would need to appoint a new editor. On 16th August 1879 WH Knight, who had been the original editor, died while still in post. JW's choice as successor was George H West, a 29-year-old journalist on the *Field*. Winder[99] reports that in the year that he took up the *Almanack* post West also became cricket correspondent for *The Times*. It had been Knight's painstaking pursuit of completeness and accuracy that had established the *Almanack's* reputation as the best of the annual cricket handbooks – and very good value; still only 1s despite now being up to around 250 pages. In the ensuing years the book stumbled a little in such matters as adherence to publication dates but it later regained its balance, made some adjustments, expanded its contents and pushed onwards.

Although JW was no longer directly involved in cricket matches he was still very much involved with cricketers. The need for his continuing efforts on behalf of CFFS was well illustrated with announcements in November 1877 that Julius Caesar of Surrey CCC was 'in great distress'. 'Julie' had been a central player in the heydays of the travelling elevens during the 1850s and 1860s but was now in declining health and had been badly affected by the premature death of his son. His needs proved to be beyond the capacity of CFFS to meet and Surrey CCC led an appeal for donations. JW was near the top of the list of donors with

---

[98] The work of publishing volumes of *Scores & Biographies* continues to this day. It is led by author/publisher Roger Heavens and supported by a group of volunteers seeking to ensure the most complete and accurate record of matches in the Victorian era by completing Haygarth's series of books.

[99] *The Little Wonder*

£1-1-0 and the subscription list in *Bell's Life* included the likes of HH Stephenson, Alfred Clarke, umpire Bob Thoms and WH Knight. Sadly, Julius did not live much longer, passing away in March 1878.

For JW a continuing task was to try to ensure that CFFS income annually exceeded expenditure. Income had become less reliable since the tensions amongst the professional players had burst into outright hostility. Matters were exacerbated by the active promotion of an alternative MCC fund. One helpful change was that the name of the MCC fund no longer included the word 'cricketers' and used 'professionals' instead. This reduced the use of words 'cricketers' fund' which was thought to have caused confusion between the funds and was reported to have acted as a restriction on donations to CFFS.

In terms of creating funds for CFFS one great resource that the player-members had was their skills. Within their ranks they had the players from whom to create the strongest teams in the land. Matches between such teams were very attractive to the cricketing public who could be persuaded to become paying spectators. The challenge was to bring together two competitive teams and arrange a stage on which they could display their talent. In the early years of CFFS this was achieved by staging the AEE v UEE fixtures at Lord's. This arrangement came to an end, firstly when MCC stopped making Lord's available and then when UEE finally stopped operating. In July 1870 as a substitute for the AEE v UEE fixture, Lord's staged a match United South of England v United North of England for the benefit of CFFS. In respect of gate receipts this match featured the additional attraction of WG Grace.

This 1870 match was a one-off in terms of support for CFFS and so JW needed a more regular and reliable stream of match income to add to the players' subscriptions and the gentlemen's donations. The solution was to come from a series of North v South fixtures. There were now two or three and sometimes more of these matches each season. Each year one of them fitted into the Whit Monday at Lord's slot which had been used for AEE v UEE matches in the early 1860s. This match was played for the benefit of the MCC Professionals Fund. Presumably some of the potential beneficiaries of this fund were also members of CFFS thus benefiting the Society by reducing the amount of potential claims on its funds.

Another of this series of annual matches was played at Prince's Ground and CFFS benefited from these matches although they also had to share the profit with individual beneficiaries. In this way they were also meeting the demand for more matches featuring the best players in the country. There were also opportunities for one-off matches such as when Surrey CCC made the Oval available for An England XI v Richard Daft's American XI (who had recently toured there). These matches seem to have served their purpose and CFFS funds remained healthy.

There is continuing evidence that JW's shop was still being used as an occasional meeting place for cricketers following the move across Leicester Square. Its popularity may well have been enhanced as the *King's Head*, run by Tom Box since 1863, was now even closer, being just around the corner in Bear Street.

Relationships between the professional players and MCC must have improved by the end of the decade since on 9th July 1883 Lord's Cricket Ground hosted the CFFS AGM. It was to be JW's last. It was well attended with their long term supporter Edmond Wilder, the president, in the chair. JW was able to lay before the meeting a cheque from MCC for £130-10-6 being the net proceeds from the recent Whit Monday match. He reported that the previous year's income had been £190-13-4 while the expenditure had been only £110-14-2. The MCC cheque would take the bank balance up to £264-11-5 and the society had £3,187-7-0 invested in consols. Altogether it was a sound financial state for the society.

Whether or not WG Grace would have been accepted as an ordinary member of CFFS is a moot point. He certainly derived a living from playing cricket – reportedly a very substantial one. However, he was classified as an amateur and these gentlemen were normally only honorary members. He would certainly have been a controversial member. He was not universally popular amongst the professional players; apparently eager to play matches on his terms and, for instance, reluctant to leave the crease if dismissed early in his innings. This tension can perhaps be best illustrated by one of the many stories about this issue. Grace had been comprehensively bowled early in an innings, two of the stumps having been taken out of the ground. As he trudged off Grace passed one of the old hands who is reported to have observed: 'Leaving us so soon Doctor, there is still one stump standing?' Whatever the truth of this account it may well illustrate the state of relationships.

Wisden's Cricketers' Almanack has been criticised for being parsimonious in its recognition of Grace's achievements. At this time the nation was in thrall to the man, at times to the point where no other player seemed to matter. If JW had any editorial input to the *Almanack's* comments, his instincts were to stand up for those being side-lined and to attempt to amend the balance. He would want to draw notice to the achievements of all players.

When the 1881 census was taken the residents of 21 Cranbourn Street were recorded as:

John Wisden	54	Head
Henry Luff	25	Clerk
Joseph H Williams	35	Packer
Ann Hemming	52	Housekeeper

Joseph Williams had been employed by John Wisden & Co at least from 1861, when he was recorded at 2 New Coventry Street in that year's census. Working for JW may have been his first employment. Henry Luff married Louisa Amelia Joynes on 31st January 1884. On his marriage certificate he is described as a commercial clerk living at 21 Cranbourne [sic] Street. By the turn of the century he was the head of a prosperous household with Louisa, five children and two servants.

Also recorded in the 1881 census was James Dean, back in his home village of Duncton where the records show a remarkably high concentration of people born either in the village itself or in one of the surrounding villages. James is described as a widower and licensed victualler. Also in the household are Jane Luff (no apparent relation to Henry) as housekeeper and two young servants. James (Jemmy) was team-mate, colleague, assistant and, more importantly, life-long friend to JW. James had been an agricultural worker (probably a sawyer) when as a 19-year-old he first played for Sussex at Lord's against MCC in 1835. Forty years later he was beyond playing or umpiring or returning to his original trade. To ensure that James was well set up for his declining years JW had purchased the *Swan Inn* in James's home village and installed him as inn-keeper. The opening dinner was held in March 1868. The inn was later renamed *The Cricketers*. For Christmas 1881 JW went to stay with James. On Christmas morning JW went to look for James in his room and discovered him dead in his bed. James had been a long time asthmatic and had died in his sleep.

21

LEGACY

Throughout its existence, John Wisden & Co had been regular, usually weekly, advertisers in *Bell's Life* and the *Sporting Gazette*, amongst other papers. While JW & Co advertised across the country and even as far north as Dundee, these metropolitan advertisements would provide a window through which to monitor the progress and development of the company. The *Almanack* for 1884 was published at the end of November 1883 but after an announcement of its publication in the first week of December advertisements for the business came to an abrupt halt, a signal that all was not well at the Cranbourn Street shop.

John Wisden died on Saturday, 5th April, 1884 at his home at 21 Cranbourn Street. He was 57 years old. The death was registered by Ann Hemming, his housekeeper, who had been 'present at the death'. His death certificate states that he died of 'sarcoma of cervical and sub maxillary glands 6 months'[100]; the last few months must have been uncomfortable.

Judging by 21st century standards, for someone who had once been so much in the public eye and who still held a national office, the notices of his death appear somewhat perfunctory. As his death had occurred at a weekend it was not until the following Tuesday 8th April that a two-line announcement appeared in *The Times*. The notice did not stretch to details of the funeral. The announcement in *Sporting Life* was in the form of a letter from Edmond Wilder and was followed by extracts from JW's biography in *Scores & Biographies*.[101] The announcement stated that the funeral would be at '2pm on Thursday, 10th April'. On Wednesday, *Bell's Life* announced the death and gave a brief summary of the phases of his career. It stated that the funeral would be at Brompton Cemetery at 'ten o'clock on Thursday, 10th April'. Any confusion about the timing may have been averted by the publication of a second announcement in *Sporting Life* confirming 2pm as the time; in this they were supported by *Pall Mall Gazette*. *Sporting Gazette's* second announcement was

---

[100] In less medical terms – cancer of the jaw.
[101] *Scores & Biographies III*, p. 404 (probably written in 1862)

immediately followed by an advertisement for the shop. Possibly picking up *The Times* announcement earlier in the day the *London Evening Standard* also announced the death. The spreading of the news outside London began with an announcement in the *Birmingham Daily Post* on Wednesday 9th where JW appeared as one in a list of deaths. The *Sheffield Weekly Telegraph* supported its announcement with a factual list of his achievements.

By the weekend, Saturday 12th, JW's death was being reported nationally. Leamington Spa had not forgotten JW and in announcing his passing the *Leamington Spa Courier* reminded its readers of his role in establishing the cricket ground in the town. During his life time the *Nottingham Journal* had given good coverage to JW and now in reporting his death it also reported on his funeral which it described as 'most unostentatious'. Also reporting his death that weekend was the *Bucks Herald*, immediately following a report of the death of the Hon Robert Grimston.[102]

There is no record of JW having travelled further north than Edinburgh and Glasgow but the citizens of Aberdeen and Dundee were informed of his passing; *The Dundee Courier* had regularly carried advertisements for the London shop.

It was a week later that the *Bradford Telegraph* announced the death and it was not until 28th that the *Liverpool Mercury* made its announcement. It had had time to think and unlike many other announcements which were merely syndicated from other publications made its own interesting comments. It observed that his bowling style would not have worked on current pitches and against current batsmen. It went on to describe JW as 'well conducted, respectable and respected. Numerous friends contributed to the success of his shop'.

JW's eldest brother, William, travelled up from his Brighton shop to lead the mourners at Brompton who included William Games, the husband of JW's sister Johanna, Henry Luff, then JW's 28-year-old principal assistant, and WH Crockford jnr whose father had been joint editor of the early *Almanacks* before cutting back to being just the printer. Crockford's were still printing the book at this time. Amongst those from the world of cricket there were Edgar Willsher, Thomas Hearne and James Lillywhite jnr, the sole survivor of two generations of great

---

[102] Robert Grimston was an Old Harrovian who helped with coaching of the boys during JW's years at the school. At the time of his death he was President of MCC – the only holder to date to die in office.

Lillywhite cricketers, who, like JW, had done great deeds for Sussex and England. JW had been a captain of the first cricket team to travel abroad and James had been England's first Test match captain when he was leading a touring team in Australia in 1877.

JW was laid to rest in the family grave which had first been used in 1868 for the burial of his sister, and sometimes housekeeper, Eliza. In May 1879 one Ann Grant had been added to the grave. It is difficult to establish Ann's link with the family.

Apart from some short paragraphs to support the announcement of the death there was little in the way of obituary in the weeks following the funeral. The first full assessments of his career did not appear until June. *The Sporting Mirror* published a one-page piece recording and evaluating his career accompanied by a lithographic portrait of JW the businessman which well-illustrated his increase in weight from the seven stones of his early playing days to a final weight of near 11 stones.

The best of the In Memoriam pieces was published by *Bell's Life* on 14th June 1884 and was written by Charles Francis Trower. The article is reproduced in full at Appendix E. As he explained, Trower had the advantage of having known JW for almost all of his life. Trower was also an historian.

The following year the first editorial page of the 1885 *Almanack* contained an obituary for JW. The text was printed within a heavy black box-border. The first two paragraphs were:

> A splendid all-round cricketer in his day: a good bat, a fine field and as a bowler unsurpassed. A quiet, unassuming and thoroughly upright man.
>
> A fast friend and a generous employer. Beloved by his intimates and employees, and respected by all with whom he came in contact.

This by no means overstated the case but was probably of a tone that JW would have found acceptable.

When the 50th edition of *Wisden's Almanack* was published in 1913 more fulsome tributes were paid to JW. Leading them was Sir Kenelm Digby who had been a member of the Harrow School XI in each of the four years during which JW was the leading coach and captain for the last three of them. He had worked with JW to develop a new structure that each year prepared a new group of boys to make up the Eleven that would play Eton at Lord's. Further tributes were given by Sir Spencer Ponsonby Fane and Canon McCormick, amongst others. All were fulsome, although it has been observed that it would ever be thus in the book that bore his name. However, it is very difficult to find mention across his lifetime of any negative comment about JW.

JW's grave was first established without a headstone.

To mark the centenary of JW's death William Gray (Chairman of Gray's) and David Frith (Editor, Wisden Cricket Monthly) jointly arranged for a headstone to be installed.

Made of polished marble it self-cleans in the rain and stands bold against a background dominated by beige and light green.

Barbara Baldwin ('Research Assistant') stands by the headstone during a visit with the author.

JW was one of the ten children of William and Mary Wisden. Two of the ten died as young children and of the remaining eight four were boys and four were girls. In general the four boys fared better in their lives than the girls. After the death of their mother, Mary (1840) and their father, William snr (1847) the children went their separate ways with only two of them staying in Brighton. William jnr had started his working life as a carpenter but then in 1856 he opened a sports outfitters in Duke Street, Brighton. The business was prosperous and in later years his household included several surviving members of the wider Wisden family. The shop finally closed around the turn of the millennium. Edwin (or Simon Edwin) worked as a carpenter in Brighton although he had moved to Stepney in London by the time of his death in 1868. After working in the City of London elder brother George Wisden emigrated to Australia where he died in 1888.

All JW's sisters eventually found their way to London, living in either central London or in the East End. It seems that the first to arrive was Johanna who at the time of the 1851 census was recorded as a dressmaker living in the Hanover Square district of London. In 1863 she married William Games, at that time described as a commercial clerk in the printing industry. In later censuses he is listed as an accountant. After a spell living in Arthur Road, Holloway the couple established a family home at Chipping Barnet where they spent the rest of their lives. Evidence from later censuses indicates that they became a prosperous family.

At the time of the 1861 census JW's sister Eliza was also in London acting as housekeeper to the household at 2 New Coventry Street. By the time that she died in 1868 she had moved south of the river to Putney. Louisa was still living in Brighton where in 1851 she married Frederick Coates at St Nicholas' Church, just up the hill from the former family home. By 1861 Louisa, her husband and six children had moved to Tower Hamlets, London. Between 1852 and 1870 she and Frederick had nine children. She died in 1871. Rosetta also spent her final days in the East End. In 1858 she had married a seaman named Alexander Grant and at the time of the 1861 census she was living alone in a house in South Shields, Co. Durham. By 1868 she was back in London and the last record of her is when she died in the London Hospital that year.

JW always had a care for those close to him, so the succession of deaths in the late 1860s created great sadness. After the death of sisters Eliza, Rosetta and brother Edwin, all in 1868 and then Louisa in 1871, JW wrote his final will and testament dated 1871.

By his will, JW left his estate to his younger sister Johanna. Griffiths & Bartlett[103] give the value of the estate as £4,233-9-9. Henry Luff purchased the business of John Wisden & Co. from the estate and so continued the emporium in Cranbourn Street. John Wisden & Co prospered under Luff's ownership. In the middle of the 20th century it was a major manufacturer and retailer of sports goods and equipment. Ironically, it was eventually subsumed into the conglomerate Grays of Cambridge which are today manufacturers of the Gilbert (rugby) footballs which were one of the first of JW's non-cricket lines. Grays had been established by Henry Gray who was a national rackets champion at a time when JW was a capable player of the game. There is no evidence that JW and Henry Gray ever played with or against each other, although Gray was a rackets professional in Cambridge in the late 1840s at a time when JW was coaching the University's cricketers each spring. Today John Wisden & Co. a is specialist division of the Bloomsbury publishing group. The *Almanack* thrives having been continuously published since 1864 making it the longest running continuously published sports handbook in the world. One provision of JW's will was no longer needed. The will provided for James Dean to remain the tenant of *The Cricketers Inn*, at Duncton for his life time. Sadly, James had pre-deceased JW.

On 21st May 1884 *The Sportsman* carried an announcement headed: CRICKETERS' FUND BENEFIT [sic] SOCIETY to say that Mr Thomas Hearne had succeeded the late John Wisden as treasurer and hon secretary of the society. When in 1889, the *Almanack* featured an appeal for the more affluent supporters of cricket to make donations to support the CFFS they were directed to Henry Luff. CFFS still had its Cranbourn Street base. The same article reported that CFFS finances were in a healthy state.

Through CFFS JW had always sought to persuade and encourage the Gentlemen cricketers to provide support for their Player colleagues in the latters' times of need. He met with success. When Richard Daft, one of the greatest professional batsmen of the later Victorian years and for many years chairman of CFFS, died in July 1900 he was a bankrupt. Lord Harris, a former captain of Kent CCC,[104] a trustee of CFFS and

---

[103] *ACS Famous Cricketers Series – No. 47: John Wisden*

[104] Lord Harris captained Kent 1871 to 1889. Harris was an excitable and voluble cricketer. On one occasion when Daft was batting and Harris was noisily fielding close to the wicket, Daft stopped the bowler mid-runup and asked for a pause 'while His Lordship regains his composure'. Clearly there was no residual ill-feeling.

grandee of colonial administration, arranged for his burial in a family grave topped with a slab of Italian marble which was so impressive that its weight eventually collapsed the grave. The CFFS continued its good work until well after the distinction between amateur and professional players ended. What was the work of CFFS is now carried on by the Professional Cricketers' Association.

John Wisden will be forever remembered as the name on the ever expanding little yellow book but in truth his legacy is so much more. He was an outstanding cricketer and a respected and effective coach. He was a natural and talented leader of cricketers both on and off the field. This led to the creation of the United (All) England Eleven. The way in which JW managed and led this team espoused a wider set of objectives than the alternative All England Eleven, and through their visits across the country greatly contributed to the expansion of county cricket in the mid-1860s. When he toured North America he helped reduce the friction between George Parr and Fred Lillywhite and when Parr was injured took over the captaincy showing great leadership and diplomacy. His shops, close to Leicester Square in central London, became an unofficial headquarters for professional cricketers, especially those based in the south of England.

In April 1963 Sporting Handbooks published the 100th *Almanack*, that completed the first 99 years of an unbroken run of publication that now stretches to 162 years. The frontispiece was a copy of Bromley's portrait of JW and the address at the foot of the preface was that of the Cricket Reporting Agency. Page xxxviii carried a report from the Cricketers' Fund Friendly Society which pointed out that it was even older than the *Almanack*. The fund now had invested assets of over £30,000 which was still managed by the combination of a panel of trustees and a committee of cricketers. Further into the book there was a one-page advertisement for John Wisden & Co Ltd, suppliers of sports equipment.

The innovations of JW's era had shown great resilience.

John Wisden – the final portrait

APPENDIX A

JOHN WISDEN'S MATCH DIARY FOR 1851

		Team	*Opponents*	*Venue*
May	5 *	AEE	MCC & Metropolitan Clubs	Lord's
	8	AEE	St Ives	St Ives
	12	AEE	Yorkshire	Sheffield
	15	AEE	Stockton	Stockton
	19	AEE	Northumberland	Newcastle
	22	AEE	Thirsk & District	Thirsk
	26	AEE	Gainsborough	Gainsborough
	29	AEE	Manchester	Broughton
June	2	AEE	Wisbech	Wisbech
	5	AEE	Oxfordshire	Oxford
	9	England	MCC XIV	Lord;s
	12	AEE	Surrey	Oval
	16 *	Sussex	MCC	Lord's
	19	AEE	Herefordshire	Ross-on-Wye
	23 *	Players	Gentlemen	Lord's
	26	AEE	Sleaford	Sleaford
	30	AEE	Derby	Derby
July	3	South	North	Oval
	7 *	England	Kent	Lord's
	10	Sussex	Kent	Brighton
	14	South	North	Lord's
	17			
	21 *	Players	Gentlemen	Lord's
	24	England	Kent	Cranbrook
	28	Sussex	Surrey	Hove
	31	Sussex	Kent	Tunbridge Wells
Aug	4			
	7	AEE	Newark & District	Newark
	11	England	Kent	Canterbury
	14	AEE	Huntingdonshire	Huntingdon
	18 *	Sussex	MCC	Hove
	21	AEE	Worcestershire	Worcester
	25	AEE	Staffordshire	Trentham Park
	28	AEE	Ilkeston & District	Ilkeston
Sept	1	AEE	Sheffield	Sheffield
	4	Warwickshire	I Zingari *(2-day)*	Leamington
	8	AEE	Bradford & District	Bradford
	11	AEE	Newburgh Park & District	Newburgh Park
	15	AEE	Scotland	Edinburgh
	18	AEE	Glasgow	Glasgow
	22	AEE	Birmingham	Birmingham
	25	AEE	Hereford	Hereford
	29	AEE	Devon *(4-day)*	Teignbridge
Oct	3			
	6	AEE	Hampshire	Southampton
	9			
	13	AEE	Sussex *(4-day)*	Hove

All 3-day games unless stated   * = *completed in two days*   *AEE = All England Eleven*

APPENDIX B

PRINCIPAL FIXTURES INVOLVING PROFESSIONAL PLAYERS 1854

An emerging co-ordinated programme of matches avoiding clashes as much as possible

UEE = United England Eleven   AEE = All England Eleven

		UEE	**National**	**AEE**
May	1-3	Sheffield XV		
	15-17	Rugby XXII		
	22-24			Upton Park XXII
	25-27		MCC v Cambs Univ	
	29-31	Cambs Univ XV		
June	5-7		England v Notts	
	12-14		MCC v Surrey	Liverpool XXII
			Kent v Sussex	
	19-21		MCC v Sussex	St Helens XXII
	22-24			West Glouc'shire XXII
	26-28	Oxon Univ XV		South Wiltshire XVIII
	29-1		Sussex v Surrey	
July	3-5		Kent v Sussex	
			Notts v Surrey	
	6-8			Sleaford XXII
	10-12	Oxon & Cambs Univ XV		Earl of Stamford XXII
	13-15			Uppingham XXII
	17-19		Gentlemen v Players[105]	Maidstone XVIII
	20-22			Manchester XVIII
	24-26	Northants XXII	MCC v Kent	Yorkshire Gents XXII
	27-29	Rotherham		AEE (N) v AEE (S)
	31-2		MCC v England	Bingham XXII
Aug	3-5	Dorsetshire XVIII		Spalding XXII
	7-9	South Hants XVIII		Stourbridge XXII
	10-12		Sussex v MCC	United Amateurs XXII
	14-16		Kent v England	
	17-19		Sussex v England	
	21-23		Notts v England	
	24-26	Young Kent XV	Surrey v Notts	
	28-30	Phoenix Park XXII[106]		Dudley
	31-2	Rochdale XXII		

[105] Dispute between William Clarke and MCC meant that no AEE players were included in the Players team. The Players still won easily – by nine wickets.

[106] The move from Dublin to Rochdale was UEE's only overnight journey during the season.

APPENDIX C

PRINCIPAL FIXTURES INVOLVING PROFESSIONAL PLAYERS 1857

		UEE	National	AEE
May	18-20		Cambs v Surrey	
	21-23	Household Brigade		
	28-30	Christ Church, Oxon		
June	1-3	AEE (CFFS Benefit)		UEE (CFFS Benefit)
	4-6		Oxfordshire v Surrey	
	8-10		MCC v Kent	
	11-13		Surrey v Kent	
	15-17		MCC v Sussex	Liverpool
	18-20		MCC v Oxon Univ	Manchester
	22-24	Camb Univ (Lord's)		
	25-27		Sussex v Surrey	Sleaford
	29-1	Oxon Univ (Lord's)		Loughborough
July	2-4		Players v Gentlemen	
	6-8		England v Kent & Sussex	
	9-11		Surrey v North	
			Sussex v Kent	
	13-15		Players v Gentlemen	
	16-18		Surrey v Sussex	Uppingham
	20-22		North v South	
	23-25		Surrey v Oxfordshire	Wakefield
	27-29	AEE (Dean's Benefit)		UEE (Dean's Benefit)
	30-2	Earl Stamford XI		Derbyshire
August	3-5		Surrey & Sussex v England	
	6-8	EW Vyse XXII		Boston
	10-12		Sussex & Surrey v England	
	13-15		South v North	
	17-19		England v Kent & Sussex	
	20-22	Reigate		Grantham
	24-26		Kent v Sussex	
			North v Surrey	
	27-29	Liverpool		Chichester Priory Park
	31-2	Cardiff		
Sept	3-5		Manchester v Surrey	
	7-9		North v South	
	10-12		Sussex v MCC	Leeds
	14-16	Birmingham		Shropshire
	21-23	Irnham Park		Stockton on Tees
	24-26	Scotland		North Shields
	28-30	Kelso		Richmond
Oct	1-3			Glasgow

APPENDIX D

CAREER STATISTICS
OF JOHN WISDEN

In presenting these statistics two objectives are sought. The first is to record JW's playing achievements season by season; a fairly familiar process. The second objective is to use the data on JW to illustrate the steady development in the presentation of end of season data during JW's playing career. The data used is that published, each autumn, by *Bell's Life*, the leading sports newspaper of the time.

Launching and developing *John Wisden's Cricketers' Almanack* was far from JW's first foray into the recording, reporting and publishing of data about cricket matches. At the same time that JW was establishing his career as a player, Fred Lillywhite was putting his training and skills as a printer to good use to create new information systems for both spectators on the ground and subscribers who followed the game from their breakfast tables. Lillywhite was often on the ground to record JW's early achievements and later became the embedded scorer for UEE. At this time he was also a correspondent for *Bell's Life*, the leading cricket reporting newspaper at the time, continuing in that role after he entered into commercial partnership with JW. In the later 1850s JW, Fred Lillywhite and *Bell's Life* were the 'holy trinity' of cricket reporting.

In general today's professional cricketers play the game in three formats[107]; each format having its own set of statistics. However in each of these formats nearly all of the players are professional cricketers and all of the matches between sides of eleven players. This was not the case in the 1850s. In the same week JW might begin with a UEE eleven-a-side match that would be deemed first-class and then for the second part of the week travel to a market town where UEE would play a team of twenty-two occasional players drawn from the neighbourhood. In the latter match wickets might be easier to take but runs were much harder to score with 22 fielders. This effect can be seen in the data that follows.

---

[107] T20 and The Hundred have been classified as the same format of cricket.

The first-class element of the averages is important as it records the achievements of JW as an outstanding cricketer who, around 1850, had a claim to be the best in the world. But equally important are his achievements while playing for, firstly AEE, and then UEE, the teams that played a critical role in developing the framework of cricket which took the game forward in the 1860s and 1870s and are still the central component of first-class cricket in England today.

In the 1840s cricket scorecards and averages were very basic and disproportionately focused on batting. During the 1850s this situation changed and the data has been arranged to display in the tables that follow this progression towards statistics closer to those published today. To better illustrate the progression a single source has been used, the averages which *Bell's Life* published each autumn from 1846 onwards. As the *Bell's Life* editor reported almost annually these averages increased in scope and sophistication year by year. I have sought to replicate the data as it was published at the time, although some of the extra detail has been omitted for ease of reading and interpretation. For instance the number of wickets taken with LBW decisions and the number of 'no score' innings have been omitted along with the numbers of no-balls and wides bowled. The intention is to make it easier to follow key features. In a few places there is reason to doubt the accuracy of a number and it is entered within square brackets. In three instances lines of data have been calculated from original data so as to have some sense of completeness. These lines of data have been entered in italics. JW's annual figures have been selected as an exemplar and to also illustrate his considerable achievements.

The tables illustrate the extent to which, for many years, batting averages were more detailed than those for bowling.

It would appear that Victorians 'did not do' decimals! If a batsman had scored 75 runs from six innings his average would be recorded as 12 with 'number over = 3'. This is similar to the answer to a schooldays long division sum, so the average has been entered as 12 r3.

During JW's playing career playing surfaces were improved and runs became easier to score and wickets harder to take. For 1846 it might be necessary for totals to multiplied by three to achieve a sort of parity with 21st century run totals; by 1863 the multiplier was probably nearer to two.

In the seasons 1844 and 1845, before *Bell's Life* started to annually publish their national averages, JW played in four matches that might, otherwise, have been included. In 1844 he played in two matches, batted in two innings scoring 13 and 0. He bowled in one innings taking 6 wickets. In 1845 he played in two qualifying matches. In the first he scored 4 runs in his single innings and had match bowling figures of 63-?-105-9. In the second match he neither batted not bowled.

Further statistical records of JW's career can be found within the on-line archive *Cricinfo* or in the ACS publication *Famous Cricketers No 47: John Wisden*.

Codings used within the statistical tables

a   Entries calculated by the author.

b   Average calculated by runs per innings (no allowance given for 'not out').

c   Only matches that had been reported in *Bell's Life*'s 'Cricket Register' were included in the compilation.

d   A new level of detail introduced by *Bell's Life*. The headings used for the various sub-sections are as per *Bell's Life*.

e   Excludes matches deemed 'second-class' (players being mainly amateurs on country grounds).

f   Settled format and pattern emerging.

g   Ignores second-class.

h   Averages record that JW did not bowl a single wide or no-ball during the season.

j   Average calculated as wickets per match.

k   Unexplained inclusion by *Bell's Life*.

m   Average calculated as wickets per innings.

n   Limited or no data available from UEE records, UEE scorebooks loaned for the process.

p   *Bell's Life* prepares whole season summary for batsmen, not bowlers.

q   There is reason to doubt figure given in brackets.

r   Average calculated as runs per wicket.

x   In accompanying notes *Bell's Life* felt the need to explain who John Wisden was.

BATTING

Year	Teams	M	Inns	Runs	HS	N.O.	Average	Note
1846	All	14	22	200	40	3	9 r2	b
1847	All	18	26	407	91	2	15 r17	x
1848	All	26	47	487	92	2	10 r17	
1849	All	27	46	511	60	3	11 r5	c
1850	All	38	60	848	100	7	14 r8	
1851	All	43	75	728	52	6	8 r50	
1852	All	20	37	507	52	5	13 r26	
1853	11-a-side	9	16	157	35	1	9 r3	d
	Odds	12	20	277	48	3	13 r7	d
1854	11-a-side	13	22	223	52	2	10 r2	
	Odds	11	16	144	27	2	9 r0	
	Overall	24	38	367			9 r25	
1855	11-a-side	11	18	420	148	3	23 r6	
	Two Elevens	13	23	178	80	4	7 r17	n
	Overall	24	41	598		6	14 r24	
1856	First-Class	11	20	292	89	3	14 r12	f
	Odds	14	27	279	42*	6	10 r9	f,n
	Combined	25	47	571	89	9	12 r7	f
1857	First-Class	18	33	425	74*	1	12 r29	
	Second-Class	1	1	18	18*	1		
	Odds	14	23	242	51*	3	10 r12	
	Combined	32	56	667	74*	4	11 r51	e
1858	First-Class	16	30	465	58	2	15 r15	
	Odds	14	25	237	35	1	9 r12	
	Whole season	30	55	702	58	3	12 r42	
1859	First-Class	17	26	343	42	3	13 r5	
	Odds	8	11	150	38*	4	13 r7	
	Whole season	25	37	493	42	[6]	13 r12	q
	North America	5	5	15	7	0	3 r0	
1860			0					
1861	First-Class	8	15	196	66	0	13 r1	
	Odds	9	14	149	29	2	10 r9	
	Whole season	17	29	345	66	2	11 r26	
1862	First-Class	4	6	46	13	2	7 r4	
	UEE	6	8	73	32	0	9 r1	
	Whole season	10	14	119	32	2	8 r7	
1863	First-Class	10	15	178	43	2	11 r13	
	Odds	14	20	124	16*	3	6 r4	
	Whole season	24	35	302	43	5	8 r22	

BOWLING

Year	Teams	M	Inns	Balls	Overs	Mds	Runs	Wkts	Wkts/M	Note
1846	All	14						70		
1847	All	17						111		
1848	All	26						245		
	AEE	1			24	15	14	5		k
1849	All	26						267	10 r7	j
1850	All	38						340	8 r36	
1851	All	41						445	10 r35	
1852	All	18						168	9 r6	
1853	11-a-side	9	16					75	4 r11	m
	Odds	10	16					106	6 r10	m
1854	11-a-side		23					97	4 r5	m
	Odds		16					113	7 r1	m
	Overall		39					210	5 r15	m

Year	Teams	M	Inns	Balls	Overs	Mds	Runs	Wkts	*Runs/Wkt*	Note
1855	11-a-side		16	1826	456	446	241	55	8 r6	g
	UEE		25	3196	799	712	419	168	4 r40	n
	Overall		41	5022	1255	1158	660	223	5 r43	
1856	11-a-side		21	2193	543	825	205	65	12 r45	
	UEE		25	3151	787	641	489	151	4 r37	n
1857	First-Class		30	2861	715	1005	318	93	10 r75	
	Odds		21	2374	593	546	323	139	3 r129	
	Overall		51	5235	1308	1551	641	232	6 r159	
1858	First-Class		20	1883	470	683	188	64	10 r48	
	Odds		22	2184	546	585	272	117	5 r0	
	Season		42	4067	1016	1268	460	181	7 r1	
1859	First-Class		21	1731	432	569	198	53	10 r39	
	Odds		12	1452	363	514	143	70	7 r24	
	Season		33	3183	795	1083	341	132	8 r27	a
	North America		8	699	175	157	98	38	2 r41	q
1860		0								
1861	First-Class		12	1176	294	418	119	36	11 r22	
	Odds		15	1675	418	593	169	59	10 r3	
	Whole season		27	2851	[718]	1011	288	95	10 r61	q
1862	First-Class		3	112	28	43	14	3	14 r1	
	AEE & UEE		8	602	150	124	74	35	3 r19	
	Whole season		13	834	208	205	102	42	4 r37	
1863	First-Class		9	598	149	246	66	9	27 r3	
	Odds		6	434	108	228	47	8	28 r4	
	Whole season		15	1032	257	474	113	17	27 r15	a,p

APPENDIX E

IN MEMORIAM

This assessment of JW's career appeared in the 14th June 1884 issue of *Bell's Life*. It was the best of those published.

THE LATE JOHN WISDEN

TO THE EDITOR OF BELL'S LIFE IN LONDON

Sir: If an "in memoriam" tribute to this excellent cricketer and very respectable tradesman has already appeared in any newspaper or periodical, none has caught my eye: one more will do no harm, and, having known him for 50 years, I may be able to add something. His father was, I believe, a carpenter in West-street, Brighton, and he was himself brought up to the trade. Anyhow he was a native of Brighton, and my first personal recollections of him were on old Lillywhite's cricket ground, then on the site now covered by the upper portion of Montpellier-terrace, when I was doomed as a schoolboy to pass part of my Midsummer holidays in Brighton, and fled for occupation and amusement to that beautifully-kept greensward, fed down by the bite of a few sheep and deer, and in which, for the moderate sum of 5s the season, one had the privilege of having one's middle stump upset by the first bowler of the age. Wisden, then a little boy of slim and slight proportions, was one's long-stop, glad to pick up an honest 6d, and silently, no doubt, taking in what he saw and learned from the great master of attack. Occasionally even then he would "send up" a good round hand ball himself (but was not yet strong enough to keep it up) in a style which foreshadowed his future greatness in the line. For I am strongly of opinion that for ten years and upwards a more successful medium-paced bowler never existed, and that his bowling averages were the very highest. With the exception of Mr Kirwan I know of no one besides him who bowled out the whole of a side in any first-class match. This he did in 1850, in North v South, at Lord's. At pigeon and other shooting his quick and correct eye enabled him to do equal execution. He was rarely seen at Lord's since he left off playing. His great friend was Jemmy Dean, whom he constantly visited and shot with at his home at Duncton, near Midhurst. He was quiet and unobtrusive in his manners, and singularly well-behaved. He was known as the "Sussex pet" when he was at the height of his fame, and contributed, perhaps, more than any one else except old Lillywhite to the victories which the county used then to achieve. I am sorry to say I have never played in any match either with him or against him, though I have done so with many of his contemporaries. But I have often watched him, and always with delight. Next to Lillywhite's his was the straightest and evenest bowling I ever remember, and was never "expensive." His run was short and his delivery graceful, and he could bowl through a whole innings without tiring; indeed, it was the commonest thing to keep him on without any change. His defence with the bat was also admirable, and as patient as Jupp's; but there was a good deal more dash about it when he was once fairly set, and in the days when "centuries" were not the common things they are now he was not without them. When "off" bowling his place in the field was short-slip, where he was as good and quick as at the wicket, never letting a ball pass him, and seldom missing a catch. It was with him good all-round cricket, and, given a choice whom I would have on my side in a single wicket match, I would have, next to W.G. Grace, named him.

He died unmarried on April 10 [108], aged 58 (after four months suffering of cancer) at his cricketing emporium, where he resided, in Leicester-square, and is buried in Brompton Cemetery. And though his contemporaries are fast passing away, or have passed away, and the great throng of cricketers of the present generation sweeping by have made his fame a thing of the past, and perhaps to some extent obliterated it, I am confident there is no one in the humbler walks of life to whom cricket, and certainly Sussex cricket, owes more, and it would be, I think, but a just recognition of his services if some tablet or memorial could be erected in his native place at the public expense.
– Yours, &c.,

CHARLES FRANCIS TROWER

JOHN WISDEN (1826-1884)
Cricketer and Almanack Publisher

A cricket ground was created near this spot in 1849 by John Wisden and his friend and fellow player, George Parr. Many important matches were played here to large crowds. Wisden lived in the town from 1848 to 1852. In 1850 he founded John Wisden & Co. probably selling sporting equipment. They gave up the lease of the ground in 1863. His obituary in his Almanack in the 1885 edition reads:

"...A quiet, unassuming and thoroughly upright man. A fast friend and generous employer. Beloved by his intimates and employees and respected by all in whom he came in contact."

As yet no tablet has yet been erected in his native place, but a plaque has been erected on the wall of *The Cricketers'* public house, at what had been the entrance to the Parr & Wisden Ground in Leamington Spa. A short ceremony and booklet marked the occasion.

---

[108] This is an error, it was 5th April. The funeral was held on 10th April.

BIBLIOGRAPHY

Books

Altham, HS, **A History of Cricket (Volume 1)**, George Allen & Unwin (1962), London.

Arnot, Chris, **Britain's Lost Cricket Grounds**, Aurum Press (2011), London.

Barty-King, Hugh, **Quilt Winders and Pod Shavers,** Macdonald & Jane's (1979), London.

Bedford WKR and Collins WEW, **Annals of the Free Foresters,** William Blackwood and Sons (1895), London.

Berry, Sue, **Georgian Brighton,** Phillimore (2005), Chichester.

Booth, Keith, **The Father of Modern Sport**, Parrs Wood Press (2002), Manchester.

Brodribb, Gerald, **Felix on the Bat,** Eyre & Spottiswoode (1962), London.

Caffyn, William, **71 not out,** William Blackwood & Sons (1899), London.

Daft, Richard, **Kings of Cricket,** JW Arrowsmith (1893), Bristol.

Down, Michael & West, Derek, **Sketches at Lord's,** Willow (Collins), (1990) London.

Frith, David, **The Trailblazers**, Boundary Books (1999), Goostrey, Cheshire.

Gale, Frederick, **The Life of the Hon. Robert Grimston,** Longmans, Green & Co (1895), London.

Gaskell, Elizabeth, **North and South,** Chapman & Hall (1855), London.

Gibson, Anthony & Chalke, Stephen, **Gentlemen, Gypsies and Jesters**, Fairfield Books (2013), Bath.

Gilbert, James, **The Gilbert Story,** James Gilbert (1957), Rugby.

Griffith, Peter & Bartlett, Kit, **John Wisden,** ACS (1999), Nottingham

Hadfield, John, **A Wisden Century,** Sporting Handbooks (1950), London.

Haygarth, Arthur, **Scores & Biographies, Vols. II to VII,** Frederick Lillywhite, London, John Lillywhite, London & Longmans & Co., London.

Heavens, Roger, **Haygarth at Harrow,** Roger Heavens (2018), Louth.

Hobsbawm, Eric, **The Age of Capital,** Weidenfeld & Nicolson (1975), London.

Hudd, Gerald, **John Jackson, The Nottinghamshire Foghorn**, ACS (2016), Cardiff.

Jenkinson, Neil, **Richard Daft, On a Pedestal**, ACS (2008), Cardiff.

John Wisden's Cricketers' Almanack for 1885, John Wisden & Co (1885), London.

Lewis, Tony, **Double Century**, Hodder & Stoughton (1987), London.

Lillywhite, Frederick, **The English Cricketers' Trip to Canada and the United States 1859**, F Lillywhite (1860), London.

Lillywhite John, **John Lillywhite's Cricketers' Companion for 1865**, John Lillywhite & Co (1865), London.

Lonsdale, Jeremy, **A Game Taken Seriously**, ACS (2017), Cardiff.

McCann, Timothy J, **Sussex Cricket in the Eighteenth Century,** Sussex Record Society (2004), Lewes.

Major, John, **More than a Game**, Harper Press (2007), London.

Marshall, John, **Sussex Cricket, A History,** Heinemann (1959), London.

Morrah, Patrick, **Alfred Mynn and the cricketers of his time,** Eyre & Spottiswoode (1963), London.

Myall, Steve, **The Victorian Development of the Clifton, Montpelier and Powis Estates of Brighton**, Pomegranate Press (2008), Lewes.

Packham, Roger, Sharp, Nicholas, Barnes, Phil, Filby, Jon, **A Pictorial History of Sussex County Cricket Club,** Sussex Cricket Museum and Educational Trust (2014), Hove.

Phillips, Giles, **On Fenner's Sward,** Tempus (2005), Stroud.

Phillips, Giles, **Edgar Willsher, The Lion of Kent,** ACS (2012), Cardiff.

Reeves, Scott, **Champion Band,** Chequered Flag (2014), Sheffield.

Shimwell, David, **Cricket and Cannons**, ACS (2017), Bedford.

Simons, Greville, **Lillywhite's Legacy**, Wisteria Books (2004), Malvern.

Sissons, Ric., **The Players, A Social History of the Professional Cricketer**, The Kingswood Press (1988), London.

Wade, Charles, **The History of the Leamington Tennis Court Club 1846-1996,** Ronaldson Publications (1996), Oxford.

West, G Derek, **The Elevens of England,** Darf (1988), London.

West, G Derek, **Days of Grace**, Darf (1989), London.

Wilson, Martin, **Lillywhite, The First Modern Bowler,** Christopher Saunders (2011), Newnham on Severn.

Winder, Robert, **The Little Wonder,** John Wisden & Co. (2013), London.

Wynne-Thomas, Peter, **George Parr – his record innings by innings**, ACS (1993), Nottingham.

Wynne-Thomas, Peter, **Cricket's Historians**, ACS (2011), Cardiff.

Wynne-Thomas, Peter, **The Old General (Life of William Clarke)**, ACS (2014), Cardiff.

Newspapers

Baily's Monthly Magazine of Sports and Pastimes
Bell's Life in London and Sporting Chronicle
Brighton Gazette
Brighton Guardian
Brighton Patriot
Harper's Weekly
John Bull
Leamington Spa Advertiser and Beck's Weekly List
Leamington Spa Courier
Nottingham Journal
Nottingham Review
Sporting Gazette
Sporting Life

Record Offices and Libraries

Brighton History Centre*
City of Westminster Archives
East Sussex County Record Office, Lewes*
MCC Library, Lord's Cricket Ground
National Archives, Kew, London
Nottinghamshire County Cricket Club Library
Sussex Cricket Museum and Educational Trust
The Keep, Falmer, Sussex
West Sussex County Record Office, Chichester
Warwickshire County Record Office, Warwick
Warwickshire Libraries, Leamington Spa

*:These centres have now combined with the University of Sussex to form The Keep.

Websites

Ancestry: www.ancestry.co.uk
British Newspapers: www.britishnewspaperarchive.co.uk
Cricket Archive: www.cricketarchive.com
Family Search: www.familysearch.org
Find My Past: www.findmypast.co.uk